MEDIA AND ETHICS

Principles for Moral Decisions

ELAINE E. ENGLEHARDT
Professor of Philosophy
Utah Valley State College

RALPH D. BARNEY
Emeriti Professor of Communication
Brigham Young University

Under the general editorship of

ROBERT C. SOLOMON
University of Texas at Austin

WADSWORTH
THOMSON LEARNING

Australia • Canada • Mexico • Singapore • Spain
United Kingdom • United States

WADSWORTH

THOMSON LEARNING ™

Dedicated to Linnea Barney and Rich K. Englehardt

Philosophy Editor: David Tatom
Development Editor: Ann Greenberger
Marketing Manager: Adrienne Krysiuk
Project Manager, Editorial Production: Erin Gregg
Permissions Editor: Shirley Webster
Production Service: Graphic World Publishing Services

Copy Editor: Keith Huff
Cover Image: Photodisc
Cover Printer: Malloy Lithographing
Compositor: Graphic World, Inc.
Printer: Malloy Lithographing

Printed in the United States of America
1 2 3 4 5 6 7 05 04 03 02 01

For more information about our products, contact us at:
Thomson Learning Academic Resource Center
1-800-423-0563
For permission to use material from this text, contact us by:
Phone: 1-800-730-2214
Fax: 1-800-730-2215
Web: http://www.thomsonrights.com

ISBN: 0-15-508256-6

Library of Congress Catalog Card Number: 2001092722

Asia
Thomson Learning
60 Albert Street, #15-01
Albert Complex
Singapore 189969

Australia
Nelson Thomson Learning
102 Dodds Street
South Melbourne, Victoria 3205
Australia

Canada
Nelson Thomson Learning
1120 Birchmount Road
Toronto, Ontario M1K 5G4
Canada

Europe/Middle East/Africa
Thomson Learning
Berkshire House
168-173 High Holborn
London WC1 V7AA
United Kingdom

Latin America
Thomson Learning
Seneca, 53
Colonia Polanco
11560 Mexico D.F.
Mexico

Spain
Paraninfo Thomson Learning
Calle/Magallanes, 25
28015 Madrid, Spain

PREFACE

Billions of human beings—individuals in every culture and subculture—must each somehow pursue their own dreams, while at the same time treading carefully so that others may also have their own freedom. This means responding to the inherent issues of privacy, deception, truth-telling and other human conflicts. The way we respond, the morality of our behavior, is critical to the quality of our lives on this planet.

Ethical issues in the media are particularly important; it is one of the few areas in ethics in which those who practice the craft are asked, even required, to think critically and make important, split-second decisions. Decisions such as whether to broadcast an interview with a bereaved family, reveal a source who has been promised confidentiality, or even accept an advertising account that may not be in keeping with a chosen lifestyle.

The media are often responsible for and most visible when responding to the multitude of situations that test tolerance and patience and our overall ability to get along with each other. Professional communicators—journalists, broadcasters, advertising and public relations people, and newly-minted cyber-communicators—are morally obligated to track their own lives, provide a viable social service, and avoid trampling others in the rush.

On what basis does the individual journalist or public relations professional make crucial decisions, such as whether to use a hidden camera during an interview (Chapter 2), whether to report a suicide (Chapter 3), or whether to warn consumers about product problems (Chapter 4)? This is where ethical decision making is of vital importance.

Media and Ethics: Principles for Moral Decisions is designed for undergraduate and graduate students as they consider how to persuade, inform, or entertain through the mass media, and as they learn to accommodate diversity and deal with ethical conflicts inherent in social interactions.

Unfortunately, media professionals often follow rules of convenience. The defense for following the rules or orthodoxies appears to be that rules are good and provide a direction. This is not the kind of reasoning discussed in this book. Rule followers require only a list of the rules, conventions, or orthodoxies to read and obey. This text supports independent thinking based on sound ethical and moral reasoning.

To encourage the reader to become an autonomous moral agent and to engage in periods of intense thought and moral reasoning, this text does not contain lists of rules, but instead, vital questions are raised about why certain decisions should be made. Readers will be invited to apply the tools of reason and the principles contained in the book, using them to trigger thought processes and to consider possible consequences. This approach leaves room for instructors to supplement this text with their own discussions, applying their own experiences and principles to discussion of the cases. It is also designed to promote a moral pluralism so valued in a dynamic, participatory society. The First Amendment and the decisions and experiences that have followed since its adoption more than two hundred years ago clearly suggest that the most contributive (and moral) professional communicators are those who regularly reevaluate their behaviors to see if they fit the rapidly changing demands of audiences. Therefore, the focus in this book is on helping professional communicators as well as consumers of mass media to become autonomous moral agents, to analyze and decide independently, to be able to make decisions, and to explain to others why those decisions are valid.

It is certainly hoped that the contents of the book will stimulate an interest in further study, and a move toward moral autonomy. An important facet of this book rests in the foundation it lays for the moral decision-making process in a First Amendment society, one that tolerates both painful disclosures of information and vigorous persuasion as a means of preserving a dynamic social system. To this end, a significant portion of the book is devoted to describing the dynamics of a social system based on the accumulation of power and a media system that should be dedicated to assuring that inordinate power does not accumulate and concentrate. These are topics one must understand in order to make ethical decisions and persuade others as to the validity of the decisions one makes.

This book does not prescribe courses of action, nor does it answer every ethics question that is likely to arise. It does, however, provide a foundation that will help a thoughtful communicator to make an informed decision.

This text provides a balance of ethical discussion and cases across mass media disciplines: journalism, advertising, and public relations. It offers the historical and social contexts for media professionals and media consumers to make solid ethical choices. The complexities of ethical decision making are highlighted, and a foundation in ethics and media allows the reader to reason, discern, and ultimately choose courses of action based on principles that are the foundations of free speech and an open information society. This text specifically explores the ethical differences, and justifications, for the information communicator (the journalist) and the persuasive communicator (the public relations and advertising professional), with attention to the unique roles and vastly different moral mandates for each area. Because of these differences, particular emphasis is placed in this text on the function of the professional communicator that requires a unique morality. So important are these concepts, the reader may find some redundancies as they are explained and illustrated. Some onlookers may find some concepts morally offensive, and difficult to understand. Yet, it is a moral structure that appears to be not only consistent with the expectations of a society that adheres to First Amendment principles, but is morally mandated for the best interests and development of that society. Professional communicators will find they occupy a unique societal position. They are morally expected to deliver on the promises of a free speech culture, yet there are no guarantees that free speech can produce these expected benefits.

PLAN OF THE BOOK

Chapter 1 ("Basic Ethics for Media Professionals") covers basic ethics. This material can be applied to specific media issues throughout the text. Included are definitions of morality and ethics plus five systems often employed for rationally justifying ethical decisions. These five systems—duty, utility, rights, virtue, and relationship ethics—are integrated throughout the text to aid the reader in making ethical decisions based on moral reasoning. The chapter ends with a description of relativism.

Chapter 2 ("Moral Obligations of the Individual Media Professional") discusses media ethics as a system that can be individualistic and designed to minimize the number of laws and regulations. By advancing the notion that rules should be questioned, the chapter also outlines a system for long-term, individual decision making in media known as the Beacon on the Hill. Individuals help determine what is harmful and what is acceptable. A well-defined personal moral theory based on sound ethical reasoning prevents individuals from blindly following the status quo.

Chapter 3 ("The Powerful Impact of Information") examines the power of communication and the ethical obligations associated with this power. If a reporter uses media power to invade an individual's privacy, gain information about a problem of importance to an audience, and then publish that information, the reporter may harm the individual but will have used power wisely to inform. When one distorts or lies about either professional or personal matters, one seriously abuses the power of communication and often fails to understand the long-term consequences of one's action. Short-term thinking involving deception can harm personal, professional, and even community relationships. Should media publish information that may shock or alter the views of a community, or should media professionals only publish information that supports the views of a community? Other uses of power in media professions are examined in terms of privacy and the importance of information.

Chapter 4 ("The Politics of Media Decisions: Who Wins—The Individual or the Community?") discusses ethics as part of a complex political system known as communitarianism and liberalism. These two systems have been operational in mass media since the first days of newspapers. The conflict between these two factions continues today in media struggle between community interests and individual rights and privileges.

Chapter 5 ("Public Perception of Media Decisions") addresses practical ethical issues faced by the individual and the community. The focus is on relationships with the community that emphasize truth, loyalty, education, and competence. Throughout this chapter, the reader is reminded of the need to develop individual moral reasoning abilities, and it is suggested that truthfulness is always an important virtue for communicators. This chapter also covers the effects of community attitudes toward media coverage.

Chapters 6 and 7 move into specific areas of media. **Chapter 6** ("Journalism Ethics") details print and broadcast journalism ethics, while Chapter 7 provides an in-depth look at the ethics of public relations and advertising. Chapter 6 discusses social responsibility in journalism with a specific and vital emphasis on the privilege granted to journalists by the First Amendment. In addition, this chapter offers significant coverage of deception, privacy, and diversity.

Chapter 7 ("Advertising and Public Relations: Ethical Persuasion") embraces the understanding that advertising and public relations—the persuasion crafts—are honorable professions and should always remain so through the use of ethical persuasion. This chapter addresses issues of loyalty, truth, the impact of lying, competition, and acceptable practices in the field of persuasion.

Finally, this text culminates with a look at the history and the future of media ethics. **Chapter 8** ("The History and Future of Media Ethics") provides an understanding of the underpinnings of First Amendment concepts and also analyzes the foundation for education in media and media ethics. This historical context arms the reader with a broader base from which to learn about the impact of ethical decisions in media. Many professional communicators have been punished for their ethical decisions, and many communicators have made money at the expense of the profession and of society. The chapter moves from the historical descriptions of libel and press freedoms to the current scholarship in ethics for communicators. The chapter ends with a view of future by discussing issues of cyberspace for professional communicators and media consumers.

FEATURES

The purposes and themes of this text are addressed not only in the narrative but in the features and pedagogy. These features provide added depth and require the reader to actively engage in moral reasoning and ethical decision making. These are unique features in a media ethics text. Making use of them will enhance the reader's ability to engage in thoughtful ethical choices related to media issues.

Moral Reasoning Questions.   Each chapter ends with several moral reasoning questions that motivate the reader to think critically about concepts presented in the chapter. These questions emphasize the theme of moral reasoning throughout the text.

Contemporary and Classic Cases.   There are over 60 contemporary and classic cases in the text. The cases cover realistic dilemmas for the reader to discuss and work through. Each chapter opens with a case that is particularly pertinent to the theme of the chapter. Additional cases appear throughout each chapter and at the end of each chapter. End-of-chapter cases are supplemented with several questions to stimulate the reader's thinking. The contemporary cases address current media ethics issues; the classic cases present groundbreaking issues in media ethics and are an essential perspective. Cases represent the media disciplines of print and broadcast journalism, public relations, and advertising.

Checklists for Ethical Decision Making.   These checklists, approximately one per chapter, are not prescriptive but offer a focused list of questions that offer significant support for the reader in making ethical media decisions.

Summary.   The chapter summary includes major concepts covered in the chapter.

Selected Sources.   A list of selected sources at the end of each chapter provides further reading for those so inclined or may be helpful for instructors who wish to provide assigned readings to students seeking a greater depth of exposure to the concepts.

Glossary.   The Glossary contains definitions of key terms that are bold-faced in the text.

Appendix: Selected Codes of Ethics in Mass Media.   The Appendix contains complete codes of ethics for many of the mass media associations.

Web Sites for Ethics in Journalism, Public Relations, and Advertising.   This end-of-book resource lists numerous web sites, including ACLU cyberliberties, Codes of Ethics online, plus sites in journalism, public relations, advertising, race, and cultural diversity.

ACKNOWLEDGMENTS

Grateful appreciation is extended to colleagues, friends, and family for the help they have provided on this book over years of discussion and challenges to its concepts. A special thanks to Ann Greenberger, our developmental editor and a patient friend. Thanks to careful reviewers for their time and energy devoted to this work: Louise W. Hermanson, Jay Black, Lynn Disbrow, Gilda Parrella, and Beth Hindman. For editing and other support we thank Steven Carter, Harriet Eliason, Robert C. Solomon, David Keller, Laura Hamblin, Nancy Rushforth, Kirk Englehardt, Deb Thornton, John Turbyfill, Donald Schmeltekopf, Jim Anderson, Scott Abbott, Kellie Englehardt, Sam Rushforth, and Brian Birch. Elaine thanks Utah Valley State College administrators and friends Kerry Romesburg, Lucille Stoddard, Jennifer Howard, Jans Wager, Melanie Hubbard, Ben Rose, Jim Harris, Eugene England, and J. D. Davidson. A special tribute to two women who continue to influence our lives: Ralph's mother Norma Barney at 92 years of age and Elaine's grandmother Cleo Hinckley at 110 years of age.

TABLE OF CONTENTS

1

BASIC ETHICS FOR MEDIA PROFESSIONALS

CLASSIC CASE IN PUBLIC RELATIONS: A MORAL CHOICE FOR THE WHITE HOUSE PRESS SECRETARY

Jerry terHorst recounts his toughest ethical dilemma in his book Gerald Ford and the Future of the Presidency. *As White House press secretary, terHorst held the top public relations spot in the country. Only 30 days into the job, he learned that in only hours President Ford would pardon former President Nixon. He handed President Ford his letter of resignation an hour before Ford met with the press regarding the pardon proclamation. In terHorst's letter, he states that "It is with great regret, after long soul-searching, that I must inform you I cannot in good conscience support your decision to pardon former President Nixon even before he has been charged with the commission of any crime. . . . I do not know how I could credibly defend that action in the absence of a like decision to grant absolute pardon to the young men who evaded Vietnam service as a matter of conscience and the absence of pardons for former aides and associates of Mr. Nixon who have been charged with crimes—and imprisoned—stemming from the same Watergate situation (p. 236)."*

At the subsequent news conference, reporters posed some interesting questions to President Ford, according to terHorst. Godfrey Sperling of *The Christian Science Monitor* asked if Ford would write a **code of ethics** for the executive branch as a way to prevent future Watergates. Ford stated that "The code of ethics that will be followed will be the example that I set (p. 191)."

terHorst noted that the pardon met all legal and constitutional requirements but that it did not pass his own ethics litmus test. He explained that he resigned from the prestigious and important position because he could not be part of an act he thought was ethically wrong. "My beliefs about the justice system are too central to my ethical value system to compromise," he said (terHorst, 1989).

terHorst's position as a high-level public relations professional was to support the views of the President and to present these views to the public. In the case of the Nixon pardon, terHorst had such strong personal feelings against it that he decided to resign rather than remain in a position in which he would be asked to condone something that was contrary to his personal moral beliefs.

What Is Ethical Decision Making?

Like terHorst, we all will make difficult ethical decisions; unlike terHorst, most of them will not be nearly as public. When called upon to make these decisions within a deadline spanning only a few minutes or a few hours, how do we know we will make the correct decision? Would a professional code of ethics help us to understand what is morally acceptable? Could another professional in the field help us to better understand the complexity of our own decision?

Justifying Our Choices

If our decision is thoughtful one, we should be able to spell out the reasons for our action, as terHorst has done in his book. Is there a rule book that spells out what terHorst should have done? Certainly, there was no code of ethics to help terHorst make his decision, and there was little time to consult other professionals. terHorst had to make his decision based on his personal **ethics** system. It was a system he knew intimately, and he implemented its principles in making one of the most important decisions of his life. He left the most visible public relations job in the country. In doing so, he appeared to publicly betray a client, President Ford, because of his own beliefs—an action approaching cardinal sin for a public relations professional.

Understanding Ethical Decision Making: Rules Vs. Principles

How are ethical decisions made? The above case is meant to demonstrate that ethical decisions can be made in at least two ways:

- On the basis of **rules**—prescribed by tradition or authority.
- On the basis of the thoughtful application of **principles** and through reason.

Individuals from each camp may disagree with the other's method of decision making or may not understand the way others function in the moral decision-making arena. If we follow rules—even if earlier evaluations have found them valid—the decision is still being made for us, and we only need endorse it with our actions. In a rules scenario, no thoughtful approach is necessary when an individual is subjected to the stress of newsroom deadlines. In this instance, moral decisions are ratifications of someone else's rules, no matter how good they are. These rules may not be appropriate for the situation when we make the decision, but the rule-following approach, at least emotionally, is a favorite choice because it assigns responsibility to others, simplifies decisions made under stress, and frees us from the consequence of blame.

LEARNING THE BENEFITS OF ETHICAL DECISION MAKING

If, on the other hand, we make decisions based on the situation before us and with extensive knowledge of the consequences of our actions as well as the benefits to others, we are more likely to be acting as **autonomous moral agents**, determining for ourselves what is right and what is wrong in our professional lives. If our decisions tend to follow rules and the authority of others, it is likely that little ethical instruction is necessary, since others tend to be doing our thinking for us and directing our actions, whether those others are our supervisors or the generations of professionals that have preceded us. Rapidly changing circumstances, on the other hand, suggest that professional communicators and society in general are best served by developing their own **moral reasoning** mechanisms and accepting responsibility for their own actions.

Communication Pressures and Ethics

This book looks at ethics from a practical, applied perspective, examining it in such a way that readers may see the relationship of the concepts to both their personal and professional lives. A society loath to make rules, one that thrives on a minimum of moral or legal restraints, expects its people to act well in order to avoid the inevitable imposition of rules to maintain **social order**.

Communication professionals have a great stake in this, particularly since the current social revolution is an information revolution. Communication professionals are the beneficiaries of an extreme view about freedom—including the view that speech ought be regulated only to the bare minimum required to maintain the peace and good order of society. Hence, journalists, broadcasters, professional persuaders (in advertising and public relations), and even those who use the new electronic technology of the Internet or cyberspace are under increased moral pressure to act well as they wield their inordinate power to control the media through which information flows. Their approach to the use of this power is especially important since they are specifically exempt from formal regulation. The First Amendment generally prohibits regulation of speech and press, which precludes licensing and the adoption of enforceable codes of ethics.

Great Power With Minimum Restraint

The media, especially cyberspace, embodies the worst nightmare come true of the compulsively orderly person: great power with minimum restraint. Beyond that, fear is widespread that the communicator will somehow manage to exploit audiences by using both those advantages and some "superior" ability to manipulate. Therefore, communicators are the subject of intense efforts to apply informal restrictions that result in self-censorship or under pressure to accept external, albeit informal, restrictions on their activities.

Clearly, professional communicators must resist succumbing to outside pressures by thoroughly understanding their roles in making thoughtful, ethical decisions. Paradoxically, professional communicators must use their freedom and individuality to distribute information that will serve the overall and long-term interests of the community, even if the vocal community appears disturbed about the short-term effects of the information.

Accepting Responsibility for Professional Moral Actions

This book intends to be an instruction manual for the development of moral agency and for helping individuals accept responsibility for their professional actions. It is based on two premises:

◆ A changing and increasingly complex world requires thoughtful people to minimize harm.

♦ Professional communicators have an extremely critical role in preserving a democratic society and therefore must not yield their autonomy to examine and act on moral dilemmas.

Indeed, the argument for communicators maintaining moral autonomy is made compelling by the rights granted to them in the First Amendment. However, when some communication professionals unthinkingly follow conventions, rules, or orders, they actually give up their First Amendment freedoms. In order for the First Amendment to be a valid protection of free speech, its defenders must themselves accept responsibility for the effects of their actions, rather than shift responsibility to others.

RESPONDING TO SELFISHNESS IN SOCIETY

CONTEMPORARY CASE IN PUBLIC RELATIONS: KATHY LEE AND CLOTHING

Kathy Lee Gifford stirred public outrage when she was forced to defend her endorsement of "sweatshop" clothing sold in her name by Wal-Mart stores. Many critics charged that it was unacceptable to endorse or purchase clothing manufactured under conditions in which workers cannot earn a living wage by American standards. Is it acceptable to support the exploitation of workers so the rest of us can have beautiful clothing at reasonable prices?

The dilemma posed by the Gifford case shows why ethics is a suitable arena for serious study. It is a classic case of virtues in competition. Pursuit of our own individual dreams, including affordable clothing, is an integral part of the American dream of life, liberty, and the pursuit of happiness. However, dignity in the workplace and the need to earn a living wage is also a laudable goal for people in developing countries. In a land of personal freedom, there must be some way in which we can organize ourselves so we can live together with the assurance of optimal, individual liberties.

The law provides a first level of assurance of basic protection, defining generally what others may not do to us. Ethics provides the second and, arguably, the most important level of assurance because it helps determine what individuals do *not* do while exercising whatever power they possess over others, whether it be lying about colleagues or profiting from unreasonably low wages paid to workers. When the law fails to protect, it is ethics that supplants the blind, selfish exercise of power with the reasoned decision making of those with power who sacrifice it in order not to victimize the powerless. In an ideal world, Kathy Lee would relinquish some of her profits to improve the standard of living of the workers manufacturing her garments.

Ethics instruction, particularly in the mass media industry, has the capability of bringing the ideal world of optimal self-determination somewhat closer to realization. Many personal protections, at least in the United States, are embodied in social and cultural "rules" that have emerged over the ages—rules that create some degree of social order by telling us how to behave toward others. For the individual exercising power, these rules reduce personal confusion over what the right thing is to do. Humans organize themselves in the ethical and moral arena without benefit of law, and it is in this arena that humans refine the protection of the powerless and help the powerful to act well. It is not a given, however, that any system will produce the desired results, culture, and moral behavior.

In the arena of unlimited individual autonomy, behaviors tend to be fairly fluid, changing with conditions and continually modified by way of trial and error. The problem is as old as human communities in which people have tried to learn to live with each other. Social organization in the United States today is the product of thousands of years of evolving civilization and more than two hundred years of trial and error. In today's media culture, we are blending law with **morality** in a democratic structure.

UNDERSTANDING THE TENDENCY TO INFLICT HARM

Formally, ethics is often defined using two fundamental, distinguishing characteristics: harm and mutual aid. Most individuals have a basic and universal aversion to harm—physical and psychological. Nobody wants to be harmed in a physical or interpersonal arena or submit to harm without consent. We need to acknowledge as a given that individuals do not want to be harmed (without consent), as well as acknowledge as a given that most, if not all, humans, particularly those in the media industries, are inclined to inflict harm on others without their consent. These coexisting realities—the universal human aversion to harm and a universal tendency to inflict harm—are the conditions that make the study of ethics necessary. Media professionals will find these clashing realities constant in their ethical decision making. For example, will a journalist's story about a politician propositioning a vice-squad member ruin the politician's career? Should the constituents of the politician know of the illegal misdeed? Should the story be buried so that the status quo can be maintained (and the power of the political leader protected)?

Developing a System of Guidance

CONTEMPORARY CASE IN MEDIA: TRASH TV

Daytime television talk shows can push the limits of social decency. It is easy to find several talk shows per day that feature guests who discuss intimate details of their lives on topics such as lying, cheating, and adultery. The person who could be most injured by this information is invited (often unsuspectingly) to appear along with the featured guest. Viewers watch the eyes and face of the injured party, while the guest is encouraged to describe any number of horrors of infidelity and weakness.

Some talk show producers have been prosecuted for their programming choices. Warner Brothers, the parent corporation of The Jenny Jones Show, *was found negligent in the killing of a guest and ordered to pay $25 million in damages plus burial costs. The case originated when Jenny Jones invited Jonathan Schmitz and Scott Amedure to appear on a program about sexual fantasy. Amedure confessed to having a same-sex crush on Schmitz. Three days later, Schmitz went to Amedure's home with a shotgun and fired two fatal shots. There were two subsequent trials, and Schmitz was found guilty of second-degree murder. Warner Brothers plans to appeal the verdict.*

Perhaps Amedure had a right to consent to baring his personal life before a national television audience, and perhaps the Jenny Jones producers could justify holding the guest up to a public examination to which he had consented, but when Schmitz was folded into the mix, apparently without his consent (and perhaps under false pretenses), *The Jenny Jones Show* and Amedure joined to inflict grievous harm (public humiliation of Schmitz) for their own benefit (personal publicity for Amedure and greater audience attraction, hence greater profits, for *The Jenny Jones Show*). On the face of it, these actions violate a basic premise of moral behavior—do no unnecessary harm.

Ethics is a system of guidance designed to assist in living within a society. A primary goal of ethics is to establish appropriate constraints on our own behavior, constraints that would lead the Jenny Jones producers to resist the cheap profit that comes from humiliating a hapless guest. Owing to a diversity of relations and relationships, we are asked to curb our inclination to do many things just because they please us. These constraints are necessary because we have conflicting interests and selfish desires that can lead to harm to ourselves and others. We are social animals, and our species would not survive if each of us lived in isolation. That we must live together triggers the positive requirement of doing good for one another. We would not need ethical guidelines if people lived together peaceably and in mutual support without harming one another. The fact that we do not so live is the major condition requiring ethics.

Ethics continually represents the tension between the individual and others. Ethics is not *just* a code for individual behavior. It is a social enterprise that consists of a system of rules, ideals, and sanctions that facilitate the basic social functions of accord and cooperation. We expect each of the social organizations to which we belong, including our media organizations, to function in ethically appropriate ways. We expect ethical behavior to be practiced by those who are members. Most individuals would feel uncomfortable if asked by a superior to perform an unethical act. Earlier, it was pointed out that Jerry terHorst was so uncomfortable with having to defend the pardoning of Nixon by the President of the United States of America that he resigned as White House press secretary. Jenny Jones, on the other hand. . .

Using Reason as a Guide to Truth

An important component in the definition of ethics concerns the concept of rational justification. Ethics falls within the discipline of **philosophy;** as such, work in the field of ethics rests ultimately on reason and its power to justify beliefs and actions. Ethicists generally hold that while reason is not the only guide to truth, it provides the best direction. Ethics involves our analysis of and reflection on moral choices and judgments. Other guides to truth may involve religion, intuition, or advice from trusted others.

However, within the study of ethics and professional media ethics, each of us must accept the difficult challenge of rationally defending our choices and actions. We often need to explain our decisions; "because it feels right" is not an appropriate justification. It is hard work to understand ourselves and to examine how our decisions and actions affect others. It is important to understand the Socratic dictum that an unconsidered life is not worth living. We must carefully consider our lives and the effect our interactions have on others.

CONSEQUENTIALISM AND NONCONSEQUENTIALISM

Consequentialism and nonconsequentialism are two major distinguishing elements of ethics. Making decisions based on long-term results or consequence of an action falls into the first category. Most of the ethicists discussed in the next section are consequentialists. To illustrate consequentialism, consider the case of Sam, who promises not to reveal a source for a story but changes his mind when his editor threatens to kill the story. Sam has made a consequential decision by revealing his source rather than binding himself to the tradition that a reporter never identifies a confidential source. He may not realize it now, but for a short-term gain (publication of the story), Sam has harmed his source and himself. In the future, it is likely this source will not trust him with further information for stories. Sam's reputation may suffer among other professionals and sources as well. He will suffer consequences for his decision.

Making a nonconsequential decision is discussed at length in the next section. Nonconsequentialism entails making a decision based on duty, or the right action, rather than on the consequences of that decision. Using a nonconsequential system of ethics, Sam would not have revealed his source; he promised not to reveal the source if given the information, and one must keep one's word.

FIVE SYSTEMS FOR MAKING ETHICAL DECISIONS

There are five common systems of ethics that seem to encompass and explain many ethical decision-making mechanisms. Each of these systems seeks to lay out foundations for what it means to act morally. The five systems we will explore are:

- ◆ Duty
- ◆ Utility
- ◆ Rights
- ◆ Virtue
- ◆ Relationships

These five systems for ethical decision making certainly do not cover all cases, they are not flawless, and each has shortcomings in its application to specific situations. Therefore, it should not be surprising that decisions based on one system will be at odds with decisions based on another and that working ethical questions through different systems will produce very different conclusions. It is likely that each of us, in analyzing our own inclinations, will relate more comfortably to one or two of these systems than to the others. Nevertheless, it is important to consider each system and to understand the similarities and differences among them as we develop our own mechanisms for making reasoned ethics decisions, both personally and professionally. We do this by challenging the mechanisms we already have in place and either changing our views or confirming their validity. This chapter helps identify and define these systems and will act as a guide throughout the rest of the book.

DUTY: WHAT IS MY DUTY?

The first system, duty, requires rule-based behavior. Certainly, before moral rules are established within a society, culture, or organization, the reasonableness of the rule or principle must be tested. For this rule to become a **duty,** we

TABLE 1.1 **Five Systems of Ethics**

	DUTIES	RIGHTS	UTILITY	VIRTUES	RELATIONSHIPS
Terms	Obligation of individual to moral rules	Obligation of community to individual	Obligation to maximize happiness	Obligation to self and community	Obligation to the relationship
Basis	Based on universal, self-evident requirements	Based on universal, self-evident prerogatives of the individual	Based on consequences of action	Based on integrity of character	Based on the social practices of care
Action	Moral action discharges duty	Moral action preserves individual rights	Moral action produces favorable consequences	Moral action improves the individual & state	Moral action produces caring relationships

Thanks to James A. Anderson for his help in constructing this chart (2001).

must understand this principle as a rational and genuine moral principle that must apply no matter what we want. The rule must be independent of our desires, and its appeal can only be that of reason itself. We learn about ethical duty from various sources, including philosophers, religions, parents, and social systems. All of these sources inform us about which actions are morally obligatory, that is, those actions we have a duty to perform.

There are several ethics systems that borrow from the duty system of ethics, but the two most important are divine command ethics, and deontology or nonconsequential ethics.

Divine Command

Divine command is a system that establishes duties for us. It is made up of those obligations pressed on us by our religious beliefs. An example of this is the Judeo-Christian doctrine of the Ten Commandments, which followers have an obligation to obey because God said they have a duty to do so unconditionally. This is known as a divine command ethics system. As with most duties, punishments and rewards are promised in this ethics system, which are generally, but not always, related to the hereafter.

Not all divine command theories trust universal rules to portray the moral truth accurately. For some thinkers, ethical truth also depends on the details of individual situations. The mysticism (personal religious experience) of Islamic Sufism, for example, which began in the late-seventh and eighth centuries, was criticized by those who feared that the Sufis' concern for personal experiential knowledge of God could lead to neglect of established religious observances. Sufis believe that we have duties that must be performed regardless of consequences and that moral knowledge results from special insights granted by analysis of their application in particular situations. A rule is not enough; one must also know its application.

Nevertheless, divine command ethics systems tend to allow, on their face, little leeway for individual variations by declaring that the duties imposed are God's commands and that violations will be punished or rewards withheld by that God. If one wants to be an obedient child, one accepts the duty to obey the commandments.

Deontology

Very different from the duty-based divine command ethics system, nonconsequentialism or **deontology** is an ethics system that is still concerned with duty but approaches it from a different perspective. The following example may help us understand the type of decision a deontologist would make:

Contemporary Case in Public Relations: The Political Bait and Switch

Kellie is a senior staff member with a major Chicago public relations firm. As part of this staff, she put together a client proposal for a two-term member of congress, Sue Sorensen. The firm is awarded the account, but now Kellie and all other members of the senior staff are put on an assignment for a major contractor in the area. Kellie believes that the firm has deceived Congresswoman Sorensen by having the senior staff put together the client proposal and then giving the actual work to some very junior members of the firm. The company has in the past used this "bait-and-switch" technique, much to Kellie's dismay. On the other hand, Kellie doesn't particularly care for the Congresswoman's brand of politics. What are Kellie's options? Which choice might be most in keeping with a nonconsequential or deontological choice?

1. *She should go along with the decision made by management, reasoning that everybody does it.*
2. *She should feel secret pleasure that the junior staff probably will not have the same type of creativity or impact as experienced senior staff, and that this person will not be reelected.*
3. *She should contact Congresswoman Sorensen behind the scenes and let her know about the "bait and switch."*
4. *Even if it jeopardizes her job, she should insist that the CEO stop this type of deceptive activity and place a senior staff member on the account.*

Kant and Deontology

The last course of action is most clearly in line with the philosophy of Immanuel Kant (1724–1804), a German philosopher who is best known for defining duty ethics through a system of thought known as deontology. He believes moral choices should be based on duty or on what one ought to do because one has a duty to humanity to do so. Kant states that we do something because it is the right thing to do, not because it appears the consequences will be favorable. One makes a choice and follows through with an action out of a moral sense of duty. Kant made a long list of duties, such as to never lie, to help others, to develop talents, and to avoid hurting others or ourselves.

He furthered this concept of duty with his notion of a Good Will, which consists of the will to do one's duty for its own sake, simply because it is one's duty. Good Will, or a sense of duty, is the only thing Kant praised as good in and of itself, independent of its consequences. Within the notion of a Good Will, an action only has moral worth if it is done out of duty, no matter what one's natural inclinations might be.

CATEGORICAL IMPERATIVE   In order to help us understand duty, Kant stated his theory in terms of what he called the **categorical imperative.** As part of this imperative he designated three duties:

1. Act on universal principles;
2. Treat individuals as an end in and of themselves—never as a means;
3. Act so as to regard oneself as being the author of or a member legislating the moral law (1785/1988, p. 7).

ACT ON UNIVERSAL PRINCIPLES   In analyzing the first concept, how does one act on universal principles? Kant is not concerned with consequences. He sought to find universal laws in morality by insisting that if a course of action were right for one, it had to be right for all. In the above "bait-and-switch" case, Kellie thinks of several options in settling the politician's account. Kellie has seen this practice with several firms, including her own, but she has always believed that it was a deceptive practice and that deception is not right. Further, Kellie does not want this politician to win the election, but she knows that her personal political views should not be part of a decision that criticizes the honesty and fairness of the practices of her firm. The long-term consequences are not the issue. Kellie does not believe that the client should be used as a means to merely making money, but she does believe that the firm should truthfully explain to the client who will and will not be working on her campaign. From this information, Kellie will determine whether she would like to remain with the firm. Kellie does not believe that she would do business with a firm that she knew deceived its clients through "bait-and-switch" methods; she could not universalize this practice.

NEVER MERELY AS THE MEANS TO AN END   The second major focus of the Categorical Imperative is to respect all persons and treat them as ends in and of themselves rather than as merely the means to our ends. This relates to human rights as well as duty in asking us to treat others equally and fairly. If the mass media treat audience members as simply necessary for profit making rather than as autonomous individuals, then the mass media would be using audience members as a means to an end.

Contemporary Case in Journalism:
Media Analysis of TV Talk Shows

If simplistic attack-counterattack television talk shows obscure the issues they ostensibly clarify for their audiences, they may be treating those audiences as means rather than ends. Audience members viewing a show promising to discuss an important issue or problem deserve to be treated as autonomous human beings and should emerge from their viewing with enhanced knowledge of the issue and a greater understanding of the social context in which that issue is being framed; they should not come away with little more knowledge than they had going in. When the chief product of an informational issues show is entertainment (sharp, emotional conflict and simplistic exchanges between participants) and not information, then these shows have not fulfilled their stated objective in that they have also failed to enhance the viewer's ability to participate meaningfully in the national decision-making process.

It may be that viewers are more knowledgeable at the conclusion of this type of program despite the poverty of content if the program is the sole contributor to the viewer's fund of information on the topic. Nevertheless, if networks and stations air these shows primarily to attract large numbers of uncritical viewers, then they are using those viewers as means to their own ends.

Kant might tell a talk-show producer, for example, that the moral law implicit within First Amendment protections of the media requires that issues-oriented talk shows place a top priority on making better social participants of their viewers. The challenge is to make the show so valuable to audiences that they will watch to learn. Staging a spectacular that will simply attract more viewers is a way of using audience members as means to the producer's end. If the audience members are better informed as a consequence, that result is secondary to the purpose of enhancing income and therefore difficult to defend in the Kantian view.

Testing the legitimacy of our duties in a free society, particularly for professional communicators, is always a problem, since competing forces have been operative all our lives persuading us as to the nature of our duties. In a free country in which legal restrictions on individuals and media are often unconstitutional, the option for leaders of all sorts (from corporate supervisors to parents) is to encourage us to practice desired behavior by framing such behavior as duty. "Do it this way because that's the way it's always been done" is a particularly common way of framing desired behavior as duty and especially troubling when encountered in the media professions.

Kant believed that everyone must have autonomy. For Kant it is unacceptable to treat individuals as objects (audiences from which a profit may be made) while disregarding the basic elements of humanity (providing at a minimum the promised service and preferably a service that exceeds the promise). There are moral constraints on how we may behave toward others, and Kant's second principle of duty is a reminder of this.

LEGISLATING MEMBER OF MORAL LAW   In the third component of his Categorical Imperative, Kant explains that we should act in such a way that we can regard ourselves as being the author of or a member legislating the moral law. Reason, he stated, is the same in all of us; hence, we will be authors of the same laws and subject to the same laws. Kant does not intend that each individual should create or invent his or her own particular morality. Conversely, it is the moral law that is universalizable. Thus, since we are each legislating members of the "kingdom of ends," Kant believes that each of us is the author of the moral law and that we make our contribution by adherence to the law. The moral law must be such that it could be legislated as the universal law for all rational beings. The ideal behind this concept is a community in which all live as moral equals.

LYING AND DECEPTION AS IMMORAL   Lying and **deception** are important topics for Kant, who believed we should universally accept the directive "do not lie." This principle is easy to accept, since most of us would prefer to live in a world based on truth telling and honesty. We certainly are unlikely to seek a world in which everyone is allowed to deceive or lie for his or her own advantage. Most relationships would disintegrate if those involved could deceive or lie whenever it seemed advantageous.

It is easy to see that most of our daily interactions would be fraught with suspicion and doubt if anyone could lie or deceive whenever an advantage could be gained. Many people may do this today, but it is still frowned on, and the social damage is easily recognized. To sanction lying results in chaos; when we cannot tell fact from fiction, both truthful and untruthful statements become unbelievable.

In the **communication** field, lies or dishonest acts, when they are discovered, result in suspicion and loss of credibility, which is the essential asset of any communicator. In the case of Jerry terHorst, because he believed President Ford's pardon of President Nixon was dishonest, he further believed that his credibility as a communicator would be compromised if he kept his post as Ford's press secretary.

Kant was an Enlightenment philosopher with a religious background, but his objective was to theorize about how individuals could make decisions without relying on religion. He believed one should not base decisions on the commands of a religious leader. Instead, an individual should engage in an action because that is the action in which one ought to engage—there is a duty to do so. Kant's theory is not concerned with consequences. If you go along with the firm's decision to engage in "bait and switch" on the Congresswoman's account, you may make more money, but you will not be acting in accordance with Kant's Categorical Imperative. His theory asserts that we make an ethical decision based on a sense of duty and a reverence for moral law.

Utilitarianism: What Are the Consequences?

Moral theories generally differ on issues they view as fundamental as well as on the kinds of considerations necessary to address those issues. Some theories are termed consequentialist, attaching value to the act's consequences. **Utilitarianism** is a brand of consequentialism that declares that an action, intention, or principle should be judged by the overall immediate outcomes. In other words, something is good if and only if it has, or tends to have, good effects. Happiness, for example, would be the end result of good consequences, while unhappiness would be the end result of bad consequences. The decision by Jerry terHorst to resign as White House press secretary can be analyzed from a utilitarian perspective.

CLASSIC CASE IN PUBLIC RELATIONS: THE RESPONSE TO THE PRESS SECRETARY'S RESIGNATION

Public reactions to Ford's pardon of Nixon were negative. Immediately, phone calls and wires were received by the White House. They were eight to one in opposing the pardon. The reactions to terHorst's decision were positive. He received phone calls, wires, and letters from people in every state of the union supporting his decision. Additionally, the Society of Magazine Writers awarded terHorst its first "Conscience in Media" medal for his "Exemplary display of conscience and courage in resigning a highly-coveted position which he felt conflicted with his integrity as a journalist."

In this context, a consequentialist could argue that terHorst made a good decision. terHorst took a very public stand against a pardon he believed to be unethical and perhaps even illegal. He believed that everyone should be treated similarly under the system of justice in this country and that Nixon should not have been given a preferential privilege. terHorst also believed that he made the correct choice; in the long run, many members of the public lauded him as a hero. He received praise as a consequence of his action. In accordance with the "Greatest Happiness Principle," his action brought more happiness than pain to himself and others. In addition, he set an important example in ethics and decision making for future White House press secretaries. It is also important to note the consequences to Gerald Ford. terHorst's decision was decidedly upsetting and difficult for the incoming President. It happened at a time when Ford needed to establish trust and credibility with the American people. terHorst's actions did not facilitate this need.

Greater Pleasure and Less Pain

Jeremy Bentham (1748–1832) and John Stuart Mill (1806–1873) stated that the good can be seen in terms of the presence of pleasure and the absence of pain—both consequences of actions. They held that we should always maximize good, or, in other words, that a moral action is one that produces the greatest good for the greatest number of individuals. As in other consequentialist theories, utilitarianism rests on an independent characterization of good results.

Bentham defined utilitarianism as that principle which approves or disapproves of every action whatsoever, according to the tendency that it appears to have to augment or diminish the happiness of the party whose interest is in question.

Utilitarian principles focus on the Epicurean ideal of doing that moral act which would bring about the greatest amount of happiness and least amount of pain. Some antagonists who did not understand the writings of Epicurus (342–270 B.C.E.) branded this the pig philosophy in which followers spent their days reveling in the warm mud of sensual pleasure. The life of pleasure for the Epicurean and the utilitarian, however, is actually a life focused on the higher pleasures—the mental pleasures. They emphasize that the lower pleasures are the temporary bodily pleasures and that an ethical/moral life would be one in which the individual pursues those long-term pleasures that can never be taken away, such as improving the intellect.

John Stuart Mill and Civil Liberties

Two thousand years later, John Stuart Mill extended the utilitarian principle to include moral action that brings about the greatest good for the greatest number of people, but he qualified this sweeping statement to rule out doing egregious harm to a few in order that a greater good could be done for the many. Mill's brand of utilitarianism, of course, underlies the principle of "majority rule." Modifying the sweep of majority rule in the United States is the constitutional guarantee of individual rights against which the majority may not trespass.

CONTEMPORARY CASE IN MEDIA: BROADCAST NUDITY

In June of 2000, a television station in London aired a live program featuring full nudity of both men and women. The nudity was not meant to be sexually provocative; it was intended to display the naturalness of no attire. The program, which aired on an independent channel, broke broadcast decency standards set by the BBC, and viewers reacted strongly against the program. The program's producers immediately apologized and promised not to broadcast full nudity again, but the courts will decide if the program will be taken off the air permanently for breach of public trust.

How does this case relate to utilitarianism? Individuals who were part of this program desired to broadcast their entire bodies believing they would be able to make changes in the acceptance of public nudity. The majority, including those governing broadcast regulations, reacted immediately to the breach, demanding an apology and bringing charges against the producers. Many civic battles center on the majority imposing its will on the minority. Minorities, including women and ethnic groups, have won many of these battles in the past quarter-century, but the battles continue, as with this group advocating public nudity. This group will have an uphill battle in working to overcome laws and broadcast regulations that restrict their activities. A primary mission of the American Civil Liberties Union is to protect individual rights from encroachment by majorities, a mission fueled by concerns similar to Mill's utilitarian reservation about the egregious harm that can be done to a few for the benefit of a greater good.

Useless Self-Sacrifice

Mill also advances a controversial view of useless self-sacrifice. In a circumstance in which one is called upon to perform a heroic yet dangerous action, Mill cautions the individual to examine the long-term consequences of a heroic act. He did not believe that one is obligated to perform acts of heroism, particularly if the results would not bring about one's happiness.

CONTEMPORARY CASE IN JOURNALISM: THE WAR CORRESPONDENT

A war correspondent in Angola sees a soldier shot by guerrilla forces. When the correspondent believes it is safe to check on the injuries of the soldier, he approaches him, finds signs of life, and begins administering first aid. At this point, tragically, the correspondent is killed by sniper fire.

This example illustrates the need to survey long-term consequences of an action before pursuing that action. It is also a sad reminder that media representatives should avoid action arenas in a war zone. The act of compassion cost the reporter his life. Applying critical thought before reacting to emergency situations could save lives, even one's own. This is a controversial concept. Many individuals believe only a monster would allow a human to lie dying nearby without administering aid. Mill did not assert that heroic effort is unnecessary, useless, or unethical; but he did theorize that one should understand the circumstances that could result in useless self-sacrifice. A war situation is always teeming with the possibility of being struck down by sniper fire. It is a challenging, difficult assignment and one in which the media employee knows the consequences of becoming actively involved in the conflict. It is unlikely that most media professionals will be placed in life-threatening and/or life-saving circumstances, but considering long-term consequences in advance could save lives or prevent fruitless self-sacrifice.

RIGHTS: WHAT ARE THE RIGHTS OF THE INDIVIDUAL?

In communities in which individualism is prized for its creative contributions, the issue of individual rights is central to the question of progress. Individuals who transgress commonly accepted boundaries of behavior are often punished for their brash behavior. During the Vietnam war, students and other activists vigorously criticized political leaders. Depending on their means of protest, punishments ranging from college expulsion to jail to death were meted out. Other activists have strongly criticized corporations. Ralph Nader, for example, condemned General Motors for its flawed engineering of the Corvair and the company's untenable recall decisions, criticism for which Nader claims to have received numerous threats. Most Americans believe that ethics should take priority over financial gain. General Motors did not break any laws by producing an unsafe vehicle; however, it did break moral and ethical laws. General Motors knew the Corvair would roll when maneuvering a curve over 40 m.p.h., yet they marketed the car as a sports vehicle. Engineers informed executives that the problems could be corrected with a roll bar and other repairs costing less than $40 per vehicle. The decision was made to pay settlement costs for deaths and injuries caused by the Corvair's flawed design rather than recall the vehicle. A similar decision was made by Ford Motor Company with the Pinto and its flawed gas tank design. Did consumers have a right to know about these design flaws before they purchased the vehicles? Should laws dictate that consumers have a right to this information before making a purchase?

The question of rights revolves around the entitlement each of us has to be free of encroachments by others and to pursue our personal goals. This clashes, of course, with the rights of others, most notably the state, which may deny our rights by requiring us to serve the interests of the state—the drafting of males into the military in time of war, for example.

Laws of Nature: The Right to Be Treated as Equals

Thomas Jefferson (1743–1826) wrote in the Declaration of Independence: "We hold these truths to be self-evident, that all men are created equal and that they are endowed by the creator with certain inalienable rights, among which are life, liberty, and the pursuit of happiness." Jefferson drew on the writings of Thomas Hobbes, John Locke, and others who had previously declared that all human beings have the same basic nature and as such deserve be treated as equals.

Hobbes (1588–1679) believed that human beings should be able to establish a social compact in which members of a society agreed to uphold certain practices. These views, based on the egoism of participants, were founded on the belief that individuals would keep social covenants out of a sense of self-preservation. Hobbes believed that individuals should have the rights in society as granted and sustained by the members of that society. Rooted in this notion is the belief that human beings are capable of rational thought; hence, law made by society is natural law. And, since natural laws apply to all human beings and are grounded in human nature, in Hobbes' view, natural law is the moral law. Through social compact, society would be based on "laws of nature." Hobbes also advocated an enforcement system to punish those who do not keep the agreed-upon societal covenants; they were to be banished from society and theoretically forced to live in a state of war. Without such laws, Hobbes concluded, individuals would be doomed to the horrors of war in a "state of nature." Despite his concerns for the betterment of society, Hobbes' most famous statement about humankind is decidedly pessimistic: ". . . and the life of man solitary, poor, nasty, brutish and short."

The Role of the Communication Professional

The issue of rights provides a compelling mandate for professional communicators to distribute information in a manner that brings rights violations into the sunshine of public scrutiny. In this sense, protected by a First

Amendment right to be left alone, communication professionals are the guarantors of individual rights in two crucial ways.

PROVIDING INFORMATION   The first method of guaranteeing individual rights is for professionals to provide the information needed by individuals in society that will enable those individuals to assert their rights through the use of adequate knowledge and to take advantage of opportunities offered by society. There are no social assurances that people will be well informed. At best, the First Amendment assures that people *may* be well informed by an unfettered mass media, but it remains for media workers to uphold that right.

PUBLIC SCRUTINY   The second way communication professionals can be guarantors of individual rights is by acknowledging the value of publicity and being aware that public scrutiny can deter those who seek to infringe on individual rights. The social condition, and participation, of both women and minority groups in this country have changed drastically over the past quarter-century partly because of a robust public media discussion that pricked consciences and stimulated public action to correct decades of rights violations involving these groups. A professional communicator considering his or her work would look to the effects of that work on the rights, and therefore the autonomy, of affected individuals and groups.

Veil of Ignorance: Understanding the Most Disadvantaged Position

The subject of rights ethics has been clarified by contemporary philosopher John Rawls (1921–). Through analysis of rights and duties, Rawls formulated a theory of justice that helps individuals make rational choices by placing each of us, as moral agents, behind a "veil of ignorance" or in the "original position." This is a position in which we have no concept of our past history, present circumstances, or future worth. In this state, moral agents are to determine what basic rights all should have in order to maintain a minimum level of dignity. As a result of this analysis, Rawls believes fairness can be attained.

Contemporary Case in Advertising: Tobacco

An advertising executive has just accepted an account for a major tobacco firm. The executive is to research, design, and prepare a tobacco campaign targeted to sell product in Asian countries. The executive is specifically told that advertisements for all age groups are to be part of this campaign. The successful completion of this account will earn the account executive and the firm an incredible amount of money.

Behind Rawls's **veil of ignorance** this account executive could see himself as a member of this Asian society, perhaps even as a child who is given a free three-week supply of cigarettes. Or this account executive could be an individual already addicted to nicotine, a national congresswoman being lobbied by tobacco interests, or even a tobacco executive.

Behind the veil of ignorance the account executive must place himself in the shoes of all the stakeholders and make the decision on the advertising campaign, knowing the addictive and other health-related harms of cigarette smoking but not knowing who he will be when he steps back into reality. The account executive may become the unsuspecting child, the parents of the child, a congresswoman struggling with tobacco lobbyists, or a tobacco executive who will profit from the campaign.

Rawls argued that we will make a much more solidly based decision if we suspend our present circumstances and are uncertain about our own future. If we understand the most disadvantaged position and work toward equalizing the disadvantages, Rawls theorizes that justice will be better served and our own future generally made more secure.

PRINCIPLES OF JUSTICE   Rawls's two principles of justice, which he states are best served by the veil of ignorance, are as follows:

1. Each person is to have an equal right to the most extensive scheme of basic liberties compatible with a similar scheme of liberties for others.
2. Social and economic inequalities are to be arranged so they are both (a) reasonably expected to be to everyone's advantage, and (b) attached to positions and offices open to all.

Rawls's plan is a concept of justice that provides a reasonably systematic alternative to utilitarianism. He believes the utilitarian doctrine provides a weak basis for constitutional **democracy** and that it cannot provide a satisfactory account of the basic rights and liberties of citizens as free and equal persons. The latter should be a requirement of first importance for democratic institutions.

Contemporary Case in Public Relations: The Gay Employee

After five years with a public relations firm, Maynard announced he is gay. He has a long-term companion, Franklin, who needs the insurance benefits Maynard's company provides to spouses and partners. Many friends are supportive of Maynard. However, some anonymous employees have left rude notes, letters, and other sentiments on his desk, in his voice mail, and in his employee mail box. Maynard has notified the human resources department about the messages, but the staff members tell him that little can be done about the harassment until they catch the individual or individuals perpetrating the problem. Maynard has been complaining to coworkers about the notes in an effort to flush out the notewriter(s). He has set elaborate traps for the perpetrator(s), but has caught no one. Maynard's supervisor has called him in. He states that Maynard's complaints to employees are causing problems. He declares that someone of Maynard's expertise in public relations should not be behaving in this manner. He warns Maynard to get back on track.

Behind Rawls's veil of ignorance, any of us could be Maynard, Franklin, or the employee(s) who are uncomfortable around an openly gay employee. Once we understand Maynard's position, we also understand that leaving rude notes is an unethical action. Maynard has announced his gay relationship in order to provide his partner with basic insurance. He wants Franklin to have the basic economic liberty of insurance. Maynard is now paying the price of harassment by others for insisting that his partner have this liberty.

Rawls's principles of justice argue that every individual should be able to have the basics of life, liberty, and the pursuit of happiness. This could include basic governmental and civic services, such as a public defense, public roads, and governmental organizing systems. He might further argue that everyone has the right to other basic social liberties, such as the dignity and safety of a place to live, food to eat, clothing to wear, educational opportunities, and job opportunities. Many individuals, such as Maynard, would add health care to this list. Others insist that health case is not a basic liberty.

Additionally, Maynard would expect that, behind the veil of ignorance, partner preference would be respected.

Behind the veil of ignorance, should Franklin, as an employee's long-term partner, though not legally a spouse, be denied the privilege of Maynard's health care plan? Should Maynard be harassed because of his committed relationship with Franklin?

VIRTUE: WHAT IS THE MOST VIRTUOUS DECISION?

We can look to ancient Greece to uncover the foundations that promote **virtue** as an ethical reasoning system. The citizens of Athens were far more concerned with the virtues and character of individuals than with an ethic emphasizing rules, principles, or notions. They believed that virtue would produce its own admirable ethic.

A Lifelong Habit

Virtue for the Greeks was not sought and practiced solely to attain individual benefits, such as happiness, integrity, freedom from harm, and honesty; rather, virtue benefitted the individual and society. For example, a Greek citizen was to be honest, not simply because such virtuous behavior is its own reward, but because honesty contributed to an honest society. A citizen was not to be only occasionally virtuous, but was to make virtue a lifelong habit. It would follow, therefore, that a person would not have to debate over whether to be dishonest because honesty would be the natural character trait developed through habit, and the individual would be surrounded by honest citizens in the same honest (virtuous) environment. In this sense, virtue is a rational activity practiced in accordance with a rational principle.

The Great Virtue Ethicists

SOCRATES AND PLATO   The great virtue ethicists were the Athenians Socrates (469–399 B.C.E.), Plato (427–347 B.C.E.), and Aristotle (384–322 B.C.E.). The first of these, Socrates, did not record his lectures and discussions; they come to us from his student, Plato. Socrates was a brilliant thinker and teacher, often living only off gifts from his students. He was accused of impiety and corrupting youth by questioning traditional values and was sentenced to die by drinking poison.

Plato, who was with Socrates through his trial and execution, was the scribe for the dialogues of Socrates. He founded the famous Academy in Athens, where he preserved Socrates' dialogues. Because Plato often used Socrates as a model in his own writings, the mix made it difficult to determine which ideas were Plato's and which were Socrates'.

ARISTOTLE   One of Plato's students was Aristotle, whose influence is acknowledged by philosophers today, and who also developed scientific thinking in physics and other sciences, making wide-ranging contributions beyond the field of ethics. He studied with Plato for 18 years, but they parted company over theory differences, with Aristotle lamenting that "Dear is Plato, but dearer still is truth."

In *Nichomachean Ethics*, Aristotle links virtues to the good of humankind, suggesting that all human activities should aim at happiness, a state with many definitions, such as health, pleasure, wealth, and honor. He believed the ultimate human happiness must come through reason; thus, the best life for a human is a life of reason. His *Nichomachean Ethics* is the first systematic treatment of ethics in Western civilization.

HAPPINESS: A MORALLY VIRTUOUS LIFE   Knowing and following correct principles are not the keys to ethical behavior, according to Aristotle; rather, Aristotle saw right action emerging from living a harmonious life—a life that balances all its aspects. That, he said, is the state of happiness. We live a harmonious life by living virtuously; a morally virtuous life is a happy life. Aristotle begins his ethical inquiry by questioning what it is that people fundamentally desire. He believes that goals such as honor or wealth are inadequate. He states that the ultimate goal must be one that is (a) *self-sufficient* (makes life desirable and lacking in nothing); (b) *final* (always desirable in itself and never for the sake of something else); and (c) *attainable.*

Being virtuous can be difficult, since in a given situation it is difficult to find the midpoint or the "golden mean" of moderate behavior (extremes tend not to be virtuous to Aristotle). It is easy to give and spend money. It is difficult to know the golden mean between miserliness and wastefulness. This is Aristotle's challenge to us—that we find the golden mean in the activities in our lives. Aristotle believed that we must choose this mean (a central position between the extremes) to govern our moral behavior, a central position that *is relative to us*, the situation we are in, and who we are. The mean, in short, depends on the concrete circumstances and the person. It may be acceptable for Jamal to eat four potatoes for lunch, since he is a large athlete with a tough training schedule. It would not be acceptable for his four-year-old daughter to eat four potatoes for lunch. The latter case would be extreme and gluttonous. The golden mean between starving and gluttony for Jamal is particular to Jamal. Application of the golden mean can work in other ethical analyses as well, such as in the following case:

CONTEMPORARY CASE IN PUBLIC RELATIONS: THE GOLDEN MEAN OF WORK

Kerry finally attained the promotion he has been seeking for years in his organization, vice president for public relations and corporate communication. Now that Kerry has this high-paying and prestigious position, he is generally putting in 70 hours per week at the office. He is doing well with his occupation, but his personal life is in shambles; his only quality family time is on weekends, and often he spends his weekends handling corporate emergencies.

Through application of the golden mean, Kerry should see where he needs more moderation in his life. Aristotle would probably advise that friendship and family are important, as are success and making a living. Using the golden mean, friendship and family should not be sacrificed for an overabundant desire for success, status, and perhaps financial gain.

Aristotle would not call living to make money for oneself and the organization a virtuous life. The Aristotelian message also argues for the creation of a community, of both professionals and lay folks at large, in which doing well is such a common event and is so taken for granted by all concerned, that one is reluctant to betray the community by not doing well. Such an environment would, at the very least, cause professional communicators to pause often in their work to seriously assess the impact of their creative efforts on the well being of the community. It would tend to recognize that in a free-enterprise society, for example, vigorous competition is virtuous, but it would also place bounds on those competitive efforts to prevent destructive communications.

Relationships: What Relationships Are Affected?

An emerging theory of ethics based upon caring, sharing, and relationships arises from the work of moral psychologist Carol Gilligan. Relationships theory strongly emphasizes connections between people and groups, rather than autonomy and separation or distancing. Gilligan believes that moral psychology research traditionally has focused on male patterns of distancing, with an emphasis on autonomy equating as adulthood.

Moral Development and Gender Issues

Carol Gilligan claimed that moral psychologists, such as her Harvard University colleague Lawrence Kohlberg, promoted decisions based on individualization as the ultimate determining factor of maturity. Kohlberg's six stages of moral development are based on models of maturity such as autonomy, which diminishes moral development based on the strength of relationships and the caring and sharing that can take place in an environment of mutual needs. According to Gilligan, today's culture and values create discrepancies between womanhood and adulthood. Kohlberg's stages of moral development are discussed more extensively in Chapter 2.

The title of her primary work, *In a Different Voice*, introduces Gilligan's belief that men have historically been the primary and dominant voice in society. She argues that the national conversation changes substantially when women's voices are added. She believes that many of women's strengths—intellect, ability, potency, power, aggression, and even anger—have largely been silent in deference to men and must become a larger part of society's voice and not silenced as in the past.

Problems Created by the Media

The media continue to create and sustain roles for men and women that are based on arbitrary concepts. Media roles depicting women, particularly minority women, are often criticized. In movies, women rarely have roles in which they are portrayed as likable, strong, autonomous, aggressive role models. Instead, the majority of women's roles have been hookers, bar dancers, helpless wives, or part-time workers. *X-Men*, released in 2000, does have several female characters that are as witty, strong, and powerful as the male characters, but the movie's title is still *X-Men*. Men rarely are given roles as nurturing attendants, but are rather given roles in which they are strong, handsome, powerful, rich, and successful. The movie model provides an impossible standard for the "normal" male; it is, nevertheless, a standard toward which to strive.

The Sundance Film Festival is a forum that encourages the production of independent movies with diverse themes. Often independent filmmakers have selected movie themes that advance the interests of women and minorities, many of which, along with the Sundance Film Festival itself, have garnered high acclaim. Increasingly, major actors have been featured in the work of independent filmmakers that push the boundaries of themes in film. Major studios often refuse to produce such films, because they believe that some filmgoers may find them offensive and consequently the studio may not make the profits needed on the film.

Ethics of Caring Through Duty

Fundamental changes are taking place through a current renegotiating of the **social contract** between individuals and their society. These changes have been in process for more than three decades and have particularly impacted the role of women in the media. The ripples of change, however, may soon become evident throughout society.

The male-dominated media, for example, has traditionally flourished in a highly competitive world in which conflict has been the currency of marketable media content, along with a certain amount of callousness toward events. As women emerge in media positions of power, particularly in management, observers are trying to identify any new outlooks women may bring to ethical deliberations. Will women simply adjust to the male conflict/callous world, or will the concept of caring come to the fore in the competitive marketplace?

The emergence of women as participants in the national conversation may mean that more moral choices are made based on an ethic of care. Consider the mother who picks up a crying infant. According to moral psychologist Nel Noddings, this act arises not out of a sense of duty or concern for consequence (two basic ethical theories already discussed), but out of a sense of care based on the relationship between the mother and the child.

Caring requires a response to the initial impulse with an act of commitment: "I commit myself either to overt action on behalf of the cared-for (I pick up the crying baby), or I commit myself to thinking about what I might do. But the test of my caring is not wholly in how things turn out, but in an examination of what I considered, how fully I received the other and whether the free pursuit of his projects is partly a result of the completion of my caring in him" (p. 83).

Noddings believes that genuine moral sentiment arises from an evaluation of the caring relationship. However, she also analyzes the effects of caring for someone who does not appreciate or want the care. The person may have a different ethic of care than that of the caregiver. Noddings believes that the future may permit young boys to develop a strong ethic of care for others and appreciate the care given them by various caregivers (p. 102).

Relationship theorists argue that this emergent ethical system is not gender-based or one to be used to exclude other systems of analysis but that it is an important way of thinking that should be included within an overall consideration of an ethical dilemma.

Communication professionals may view themselves as caregivers. As caregivers, they should be considerate of the structures and relationships they affect with the dissemination of messages. Relationship awareness would prevent, or at least reduce, the unnecessary splintering of alliances.

Contemporary Case in Publishing: Seamless Structure?

Seamless Structure *is a successful architectural magazine. Now in its tenth year of publication, it is experiencing some growing pains. Five of the original founders of the magazine seem to be out of touch with the scholarship and aesthetics coming from most universities. All five are in senior-level editorial positions, and the publisher, Janice Walker, believes that all five should retire. Two professional consulting firms have recommended fresh, energetic makeovers, and Janice believes she needs new professionals to continue the magazine's success. None of the five wants to leave. There is a strong bonding of the entire staff. If Janice asks these five to retire early, there is a threat that several of her prominent writers, photographers, and designers might resign in protest.*

A relationship ethic is helpful in assessing options for Janice as a publisher. Is her first duty to make money for her shareholders? What are a publisher's duties to employees? Will the magazine lose money unless it has new professionals to give the magazine an updated look? Is it acceptable to force workers out because of age? Is it acceptable to threaten a walkout in response to the forced retirements? A **relationship ethic** clearly places the employee relationships before the cost-benefit analysis of the magazine's new look. However, the five employees have a responsibility to carefully assess their performances and determine whether they are hurting other members of the magazine staff with outdated ideas, designs, and photography. Janice Walker has a responsibility to carefully work through options for the five that could include them staying with the magazine in less senior positions.

She also needs to rationally justify her decision that their work is stale and outdated. The five know that if they are fired or forced into early retirement, several members of the staff will walk. They should carefully assess the professional and personal harms that could come to these staff members. Under a relationship ethic rubric, Janice needs to discuss long-term options with each editor.

RELATIVISM: MORAL RULES VARY AMONG CULTURES

The final section of this chapter examines the nature of **relativism.** Other chapters will detail the extensive use of this form of ethics in the media professions. Ethicists often use the terms *descriptive statements* and *prescriptive statements.* A descriptive statement tells us what the facts are. A prescriptive statement tells us what ought to be. It is easy to describe what others do and what they value. But it is a substantial leap to tell others what they ought to do and value.

In ethics we often mix descriptions with prescriptions. Within ethics we are not just describing or trying to understand ourselves and one another, but we are also trying to do what is right and live a happy life.

But who gets to define what constitutes living right and having the happy life? Who defines who you are; what is your true essential self? Some ethicists state that there are universal moral rules that must be applied in all cases at all times. Moral rules, as we noted earlier, outline the conditions for society to exist. But we also note that some moral rules may be given a more important role in some societies. The moral rule "don't steal" is very important in some communities. However, we know that some cultures do not have the same notion of stealing; in fact, since personal ownership of property is nonexistent in some cultures, the concept of theft is not understood.

What Is Correct Behavior? Understanding Diverse Cultures

Is it correct for you to extend your notion of moral rules to people across the world living under different religions or sets of social mores? A branch of ethics, relativism, rejects the notion that there are universal moral rules. Relativists argue that ethics are relative to a culture, a history, and a situation.

Anthropologist Claude Levi-Strauss stated that "When I witness certain decisions or modes of behavior in my own society, I am filled with indignation and disgust, whereas if I observe similar behavior in a so-called primitive society, I make no attempt at a value judgment. I try to understand it." There is a difference between what anthropologists would consider proper behavior and what ethicists would consider to be a moral rule. An ethicist who is a relativist would say that it is essential to understand the culture and history of any choice—whether it be your own or someone else's. Is the choice a political choice? Is the choice based on power? Is the choice based on understanding and working through differences?

ETHICAL RELATIVISM

The reach of mass media has made the world a much smaller place. We know that variations in moral rules exist from society to society. We know that some societies encourage their elderly to leave the tribe and enter the world of death, perhaps through starvation or exposure to severe weather conditions. In other societies, the elderly are given every life-sustaining treatment—to do otherwise might be considered murder or manslaughter. That the idea that what is right may vary from community to community is a threatening notion to some moralists. On the hopeful side, relativism can encourage the acceptance of disagreement and thereby reduce hostility. We are a diverse and multicultural society. Differences among cultures are often more pronounced than the similarities, and historical differences are often more severe than the similarities.

In this book, we favor ethical relativism—not an extreme relativism that suggests "you do your thing, I'll do my thing, and life will be nice," but an ethical relativism that encourages discourse among differing points of view. In the best sense, ethical relativism should involve cultivating and fostering understanding and arguments of a moral nature rather than shrugging off an area of moral conflict by stating, "We disagree, so let's not discuss it." Ethical relativism should never be used as an excuse for circumventing an understanding of the ethical issues in one's life. Ethical relativism encourages us to appreciate differences and to listen to the voices of others.

We as individuals are cultural products. Culture provides our language and hence directs our actions. Our actions are not inventions but often routines that we perform for ourselves and others. If being professional communicators grants us any ability to make a difference in understanding our reactions and choices, particularly in the context of culture and history, then ethical analysis is demanded within the media. Ethical analysis is also demanded among media professions when we consider what we proffer to be truth and how we work through the power aspects associated with that truth.

COMBINING ETHICS SYSTEMS

CODES OF ETHICS

Codes of ethics can be a combination of ethics systems. They move us toward a defined set of rules. When a code of ethics is determined by professionals, politicians, or others, it is expected that those falling under the rubric of the code will obey it. Some professions strictly adhere to codes of ethics, while others use them as mere window dressing. Whatever the case, the adoption of codes of ethics is not a new way of defining which practices are ethically acceptable.

The ancient Babylonian Code of Hammurabi, using a combined duty and rights ethics as its foundation, was drafted sometime between 1792 and 1750 B.C.E. and specified that the strong shall not injure the weak. It combined codes from ancient Sumerian and Akkadian laws to codify acceptable behavior in most Near Eastern countries and covered legal matters, such as false accusation, land and business regulations, family laws, wages, trade, loans, and debts. The massive document, which also detailed some acceptable practices in medicine, was based on the premise that to have a society that functions fairly and peacefully, we all have duties to one another. This code anticipated a social order based on duties backed by the authority of the Babylonian gods and the state. It was not to the advantage of everyone to obey this code, but it was quite successful because it did establish rules that everyone obeyed out of a sense of duty.

Codes of ethics continue to have the same function today as they did in ancient Babylonia. Many professions and practices have established codes of ethics, some of which include penalties for violations. These codes of ethics are often outlined as duties to the profession, duties to patients, duties to other practitioners, and duties to society. Transgression of codes of ethics for physicians or lawyers, for example, can result in banishment from the profession, with consequent inability to practice.

Nonbinding Codes of Ethics

Although communication industries have codes of ethics, the First Amendment to the Constitution does not allow these media codes of ethics to have the power of binding moral rules, meaning that a communication professional cannot be banned from the profession for transgressing the moral rules. Many people want the various areas in the communication field to have binding codes of ethics. It is one of the great debates in the field. When codes of ethics are nonbinding, moral decisions are made solely on the basis of ethical duty; codes of ethics act as another source of guidance. The media professional rationally justifies the acceptance and practice of the code, but the code is not enforced legally. This permits media professionals to make unilateral or personal decisions that may conflict with the duty-based code of ethics of the profession.

When Gerald Ford explained that "the code of ethics that will be followed will be the example that I set," he established a personal rather than rational model for ethics. Ethics codes are written and revised when necessary, but they cannot cover all situations in which professionals encounter problems. Codes of ethics outline prescribed actions in common areas of ethical trauma. It would be difficult for most of those on Ford's executive team to confer with him regarding the acceptability of a particular action being considered or to watch his actions at all times and rationally understand why a particular choice was made. The useful code of ethics rationally identifies moral principles that must be maintained within the profession, urging practitioners to consider these principles and to give them priority in decision making. The final section of this book contains lists of various media codes of ethics.

Summary

Jerry terHorst made a difficult ethical decision and was highly praised for it. The other cases in this chapter involving Kellie, Kerry, and Janice involve decisions being made in a less public arena, but moral decisions nevertheless, the consequences of which could remain with them for the rest of their lives. How would they know the difference between a difficult problem and an ethical problem? What systems of thinking would help them reach acceptable solutions? Can they rely on a professional code of ethics for guidance? Could another professional in the field help them to better understand the complexity of their decisions? If their decisions are thoughtful ones, they should be able to spell out the reasons for their actions, just as Jerry terHorst did in his book.

We discussed in detail the definitions of ethics and morality, as well as the five philosophical systems for making decisions relating to ethics problems. In all of these systems, rational justification is necessary. Each of these five systems (duty, utilitarianism, rights, virtue, and relationships) serves as a basis for questioning ethical behavior. Each system has philosophical support. In addition to the five systems of ethics, we also detailed ethical relativism and its potential impact on decision making within the media professions. The final section discussed codes of ethics. Detailed media codes of ethics are found in the Appendix.

The next chapter argues that an individualistic ethics system is needed within the media professions because authoritarian or rule-based ethics hamper creativity, progress, and First Amendment privileges. Strong emphasis is placed on the importance of the individual having the power to make principled, professional decisions. In response to asking "What is the right thing to do?", the authors suggest an ethical system known as the "Beacon on the Hill," a guide for ethical decision making that may help the individual make decisions within a range of morally acceptable goals.

Moral Reasoning Questions

1. Kant believed the duty to tell the truth always prevails, since lying cannot be universalized as a virtue. Do you agree with Kant? Is there a situation in which you believe it is morally acceptable to lie? If so, explain under what conditions it is ethical to lie.

2. It is possible that the most interesting lists of duties we encounter in the media professions are those based on tradition: "It has always been done this way." Choose one of the media professions (e.g., journalism, public relations, advertising, or entertainment) and provide an example of a situation in which you feel is not morally acceptable to do something the way it has traditionally been done. As a media professional, how would you handle this situation?

3. Examine and explain how making a moral decision based on duty could conflict with a decision based on rights. Write a case citing this difference.

4. Examine and explain the fundamental tenets of Kant's Categorical Imperative. Why is this a system of nonconsequentialism? Write a case illustrating how you have used a nonconsequentialist system in making a professional decision. (This could be a case involving lying.)

5. Describe your personal approach to moral decisions. Examine your beliefs and describe them in terms of the five ethical systems.

CONTEMPORARY CASE IN PUBLIC RELATIONS: THE PRESS SECRETARY

Shondra is a press secretary for Congresswoman Martinez. Shondra has an assignment to work with minority issues. The congressional district is very poor, but the congresswoman does not follow through on any of her campaign promises to her minority constituents. Instead, she sends Shondra to visit with minority groups. Shondra's instructions are to explain that employment, health care, and housing issues are the congresswoman's first concerns. To Shondra, the Congresswoman's first concern appears to be fund-raising for reelection. In addition, the Congresswoman seems to associate exclusively with white, male businessmen, particularly those in the defense industries. On the one occasion Shondra confronted the Congresswoman, she was chastised. The Congresswoman told Shondra that it was only by associating with these businessmen that she could make any meaningful changes for her constituents.

1. *How should Shondra respond to the Congresswoman? Should she continue to report that the Congresswoman is working on issues of employment, health care, and housing?*

2. *What are the problems associated with making false commitments? How is Shondra responsible for making false commitments?*

3. *How are Congresswoman Martinez's constituents harmed by the misrepresentations? What future harms may occur if she continues to ignore her commitments?*

4. *Is it possible that the Congresswoman is working on secret minority issues with the businessmen?*

5. *Should Shondra resign? Why or why not? How does her situation compare to that of former press secretary Jerry terHorst?*
6. *Which ethics system would you use to help determine the right thing to do?*

CONTEMPORARY CASE IN JOURNALISM: THE INCOMPLETE STORY

Jeff is a reporter for a metropolitan newspaper. He covers the second largest county and city in the state. A professor from the local college calls Jeff and complains that he is unfairly under impeachment proceedings as president of the college's faculty senate. He explains to Jeff that as senate president he has ruthless enemies who will do anything to ruin his career. He tells Jeff their names and gives Jeff the name of another professor who will verify his story. Jeff likes this story. For years he has believed that the named enemies were arrogant, unapproachable snobs. He had called one of the accused professors, a media expert, twice asking for opinions on stories he was writing, and the professor did not return his phone calls. Jeff runs the story using only two sources—the faculty senate president who is under impeachment proceedings and the friend of the senate president. A passage from Jeff's story reads "That media professor has made many enemies, is a ruthless backstabber, and everyone knows to look out for her. She has a personal grudge against the faculty senate president." Jeff does not give the name of his source, but identifies it as "a long-time professor at the college who asked to remain anonymous on the grounds that his job could be threatened by this powerful professor." Jeff's editor does not see the article until the following day and is furious with Jeff's reporting. Jeff replies, "Oh, we're covered; I didn't use the name of the powerful media professor."

1. *What are the ethical problems in Jeff's story? Is it ethically acceptable to tell only one side of a "political" story?*
2. *What are the problems with Jeff's theory that if the accused is not formally identified by name in his story, then it is acceptable to run the quote about her?*
3. *What makes it ethically acceptable to run a harsh, anonymous quote such as the one Jeff used in his story? How would John Rawls respond to Jeff?*

4. How much damage has Jeff done to the "unnamed" media professor? Can he repair the damage? What would Aristotle say about Jeff's professionalism?

5. Which systems of ethics would you use to address your beliefs on these issues?

Selected Sources

Anderson, J. A., & Englehardt, E. E. (2001). *The organizational self and ethical conduct: Sunlit virtue and shadowed resistance.* Fort Worth, TX: Harcourt College Publishers.

Baker, L. W. (1993). *The credibility factor: Putting ethics to work in public relations.* Homewood, IL: Business One Irwin.

Denise, T. C., White, N., & Peterfreund, S. P. (1999). *Great traditions in ethics.* (9th ed.). Belmont, CA: Wadsworth Pub Co.

Englehardt, E. E. (2001). *Ethical issues in interpersonal communication: Friends, intimates, sexuality, marriage, and family.* Fort Worth, TX: Harcourt College Publishers.

Finnis, J. (1983). *Fundamentals of ethics.* Oxford, UK: Clarendon Press.

Gilligan, C. (1982). *In a different voice: Psychological theory and women's development.* Cambridge, MA: Harvard University Press.

Gilligan, C. *In a different voice: Sixteen years later.* Address to Utah Valley State College, Orem, Utah, November 1999.

Hobbes, T. (1651/1921). *Leviathan.* New York, NY: Everyman's Library.

Kant, I. (1785/1959). *Foundations of the metaphysics of morals* (L. W. Beck, Trans.). New York, NY: Liberal Arts Press.

MacIntyre, A. (1988). *Whose justice? Which rationality?* Notre Dame, IN: University of Notre Dame Press.

Mill, J. S. (1897). *Utilitarianism.* London, UK: Longmans Green.

More, T. (1516/1964). *Utopia.* New Haven, CT: Yale University Press.

Noddings, N. (1984). *Caring: A feminine approach to ethics and moral education* (pp. 82–83). Berkeley, CA: University of California Press.

"Notes on People," *The New York Times,* 5 October 1974.

Railton, P. (1996). Moral realism: Prospects and problems. In W. Sinnott-Armstrong & M. Timmons (Eds.). *Moral knowledge? New readings in moral epistemology.* (pp. 49–81). New York, NY: Oxford University Press.

Rawls, J. (1999). *A theory of justice* (2nd ed.) (p. 53). Cambridge, MA: Harvard University Press.

Schmeltekopf, D. (1994). Morality. In E. Englehardt & D. Schmeltekopf (Eds.). *Ethics and Life*. Dubuque, Iowa: William C. Brown.

Snyner, J. W. (1989). "Hammurabi," In *The World Book Encyclopedia*. Chicago, IL: The World Book Encyclopedia.

Solomon, R. C. (1989). *Introducing Philosophy*. (4th ed.). San Diego, CA: Harcourt, Brace, Jovanovitch.

terHorst, J.F. (1989). "Gerald R. Ford—Restoring the Presidency," Hofstra University Forum, April 8, 1989.

terHorst, J. F. (1974). *Gerald Ford and the future of the presidency*. New York, NY: The Third Press.

2

MORAL OBLIGATIONS OF THE INDIVIDUAL MEDIA PROFESSIONAL

CONTEMPORARY CASE IN BROADCAST JOURNALISM: THE HIDDEN CAMERA

Two television reporters receive a news editor's memo outlining a story idea on a physician, who may be overprescribing diet drugs. The editor closes the story memo with the following: "This is a good story for using a hidden camera." One reporter arranges to rent a small video recorder. She intends to conceal the camera in a personal planning notebook and carry it into the doctor's office to ask for diet pills. The second reporter asks the news editor whether the use of a hidden camera is appropriate in this situation, since it invades the privacy of the doctor being taped. Additionally, disclosures from the taping would inevitably be very harmful to the doctor's reputation. The facts of the story may not warrant such a strategy.

If the first reporter had asked, she would have been told that the Radio-Television News Directors Association ethics code permitted surreptitious taping of subjects. The second reporter started a newsroom discussion regarding whether such a strategy would improve the ability of audience members to relate to their world. He then compared the potential benefits of the story with the harm the taping and disclosure would certainly cause the doctor. The first reporter did not, perhaps, even recognize a moral problem with taping the doctor, since such tapings were allowed by an ethics code, and the news editor had given it a blessing with the memo. The second reporter was concerned about the effects of his actions, for if the discussion determined that the information to be obtained was so valuable for the audience that the doctor's reputation could legitimately be harmed, the taping might indeed be justifiable. On the other hand, if the news editor had targeted an insignificant topic, but one that would titillate the audience, the reporter might try to talk his superiors out of the hidden camera ploy, arguing that the harm was not offset by a good.

UNDERSTANDING ETHICAL DECISIONS

In the previous chapter, ethics and morality were formally defined. Philosophers who have made significant contributions to the field were identified and their respective theories explained. The theories were placed within five systems, with a sixth system—relativism—ending the formal theory section. Formal theory is important in this book, but we are now moving away from these formal theories, rules, and guidelines. We are asking the reader, as an individual moral practitioner in the media professions, to avoid authoritarian stands and allow for individual freedom in making ethical choices.

An ethics system that emphasizes the individualist approach is designed to naturally minimize the number of laws and regulations. It gives people much more freedom, but also more moral responsibility, creating greater obligations for thoughtful behavior than does a more authoritarian culture. Ethics in an authoritarian culture consists primarily of learning and following rules, generally with immediate penalties attached for wrongdoing. In a more individualistic culture, ethics generally has neither the dogmatic flavor of the authoritarian, nor the threats of swift-and-sure punishments common to more rigid cultures. Such latitude, of course, produces free-society behaviors and events that often make society appear chaotic and even out of control. Yet, all are normal and even healthy manifestations of a pluralistic, individualistic society.

The attraction of authoritarianism is the security of knowing the limits for individual behavior. The security of limits, however, seems to doom authoritarian cultures to limited development, creativity, and progress. By most measures, authoritarian cultures lag behind the pluralistic in living standards: life expectancy, literacy, education level, per capita income, infant survival rates, and other measures of the quality of life.

Certainly, group behavior is important, but such emphasis often produces a social paradox in which the primary consideration for many as they make decisions is not based on "what is the right thing" to do, but on the group-oriented concerns about how others will react or what is best for the group or concern for rules or guidelines, all of which may prove wrong when ultimately compared with what would have been the right action. It should be noted that groups generally base their rules on their view of the right thing to do at the moment of adoption for the immediate time and place.

Even if the rule is a good one, its validity may be questioned when time and/or place change. In advertising in the 1950s, for example, it was an entrenched practice that competitive product names were not to be mentioned in comparative ads. Therefore, an Alka Seltzer antacid was compared with Brand X rather than the brand name of its competitor. This practice was accepted until an ad comparing the characteristics of several specific automobile brands was successful for the brand advertised. Since then, Brand X has fallen into disuse. Whatever the value of the brand-naming prohibition, individual, pluralistic flexibility allowed it to be challenged, and it was discarded. A basic premise behind looking at individual action is that one may behave differently than one's fellows and still be morally correct.

Such a premise is a benchmark of pluralistic social principle, creating an immediate division between absolutists and the alternatives of relativism and moral **objectivism.** Absolutists believe in a single answer to a moral problem that cannot be overridden by any other principle or by society's views.

FULFILLING A MORAL OBLIGATION TO ACT WELL

The American system gives inherent power or what could be termed individual rights to each individual, expecting that the power will be used well. Indeed, the system in the United States gambles the future of society on the expectation that individuals will act well, strengthening rather than weakening the system for selfish reasons. Such a system places the professional communicator in a unique position to help empower many individuals to act well by providing them with the information they need to contribute to the great social decisions of the day.

Therefore, one might say that in return for First Amendment protections, a professional communicator has a moral obligation to act well in ways that will strengthen society. It is this requirement to act well that demands individual thought and application of principles, for opinions will differ drastically in a pluralistic society over what it means to act well. For the communicator, the feat of acting well revolves around practices involved in the distribution of information, for it is information that makes possible a viable, dynamic individualistic society.

What's So Great About Theories? The Benefits of Moral Theory

The previous chapter may have been your first formal discussion of foundational theories in ethics. Like some students, you may have scant regard for the concept of theoretical thinking, yet tend to be a theorist in many daily activities. For example, in crossing a busy street, I theorize about how to get safely across without being hit by a vehicle. I apply traffic knowledge gained throughout my life to estimate when I may safely cross. Clearly, we fear for small children who do not have the background and experience to be good theorists and estimate traffic flow, so we issue the blanket order to stay out of the street. As they grow older and wiser, it is easier for them to calculate the theoretical odds of crossing a street safely, so we worry less about them.

We, in fact, form a theory about street safety that informs our judgment as to when to make the dash and how quickly to hurry. We have a vested interest in forming a good theory because our safety is at stake. Therefore, we each have a *personal traffic theory*. No matter how we feel about autos, street crossings, and theories, we must cross the street safely. We must look rationally at the process. Whether I detest streets and/or autos has no bearing on my decision as I find myself needing to cross the street. I still must treat them realistically.

To an even greater degree, I am likely to have strong views about matters upon which I must form moral decisions, making it necessary for me to take extra care in being rational about my professional ethical judgments, perhaps discounting many of my personal feelings in the process.

Developing a Personal Moral Theory

A **personal moral theory** is our own formal recognition of the structure through which we engage in moral reasoning and by which we make the more significant moral decisions of our lives, particularly professional decisions.

That theory may be structured in a way most convenient to us individually, but it ultimately should provide a relatively clear pathway to both recognition of moral issues and decisions about them. It should also require us to look realistically at our own values, priorities, moral principles, and our roles in society.

A logical structure for my moral theory may start with the views I have of an ideal world, a world I might want for my grandchildren. That would be a world in which they would be relatively successful, but also a world in which they have the freedom to fulfill their potential. This is an ideal toward which I can contribute professionally. Therefore, I need to assess my basic approach to ethical decision making and my feelings about the nature of the human being as well as prioritize my values and moral principles. Doing this does not assure me that I will make good ethical decisions, but it will help guide me through systematic consideration of the issues.

In an orderly process, it helps to spell out a Beacon on the Hill as a distant objective (the ideal world of my grandchildren might be a good one). This should cause me to assess, and perhaps challenge, my deep feelings about the value of information and the role of information flow in society, my feeling about the nature of my fellow human beings, my moral inclinations, how I feel about social order, and how I arrange my values and principles.

FINDING AN ULTIMATE GOAL: YOUR BEACON ON THE HILL

The first major step toward developing a personal moral theory is to decide on your ultimate goal. This may be referred to as your Beacon on the Hill, an icon to represent what you conclude is the best your profession, and you as a professional, have to offer the society you serve.

The First Amendment provides each individual with the right to make decisions in accordance with a personal morality, not as broadly defined by a profession as to what is moral. The individual is the source of the moral fortitude, not the code of ethics set up by a particular profession.

It is important for media professionals to develop a personal moral theory to help make decisions when difficult moral situations arrive. Think of the Beacon on the Hill as a towering mountain, a mountain of Individual Responsibility, with a beacon light on top that illuminates the surrounding countryside. To reach this beacon at the top of the mountain, one must find a path of moral reasoning. This pathway up the mountain is filled with obstacles, such as rules, tradition, social pressure, and codes of ethics. The way through these obstacles is by applying values and principles and by understanding harm, loyalties, and competing virtues. As opposed to turning oneself over to the rules and becoming someone else's creation—even if this is the easy path—the pathway to the peak, though fraught with perils and uncertainty, is one of independence and self-control.

One Beacon on the Hill may be a professional committed to a world in which information flows freely, making a reality of a fortunate society of well-informed people whose decisions can realistically be expected to be based on solid and diverse knowledge. In an open society that cannot guarantee truthfulness in media, the world to which this Beacon on the Hill might be expected to contribute would also expect people to develop mechanisms for evaluating the cacophony of messages and appeals for their favor. Dispersed information would range from the availability of in-depth reports about political candidates to conflicting data about consumer products (automobiles to laundry detergent, for example). In this way, when electing political officials and buying products, people would be able to make informed decisions that would serve them well.

This would create, of course, a world in which all would have to tolerate a great deal of information that might displease or even disgust, as well as the recognition that valuable data for one person is distasteful to another. To carry this view to its logical conclusion, it would mean, as a professional persuader, that I should accept an obligation to distribute information and to be professionally persuasive about subject matter with which I may personally disagree. Although I do not smoke and am persuaded that smoking is dangerous to the health of a smoker, I may still be compelled to promote tobacco products or other products I personally find repugnant on principle as long as these products are legal. Or, personal feelings aside, it may be that I would find adequate reason to refuse to promote legal products.

As a professional persuader, my refusal to promote some products or ideas may signal that I do not have sufficient respect for audiences to allow them to be confronted by some information, fearing that they have no ability to make rational decisions on their own. In the ideal world of the Beacon on the Hill described above, communicators would respect their audiences, be very reluctant to violate the national social premise of people as rational beings, and be very reluctant to make significant decisions for them by manipulating or deleting information they may need.

The world described above would require me as a professional communicator to appreciate the value of pluralistic information, to trust my fellow human beings with such information, to value the importance of competition in a dynamic society, and to maintain a reverence for truth. A journalist working under this Beacon on the Hill should have a primary loyalty to his or her audience. Ethical positions defined in the Beacon on the Hill elements listed above, of course, have a significant impact on a communicator's role and on the decisions he or she would make. The journalist who ignores stories known to be important to an audience because information would be difficult to gather or would be critical of the interests of the subject of a story, would violate the Beacon on the Hill's tenets by showing greater loyalty for a subject than for the audience one is supposed to serve. Trying to make this case to the subject of a story, at the very least, is something that needs advance thought and the perspective of a personal moral theory because a journalist can easily yield to power in order to avoid punishment unless prior thought has created a determination to follow through on decisions of conscience.

Certainly the Beacon on the Hill will be made up of a bundle of altruistic goals because the very nature of ethics is positive in that it suggests sacrifice to help others. Even if I cannot subscribe to the goal or task of helping others, it is difficult to defend morally a goal that will result in harm to others without some substantial compensating benefit to society or even to those harmed by my actions (a surgeon's patient who must suffer in order for the greater good of improved health to occur, for example).

Moral Goal to Do Good

In other words, *my moral goal should be to do good, but if I cannot do good, I should not do unjustifiable harm.* Remember, as an autonomous moral agent, my moral goal should be uniquely mine, though it will have many elements in common with the moral goals of other professionals and with the profession to which I belong as a whole. Ideally, the Beacon on the Hill should direct me toward engaging in those acts that will, by informed agreement, produce a better world. As a practical matter, I must recognize that my Beacon on the Hill will be partially idealistic and partially practical. I must be a good professional while still meeting family and other obligations.

The professional thrust of my Beacon on the Hill may be to contribute to a well-informed society based on the premise that the more information available to society, the better that society will be and the greater will be the self-determining power of individuals in that society. This is a media profession goal that may not be as easily achieved as it may appear, for there will be myriad pressures on me to stray from that resolve.

The Persuader's Goal: Choose from a Variety of Moral Goals

A persuader's goal may be to improve the world by assuring that a client's ideas or products have a fair and complete hearing in the Marketplace of Ideas, a hearing enriched through full but not damagingly misleading information. Or, I may adopt as my Beacon on the Hill the belief that my client deserves the best, most vigorous representation I can provide in the competitive arena, representation that is willing to take risks to advance my client's interests because that is how society is strengthened and enriched. Still, the question of assessing damage is important.

At the least, my Beacon on the Hill may be one in which I am determined to provide information or information services that people will pay for, as long as it does no significant harm. These Beacon on the Hill possibilities bracket the range of morally acceptable goals. The first and second options are altruistic in that they seek to contribute to a better society. The third is merely a holding goal that consciously contributes little; it does no damage, but it does allow me to earn a living in my chosen field.

DEVELOPING A HIERARCHY OF PERSONAL VALUES

The next step in building a personal moral theory is to identify and prioritize personal values, evaluating them in the light of those areas already discussed, so I can confidently support my own actions as being based on well-founded values. Two areas of particular importance to a professional communicator as discussed above are the values of truth telling and individual free agency. These are important as I consider decisions about whether to control information another receives, or whether to distribute information with which I may disagree but that audiences have a right to receive and to consider.

Pressures on Values

Soul searching about one's values is important because what individuals say about their values may not square with how they act on them. To *say* I never lie is relatively easy, for example, but when the boss is signaling to tell the caller that she is not in, truth on my value scale is tested. Or, I may declare my commitment to the importance of distributing information, but when it comes to writing a story about my brother's arrest for embezzlement, my actual priorities may be revealed. Or, when I feel the pressures of the community opposing the running of a suicide story, I may find other values (avoiding conflict in this case) may supersede the value I place on information in the community. It takes a serious effort to realistically identify the truth of a value system and to assure that values are consciously considered in the moral decision-making process.

Individual hierarchies are demonstrated by our decisions. If, for example, the military general accepts the basic function of protecting his nation, his unique value inventory will revolve around the demands of the function, which may include fairly indiscriminate killing of others, and possibly sacrificing of lives of the general's own troops, even his own friends and family. An overly sensitive humanitarian who places a high value on individual lives will have a difficult time ordering his troops to charge heavily fortified enemy positions. Because of values, it is not likely that a humanitarian will become a military general or that a military general will put aside basic feelings about killing. However, a military general's loyalty must be to the sacrificing, rather than preservation, of lives, when necessary. His humanitarianism may cause him to weep at the sacrifice, but his duty requires the sacrifice, nevertheless. A humanitarian diplomat, on the other hand, will make extraordinary efforts to find negotiated solutions to international problems, avoiding war, death, and destruction whenever possible.

The communication professional accepts the basic function of distributing information, even persuasive information. The communication professional's value system should focus on that, even in the face of strong restraints that discourage the distribution of information. A professional persuader places a higher value on the one-sided presentation of the advertiser at the expense of a broad-based, even-handed presentation that offers pros and cons. In this regard, journalists and persuaders have very different functions. A journalist would generally expect to favor pluralism, in fairness to an audience, while in advertising and public relations the primary loyalty is to the client, with its consequent one-sided persuasive message.

Values on Several Levels

Prioritizing values on several levels will help calibrate a professional's approach to the communication industry. As an example, if I value activities outside the profession (family, social or service groups, fishing, hunting, etc.) more than I value the minimum performance of my job, then I may seek a steady, 9-to-5 type of position for which routine assignments do not drain my personal resources (time, emotion, etc.), leaving me free to pursue other activities once I've spent the requisite time earning a living.

Conversely, and at the other extreme, I may push other activities to the background and allow my professional work to consume me, excluding other considerations.

In the latter situation, I value my work more than other activities, perhaps even more than my family. This is not a commentary on the rightness or wrongness of either position, but a description of behavior that tends to illustrate value orientations. Day-to-day decisions will also be triggered by my value orientations. If I have strong feelings about what social outcomes ought to be, I may elevate that value over one that respects the agency of my audience in making decisions by reducing pluralism in my directed messages. Such an orientation during a political campaign, for example, may cause me to favor one candidate over another with uneven or unfair coverage. Because this may be such a deep-seated reaction, I may be under the illusion that I am acting professionally and favoring no one.

It has been noted that ethics decisions most often must be made when two virtues come in conflict, rather than in matters of right or wrong. Thus, moral reasoning may come down to the question of whether we will look at consequences in our decisions, or whether we will follow our duty line, tradition, or rules and not worry about the consequences.

As a practical matter, as we formulate our personal moral theories, we will find consequences looming larger and larger in our thoughts. It is simple to declare that we have a duty to keep our audiences well informed, but we may also have a duty to do no harm; alternatively, we may have accepted a personal value that we will avoid conflict.

When we make a decision, however, it will most often be based on a regard for relative consequences, and it is here that prioritizing values becomes important to assist in avoiding the selfish responses that often come from wanting to avoid immediate and proximate unfavorable consequences.

Examples of Values

For example, when a member of my close-knit church group, who is also a highly visible African American business figure in the community, is arrested for soliciting a prostitute, my hierarchy of values springs to action if I am an African American newspaper editor.

First, my newspaper has a policy of publishing the names of people who are arrested and charged with such crimes, so it would appear to be my duty to publish the story. Second, however, my family and my friends remind me that I have a duty of loyalty to them that would prevent publishing a name that not only would bring public embarrassment to a good friend, but would create a publicly embarrassing situation for my church group. Third, and not least, the friends in my church would argue that friendship and loyalty were created just for the purpose of avoiding the problems I would cause by printing the story and that if the story were to be published I would be punished by the group as unworthy to be one of their number, particularly since this minority group has had an uphill battle in earning respect and credibility in the community.

All three are worthy virtues: *informing the community about its environment, avoiding harm and embarrassment to a prominent person, and demonstrating my loyalty and friendship to a group of people that I value highly.* As is most often the case with communications ethics decisions, I cannot give all three virtues equal status, so something will have to give. It would be helpful if I had worked out a hierarchy in which each of the virtues had a place when this type of situation arose, which is the purpose, of course, of developing an early personal moral theory.

Consequences

If I am concerned about consequences, I might reason something as follows: If I truly believe that information is critical to the community and that my job is the key to providing the major elements of that service, then the community has a right to know most of what I know as a journalist (that's what they buy their newspapers for), and publication of the story would produce beneficial informational consequences and publishing would top the hierarchy. Professionally, I will have done my job, with the consequent damage being more than offset by the advantages of a well-informed community. If my job as a journalist is secondary and my racial group and my family take priority, the virtue of preserving them will subsume my professional obligations. The consequence will be a less-informed community, but an unbroken relationship bond will still exist. It is not that it is either right or wrong to publish or not publish, it is that consequences will flow from whatever I do. If I do not publish the story, a false image of an important member of the community will mislead other members of the community in their dealings with him, but my friends will still include me in their circle and my family will be happy. If I publish the story, however, my community will be better informed. Although much of the community may be critical of the newspaper for publishing such a story, the community will have a more realistic image of one of its prominent members. Nevertheless, I am likely to be in deep trouble with my friends and church associates for drawing a dark cloud over their association and inflicting harm to the racial image of our church and group. These consequences, and others not mentioned, are those considered by the consequentialist who must make a decision that will either serve personal or professional purposes.

Duty

If, on the other hand, I feel it is my duty, whatever the consequences, to follow the rules of the newspaper and publish the story, then I will not be concerned about the consequences my friends and family might visit on me. Presumably, the rule was made, and it is valid, to assure an informed community. I can always tell my friends that "it was out of my hands, and I had to follow the paper's rules." Or, I may feel it my duty, no matter what my job responsibilities call for, to remain loyal to my friends and my family and protect those to whom I am loyal from unwanted publicity, no matter how truthful that publicity may be.

One big question to be answered here is whether we, as Kant suggests, are willing to universalize our behavior. That is, am I willing to grant any journalist the right to protect friends by leaving important stories out of the paper? If my brother is running a scam and bilking people of thousands of dollars, shall I sacrifice the community and protect my brother so he may continue to victimize others? The actions of a journalist or other communicator who protects friends and acquaintances at the expense of the community at large are difficult to justify. When one becomes a journalist, it is assumed that one accepts the moral obligation to inform the community, even though such actions may lead to friction with friends and others.

Thus, a journalist who fails to report stories for personal reasons tends to do a double harm. First, the story is not published, and the community is less well informed; second, the journalist occupies the professional space of someone who might keep the community informed on this and other matters. Most moral philosophers would argue that we need to place as much value on those we do not know (the community) as we do on our friends. Therefore, while to kill the story of the friend may not be the wrong thing to do, the decision to do so must override the primary obligation of a journalist to distribute information and inform the community, which itself should override personal concerns if society is to flourish.

In addition to providing information, maintaining relationships, and avoiding conflict (the three virtues just discussed), it is important that the communication professional consider a number of other virtues and values in the formulation of a personal moral theory.

We have already discussed respecting equally one's audience and friends, we have listed the values that must be considered and understood as a part of a personal moral theory, and have suggested that most decisions ought to be based on consequences rather than on rules and duties. Professional communicators working under privileges granted them by the First Amendment should define thoughtfully their own professional moral rules and, because of the service they render to society at large, should seriously consider where their loyalties lie in given circumstances. Other elements of a personal moral theory with which we need to wrestle include personal feelings about the rights of individual citizens to be free agents (an ability that requires full information) and the determination to be a competent communications professional (it is difficult to be moral without being competent and able to find jobs when it is necessary to move for principle's sake).

Each of these values, principles, and concepts is important to consider when professional communicators are called upon to make moral decisions, and each should be invoked, in addition to other questions, for the cases presented later in this book. It is only through thought and testing that a personal moral theory takes shape in our minds. Once formed, adhering to one's personal moral theory is a question of will, for professional communicators, while having the power to do good and contribute to a better society, also have the power and are likely to do harm if a carefully considered personal moral theory is not in place.

WHAT IS MORAL MATURITY?

In looking at moral development, former Harvard psychologist Lawrence Kohlberg presents a hierarchy of virtues that to him appears to be universally viable. Although his ideas are regarded as controversial by feminists and other scholars, Kohlberg considered autonomous moral thought and action as mature goals for the individual.

KOHLBERG'S SIX STAGES

To determine where one is in terms of maturity, Kohlberg developed six stages or levels of maturity.

Avoiding Punishment

The first stage is a childlike stage, which nevertheless has many adult adherents, involving compliance to rules for fear of punishment, the morality of arbitrary fixed rules, obedience to power, and avoidance of punishment. Parents of unreasoning children effectively deter them from going into a busy street with the threat of a spanking or other punishment. The child is too young to comprehend the severe consequences of running into a street, so punishment is the only effective deterrent. In adults, this stage is reflected in the fear of being fired, not receiving a pay raise, or even losing friends. When President George Bush, Sr., reflected on raising taxes despite campaign promises not to do so, he expressed regret because "the public punished me for it." Rather than the action being ill-advised because of the social consequences, the reason given was that punishment resulted, making it wrong.

Expecting Reward

The second stage, also a self-centered one, focuses on the expectation of reward and demonstrates some moral maturation from the first stage, but not much. It is a stage of behavior that serves one's self-interest, an egoistic stage, or the interests of one's equals. A telemarketer is willing to push products on vulnerable respondents in return for pay. The respondent is not viewed as the equal of the caller and therefore is exploitable for a reward. Similarly, cheating on an exam is not viewed as harming an equal, and it results, if successful, in the reward of an improved grade or score.

The first two stages are basic visceral responses to threats of survival and use power to advance one's own position. Both stages are understandable for children (be good for a few minutes, and I will give you a cookie) and tend to be deplorable in adults.

Conforming to Group Expectations

The third stage focuses on others rather than merely the self. The focus, however, is shallow in that behavior is channeled toward how to get along with others. Typically, this is the morality of teenagers who become sensitive to peers and wish to have those peers think well of them. While parents tend to control the behavior of children through the first two stages, some control is lost as a youngster seeks the approval of peers. In adults, such behavior is typically triggered by the concept of professionalism. For example, Joe does what the group expects of him despite his personal feelings, and a television reporter may adopt the tactics of pack coverage of a celebrity or murder suspect because other reporters are doing the same. At this stage, very often, the joining of professional or social groups is important for the emotional support provided by the company of like-minded individuals. In return, one is expected to conform to group expectations as a condition of continued membership in the group. Many of us need the supportive reinforcement of groups, a need that gives such groups the power to influence our behavior. When we do a story because it will win us a professional prize, or when we engage in an action because it is performed by others within the group, we may be justifying our behavior not on the basis of whether it is correct, but on the basis that since others we admire do it, so also may we. Television news stories, for example, tend to require graphic visuals in order to attract viewers. Despite loss of audiences, this premise has never really been challenged in the industry and has become embedded conventional wisdom that governs unthinking television news staffs.

Following Rules

Stage four is also oriented toward others, in that one acts according to a Hobbesian social pact, requiring one to follow the rules that produce an orderly society, assuming others will follow the same rules. What is "right" is defined by categorical social rules binding on all, while violation of the rules is viewed as harmful to society. Presumably, one may not agree with the rules, but a person in this stage accepts the obligation to follow the rules for the good of all. Duty, rules, and law are strong motivators in this stage of moral development. This is the adult stage toward which much social conditioning, to be discussed later in the book, is aimed as individuals grow and mature. Effective social conditioning produces behavior that enhances the social order. This is sometimes called the Law and Order stage.

Behavior at this stage causes pedestrians to stop at crosswalk lights signaling to not walk, even though no cars are coming. At stage one, we may not cross if there is a policeman nearby for fear of being caught; at stage two, we are rewarded for walking by progressing more rapidly toward our destination. At stage three, if others at the crosswalk will go, so will we, safely in the company of the group; at stage four, we will not walk because it is our duty to obey the light that says "Don't Walk."

All stages of moral development produce positive consequences and negative consequences. It is important to understand these stages in order to be able to evaluate the stage in which one is operating. Behavior in these stages is indicative of a state of mind that generates behavior mindful of long-term consequences and implications.

Becoming an Autonomous Moral Agent

Stage five is the first stage of the autonomous moral agent, the stage at which one has matured into thinking for oneself and developing one's own moral mechanism. At this stage, one develops a contract with society and a commitment to utility. At this stage, one does not commit to perpetuating society, but to shaping society for its original purpose, helping individuals to develop themselves. Thus, laws are to be obeyed. The stage five person, however, also commits to seeking alternatives that will help society, rather than viewing laws as the final response to a problem. The underlying theme of stage five actions is that individuals are viewed as ends in and of themselves, rather than as means to ends. Thus, laws are evaluated according to their treatment of people and their aspirations.

Valuing Human Beings

The final stage, stage six, is that of adherence to universal values, valuing human beings and rising above laws. If stage five actors are active in ongoing negotiations of the social contract, the "Moral Hero/Heroine" of stage six has the unique characteristic of standing outside the bounds of the contract, always at odds with the status quo, and using extraordinary means to force changes in the contract. These "Moral Heroes," many of whom are reviled in their lifetime, can only be recognized as such after their deaths. Moral heroes include Susan B. Anthony, Mahatma Ghandi, Jesus Christ, Martin Luther King, and Sojourner Truth, whose nonviolent protests changed the shape of the world's societies.

As we indicated earlier, Kohlberg's stages are particularly useful in determining our own motives for making moral decisions by helping us figure out whether our motives are selfish or are morally defensible in that we either help or refuse to needlessly hurt others. At stage five, we think and act on our own volition and use our own mental resources to act in ways that will safeguard basic rights as we try to right wrongs by engaging in renegotiation of the social contract.

MORAL MATURITY IN THOUGHT AND ACTION

Additionally, the Kohlberg model or theory is useful as we probe our motives and perhaps push ourselves toward a moral maturity in thinking and action. He lists ten areas in the order in which he sees most moral societies establishing their priorities, declaring that commitment to life is the most important virtue and that the virtue of punishment the least important. Significantly, liberty and truth also rank above the "social" virtues of contract, law, and so forth. His list of common virtues and their order of importance is as follows:

1. Life
2. Liberties
3. Truth
4. Contract
5. Law
6. Character
7. Authority
8. Affiliation (Loyalty)
9. Property
10. Punishment

This series reorders some popular virtues, such as loyalty, law, property, and authority, placing them low the list. On the basis of Kohlberg's list, for example, life and liberty are not put at risk by my telling the truth about my boss being in when he has told me to tell the caller he is out. Whether I do as I am told, of course, will depend on whether I have the moral maturity to determine that I will not lie and accept the consequences. Alternatively, of course, I can accept the rules that the boss lays down and consider my moral integrity in the context of these rules. I should place truth well above loyalty (company) or even authority (he is the boss).

Kohlberg's list of common virtues may be useful for situations involving personal behavior, but it may not, beyond the concepts of truth and loyalty, take into account professional values appropriate to the industry.

A way of testing Kohlberg's six levels of moral development previously discussed comes as we look at our own views of professional virtues, see what our reactions are, and determine our own personal ordering system for them. It is likely that we are not looking at doing right or doing wrong as we consider these virtues, but rather we are looking at how our personal systems treat the virtues when they conflict with each other. As we have seen, when a supervisor wants us to tell callers she is not in, we have a conflict between the virtue of truth telling (very high on Kohlberg's list) and the boss's rules of loyalty or law (both lower on the list). A morally mature individual will seek to avoid having to lie, while one who dreads punishment if he or she does not lie will, indeed, lie for his or her boss. Conversely, one may accept telling lies as normal job behavior that everyone agrees to in order to stay in good standing in the company and maintain the orderly functioning of the company.

For a communication professional, of course, the question of whether to tell the truth or deceive in any circumstance is critically important in situations in which truth telling should win. Yet, there are other areas and virtues that raise questions about whether certain information will be distributed at all, how one looks at the effect of information on individuals and communities, and whether to try new techniques in gathering and distributing information.

Therefore, here is a list of virtues that come into play as professional communicators make ethics decisions. It is not a comprehensive list, but it contains the seeds of conflict among the virtues to provide an opportunity to test individual moral levels.

1. **Pluralism, Self-Determinism, and Persuasion.** How much do I value a broad range of views being available to others, even views with which I may strongly disagree and *know* are wrong? Am I willing to allow others to make their own decisions even if they are decisions I detest? Will I leave decisions to be made in the marketplace of strongly persuasive messages?

2. **Law (Rules) and Punishment.** How much do I value the predictability of conformity and the comfort of an orderly environment, knowing others will behave as the mores say they should? Am I tolerant of rule breakers, or do I insist on punishment?

3. **Tradition and Elitism and Change.** To what degree do I believe that behavior today ought to mimic the behavior of those who have gone before me? Do any deserve to be treated with deference and respect because of their social position? Shall I refuse to criticize or publish damaging information about leaders because I value the order that results when leaders are revered and followed? Do I resist trying new things or adjusting to changing conditions?

4. **Disclosure.** Do I feel that information is generally proprietary and should be protected, or do I see the maximum distribution of information, whatever its effect, as desirable?

5. **Loyalty.** When I receive conflicting signals, to whom and under what circumstances do I owe my basic allegiances?
6. **Individualism/Communalism.** To what degree do I value the rights of individuals to act in their own ways, even though such actions may upset or outrage the community by violating community standards? Or, how highly do I value being a team player and cooperating?

SUMMARY

This chapter focuses on the need to minimize the number of rules and regulations that could constrict media practitioners from fully performing their important roles as communication professionals. Authoritarian cultures can use ethics to force professionals to learn and follow rules. This chapter encourages a model entitled the Beacon on the Hill, in which the media practitioner sets high ethical standards professionally and personally and follows them as one would a beacon on a hill. To facilitate this notion, we use a model and theory by Lawrence Kohlberg, which lists stages of moral maturity and development. The highest practical level of moral thinking, or stage six, is evidenced when the individual not only understands the need to shape society with ethics, but also to help other individuals to develop themselves. This individual understands that rules are to be obeyed but also seeks alternatives that will help society, rather than accepting laws as the final response to a moral problem.

This chapter also features a virtue checklist for ethical decision making, which is intended to facilitate an individual's decision making process based on one's personal value structure. Understanding priorities is integral to this theory. Prioritizing values on several levels should help calibrate a professional's approach to the communication industry. Professional communicators working under the privileges guaranteed by the First Amendment should define their own professional moral code and seriously consider their many loyalties.

Chapter three is designed to further prepare the media student for the many challenges that exist in the media profession. It discusses the notion that the power of controlling information is one of the most profound an individual possesses. Information is the taproot of wise decisions and of participation in a democratic society. The chapter focuses on the morality of media workers who are the first line of defense in a society in which decision making is an individual right.

MORAL REASONING QUESTIONS

1. Why are questions of harm and mutual aid fundamental to the study of ethics?
2. Why is ethics called the study of morality and moral behavior? Why is rational justification essential to this process?
3. Give an example of a moral behavior that was acceptable forty years ago but is no longer accepted as moral today.
4. How is decision making facilitated by looking at the long-term results of an action?
5. How does one determine the rightness of an action?
6. As a mass communication professional, you may do something that harms an individual but brings an overall good to society. Define a situation that could involve this type of harm and benefit. Explain how you are prepared to make these types of decisions.

CONTEMPORARY CASE IN PUBLIC RELATIONS: RACE AND CULTURE SHOCK

Regina has worked with a major advertising firm in Washington, D.C., for ten years. She received a promotion and relocated to Orange County, California. After a month in her new position in California, she describes her feelings of "culture shock" to a friend in Washington, D.C. "I am the only black in the office here, and it's worse than that. I think I'm the only black woman in the town of Corona Del Mar where I live," she lamented. She explained to her friend that Washington, D.C. gives blacks a sense of false security. "Because there are so many blacks in the workforce in D.C., you think other U.S. cities have the same level of integration. Well, it just isn't true." Regina now suspects that her promotion was one of pure tokenism. Her campaign assignments are not as meaningful as the ones she had in D.C., and she believes she is proving herself all over again to company leaders in California. "If I were a white male, I'd be accepted and working on accounts of my choosing. I'd also blend into the corporate culture better. They'd even invite me to play golf," she added.

Regina now wants to move back to Washington, D.C. Her cultural life is superior there, and she believes she understands the D.C. advertising market better than the California market. The firm insists she stay in California, re-assuring her that she will love the "warm climate."

1. Should Regina stay in Orange County, Ca.? Why or why not?
2. Has the firm harmed Regina by moving her into a culture very different than her own?
3. What type of assignments could Regina be given to make her part of the California team?
4. Does the California group have any responsibilities to make Regina happy or pleased with her promotion and surroundings?
5. Has race helped or harmed Regina's career? What are the problems with a "token" promotion?

CONTEMPORARY CASE: PERSONAL MORALITY

Your brother-in-law worked for you for two years, and a potential employer has asked you for a letter of recommendation for him. Your brother-in-law is out of work and has been asking you to reemploy him, but you have declined to hire him because he was only marginally competent at what he was doing for you, and you feel he was lazy. Yet, your sister has tearfully reminded you of your obligation to the family to give him a job in order to keep her family together.

1. What is your obligation to the potential employer? Why?
2. Would you act differently if the potential employer were a good personal friend?
3. Is your obligation greater to your sister or to the potential employer? Why?
4. Is the broad but minimal social harm that would come from being untruthful offset by the immediate benefits to your sister's family?
5. What would your reaction be if you were the brother-in-law and your wife's brother refused to recommend you in glowing terms?

SELECTED SOURCES

Abdul, A. (2001). *eBlack: A 21st Century challenge*. An address to the national conference of the American Association for Colleges and Universities, New Orleans, LA, January 2001.

Davis, J., Hirschl, T., & Stack, M. (1997). *Cutting edge: Technology, information capitalism and Social revolution*. London, UK: Verso.

deToqueville, A. (1840). *Democracy in America*. (H. Reeve, Trans.). London, UK: Grosselin Publishers.

Miller, S. (1996). *Civilizing cyberspace: Policy, power, and the information superhighway*. Reading, MA: Addison-Wesley Longman, Inc.

Perelman, M. (1998). *Class warfare in the information age*. New York: St. Martins Press.

Schmeltekopf, D. (1994). Morality. In E. Englehardt & D. Schmeltekopf (Eds.). *Ethics and Life*. Dubuque, Iowa: William C. Brown.

Schuler, D. (1996). *New community networks: Wired for change*. Reading, MA: Addison-Wesley Longman Inc.

3

THE POWERFUL IMPACT OF INFORMATION

CONTEMPORARY CASE: POLITICAL ATTACK ADVERTISING

A recent survey suggests that certain types of political advertising can affect voters and voter turnout. Researchers conducting this survey found that people believe political attack advertisements are not effective. Most voters are not comfortable with candidates who attack their opponents personally and only occasionally on issues. These researchers from the Annenberg School of Communication caution against the use of the term attack. *Attack is often used in terms of personal information, whereas* contrast *is used in terms of policy information. President Bill Clinton perfected contrast techniques in 1992 and 1996 campaigns. Contrastive advertising is sometimes labeled* attack *advertising, but the informational tone is clearly different. The contrastive format is intended to present voters with a choice between two positions on important issues. Professional advertising communicators can help their clients understand how contrast formats have positive effects on voters. Would this make campaigning more ethical, or is it just another voter persuasion method? (Jamieson et al., 2001).*

Clearly, it is most desirable for a professional communicator with a tremendous potential for affecting society to opt for a goal that is socially productive. After all, the goal of a media ethics course is to help thoughtful people learn to act well and overcome selfish and emotional tendencies in wielding power over others. As the above case demonstrates, information is powerful in its diverse uses. A purely egoistic goal is unacceptable, since it does not meet the demands of sacrifice required of an autonomous moral agent.

Merely seeking riches or status has earmarks of moral corruption. Seeking riches or status while doing well morally, however, may be acceptable, desirable, and even necessary in a free-enterprise society.

This chapter focuses on the importance of assessing the long-term consequences of moral choices when working in the media. Media professionals often underestimate the power granted them as disseminators of information. The First Amendment allows for immense discretion as information is dispersed via newspapers, magazines, broadcast outlets, the Internet, and through other advertising and public relations outlets. The power of disbursing information is often open to abuses such as deception. The first two chapters focused on traditional forms of ethics and on identifying a personal moral system for making decisions as a media professional. This chapter celebrates the freedoms of the media professions and advises on the importance of assessing the long-term consequences of each decision. Power is part of every media decision, and it should not be carelessly exercised.

What does it take to become secure in ethical decision making? Should a personal system of ethics be developed and relied on? Alternatively, should we adopt a professional code of ethics that tells us how to respond to difficult ethical dilemmas? An early step professional communicators may take toward becoming thoughtful moral agents is to decide whether their decisions are based on sound moral principles. Media professionals have the choice of traveling several roads when making moral decisions. Paradoxically, it is possible to travel more than one of those roads at the same time.

Chapter 2 discussed identifying a Beacon on the Hill as a guide for moral behavior in the lowlands and suggested that, if each member of society behaved in accordance with his or her Beacon on the Hill, an ideal world would result. An ideal such as this may be inspiring, but it is not particularly functional; intermediate, practical goals are required to guide professional communicators in steps toward such a desired, albeit seemingly elusive, Utopian objective.

In order to understand how a professional communicator may eventually reach the more desirable but abstract and distant goal of the realization of an ideal world, one must first understand the system in which one works. In the American participatory social system, a set of complex assumptions is in place to allow for the freedom of speech. In this chapter, we explore goal setting in the jungle of such a participatory social system, for it is only in this way that we can feel justifiably secure when making moral decisions.

A ROAD MAP FOR MAKING ETHICAL DECISIONS

Destination is essential to preparing for any journey. A Florida resident off to unknown parts, for example, who takes along only the accustomed light clothing and ends up outdoors in Maine in mid-winter knows the foolishness of not preparing and making good decisions, even in the absence of adequate information. Even on a wilderness hike the focus is on what is ahead in landmarks, distances, and terrain emphasizing the process of orienting to a distant location.

Similarly, we should detail a system of ethical planning. Just as one would not venture on a vacation without proper planning, one should not venture out into the world without a personal moral code. But how does one identify a personal moral code that would function well in media professions?

Identifying the long-term consequences of a decision is essential in moral reasoning. An autonomous moral agent needs a benchmark or perspective that provides the necessary tools for making decisions that consistently help to achieve his or her goal. These critically important tools, teamed with reliable information, can assist autonomous moral agents in dealing with morally complex issues.

IDENTIFYING THE MORAL GOAL

When traveling, you know you have achieved your goal when you have reached your destination. In moral reasoning, however, one's goal is more abstract and must be identified with great care, for moral actions help determine the shape society will assume. The moral actions of 280 million people in the United States combine to determine our overall social and cultural environment.

Carrying the traveling analogy further, just as you may not bother to pack warm clothing for a trip, people often neglect the preparation process in moral reasoning and find themselves facing the consequences of faulty decisions. Moreover, just as you may not want to trouble yourself preparing for a trip but decide to take the trip anyway, people often say they will let their native intelligence or intuition guide them when making moral decisions. In other words, although people want the freedom and luxury to make moral decisions, they may not make the effort to prepare themselves so the decisions they make are good ones. Reliance on undeveloped judgment or feelings as a guide to good decision making is as risky as packing shorts and tee shirts for a winter hike in Maine.

The basic problem with relying on undeveloped moral judgment is that, being concerned with only the immediate effects of decisions, the potential long-term consequences of what we do are frequently ignored. Making moral decisions based on undeveloped moral judgment often gives priority to the here and now rather than more important long-term consequences, such as "How will this decision shape the world or even my world in the future?" As with travel preparations, one who fails to prepare for making moral judgments soon finds oneself having to make them anyway—and facing the consequences, a choice that inevitably sacrifices long-term rewards for short-term gratification.

THE SHORT-TERM BENEFIT

For example, suppose you tell a caller that your roommate is not at home, even though this is not true; since your roommate does not want to deal with a troublesome phone call, you get the short-term benefit of his or her gratitude. On the other hand, you have molded (even though ever so slightly) the way the world will look at the important element of truth telling, contributing to suspicions about personal honesty. In this scenario, you have even sown seeds of suspicion in your roommate, who for all his or her gratitude will not quite be able to trust you in the future. In some ways, you have sold a bit of your soul for a brief moment of approval from an acquaintance. Yet to have told the truth and required your roommate to deal with the caller would certainly have placed serious stresses on your relationship.

Most of the decisions we are called upon to make are not matters of immediate life or death; instead, they are frequently made in the context of immediate convenience in which we choose between our own convenience at someone else's expense and self-sacrifice that may make the world a slightly better place for both ourselves and others. Certainly, if we believe we cannot survive the immediate future, then long-term consequences have no importance or value.

Problems With Short-Term Thinking

One of the problems with short-term thinking is that decisions made in this context are likely to be either *selfish* or *emotional* or both. Problems of immediate consequence most often cause us to react instinctively to protect ourselves. Concerns about these consequences are likely to outweigh the distant effects we feel can be better dealt with later.

A small child who breaks a vase, for example, intuitively denies having done it as a short-term way to avoid immediate punishment, unable or unwilling to be concerned about the long-term consequences of lying. Consideration of the latter is a benefit of character development that comes from recognizing the general importance of truth telling, however inconvenient. Adults often find it more desirable to lie as a way of avoiding consequences than to consider the long-term and far more significant damages wrought by lying and being known as a liar.

For example, the personal consequences of telling a caller that your boss is right here when your boss, on your first day on the job, has just told you to tell callers he is not in are so immediate that they shove the generally more important principle of truth telling to the background. You *know* you are going to pay an immediate penalty for telling the caller your boss is here. Your boss will likely become angry and may even fire you. At the very least, your loyalty to the company (your boss) is suspect from then on. You recognize this as you answer the phone and, having less loyalty to the caller than to your boss, you are most likely to lie at the expense not only of the caller but also the socially critical moral principle of truth telling. At that moment, you are not so concerned about the social values of truth telling, but more about the personal consequences of offending your boss. If you fail to recognize that by doing your boss a favor with a lie, you have also sown the seeds of suspicion in that he will wonder whether a new employee who is so readily willing to lie can really be trusted in the future, then you have not completed the preparation necessary to be an autonomous moral agent.

CONTRIBUTIONS TO HARM

This example, of course, highlights a personal and possibly insignificant consequence of a selfish and apparently harmless moral decision. On a larger scale, however, you have contributed, perhaps only slightly, to a social climate of distrust in which both the caller and your boss lose some of their willingness and ability to trust others and to be honest with them.

Lying for your boss, then, may be the moral equivalent of thoughtlessly packing shorts and tee shirts for that winter trip to Maine, a situation in which today's actions are not adequate for tomorrow's needs. Every society needs moral behavior today, behavior founded on a sense of trust between human beings, particularly if we would like to create a society in which our progeny and we can flourish.

A society that treats people well and allows them to accept the utterances of others with confidence is a society that does not consume its creative energies perpetually trying to distinguish truth from falsehood. All of us develop the skills needed to analyze advertising and other persuasive messages for their general accuracy—including proposals of marriage or entreaties to buy a used car, but there is a range of other situations in which we have a moral right to the truth from our correspondents. Certain circumstances, however, qualify our moral right to the truth. For example, a competitive society must have some tolerance for deception in the name of competition. Whether a competitive society should tolerate *any* level of deception in the name of competition, however, is an interesting issue that merits a discussion of its own.

PREPARING A PERSONAL MORAL THEORY

How, then, should one prepare for this abstract trip into the territory of moral reasoning and applied principle? What must one know in order to plan carefully when making ethical decisions, particularly professional decisions in communications fields? One way to prepare and plan involves systematically building a *personal moral theory*, a reliable vehicle that is equal to the hardships of the journey. For example, it is important not only to know what the long-term personal consequences of a falsehood may be but also to know the long-term social impact of habitual, though casual, lying. The professional communicator, of course, must also examine the entire environment of information and the impact of falsehood when building a personal moral theory, but there are many other issues involved, such as loyalty, respect for the rights of others, attitude toward distribution of information, and **privacy** (the right to be left alone).

A personal moral theory requires each of us to identify a desirable moral goal toward which we will strive when making professional decisions: a goal that lies beyond our immediate concerns. Self-examination is needed to inventory our own basic belief and value system; in doing so, we challenge those values that may be unsound and begin to establish a hierarchy of priorities for that system.

IS THIS INFORMATION IMPORTANT TO DISTRIBUTE?

Once you have decided to contribute to the fostering of a well-informed society, you must make basic decisions about the relative importance of which information to distribute to society, especially when there is a clash of values. It is also important to deal effectively with the social conventions that would restrict information distribution. In addition, many beliefs formed in childhood as well as those formed later in school need to be challenged and even changed in light of the new understanding and independence that result from becoming an autonomous moral agent willing to accept and wield the power of the communication professional.

Professional Obligations: Minimize Harms

Much early social conditioning, for a variety of reasons, not only does not prepare one to be a professional communicator, but it may actually inhibit one from fulfilling professional obligations. An example, of course, is the laudable principle of *do no harm*. While an intuitively attractive mandate, it may be unrealistic, not only in the communication industry, but also in many other professions. By the same token, we likely find it emotionally uncomfortable to recognize that we do indeed do harm as professionals—yet another consequence with which we have to concern ourselves as a part of the maturing process.

As a professional communicator, one soon recognizes that one walks the median strip on the freeway of social interaction (*media* in this context means the middle or intervener). *Media*, incidentally, which now popularly refers to the means by which information is transmitted (radio, TV, newspapers, and the Internet), at one time referred to a voiced stop (in music and phonetics) and the middle layer of an artery or lymphatic vessel (in physiology). It is in this role as median, or mediator, from which the professional communicator must draw ethical mandates.

Communication media lie between sources and audiences. In such a bundle of roles (with multiple courses of action and multiple audiences), distribution of information is at once harmful and beneficial. The challenge to the professional communicator is to do as little needless harm as possible and to decline to do such harm to the powerless.

If one will do harm, as well as good, as is usually the case with professional communicators, one must be prepared to understand in which areas of harm it may be desirable or acceptable to do so and in which areas it should be avoided. The thoughtless communicator may not distinguish between the two, often harming the powerless in the social structure and strengthening the position of the powerful and thereby doing harm to no good purpose. This is the course of action that thoughtless communicators will often take, since social institutions tend to condition people to help the powerful maintain power.

In many communities, medical associations and state authorities are reluctant to disclose the names of doctors who have run afoul of the rules for practicing good medicine, and doctors are often reluctant to testify against colleagues charged with malpractice. The operative rationale, in these instances, is that the professional reputation of a doctor is such a critical element of the doctor-patient relationship that the profession is reluctant to publicly name physicians who have been found to have transgressed the rules. They argue that patients need to have confidence in their doctors and that such confidence cannot be maintained when they are made aware that their particular doctor has been disciplined. Similarly, it is argued that any disciplinary action against a physician hurts the entire medical profession and damages doctor-patient relationships in life-or-death situations. As a result, public relations workers frequently discourage the media from disclosing this information, and journalists often collaborate to protect the fragile doctor-patient relationship. Few, however, argue for the rights of the powerless who, in life-or-death situations, sometimes find themselves trusting doctors who may not deserve that trust.

CONTEMPORARY CASE IN JOURNALISM: THE MINORITY REPORTER AND THE POLICE

A minority reporter with a metropolitan newspaper wrote several stories that criticized the city's practice of racial profiling, resulting in heated discussions between the reporter's editor and police. One night, the reporter was stopped by police and arrested for solicitation of a prostitute. The reporter stated he was working on a story. He also stated that racial profiling was part of the story. The police officer had witnessed the reporter engage in a sexual act with the prostitute. He informed the reporter of what he had seen and attempted to restrain him. As the reporter attempted to drive away, the officer jumped on the hood of his car and rolled to the windshield to avoid being hit. The reporter was then arrested and taken to jail. The reporter's newspaper did not run a story about their employee's run-in with the police. The police, however, fed the story to the competing newspaper's police reporter, and, two weeks after the incident occurred, the competing newspaper ran it.

This case clearly illustrates abuses of power. The reporter had researched and written stories that detailed a significant problem of racial profiling by police in the city. The police denied all allegations in the reporter's stories. The first abuse of power occurred when the reporter lied to police after being caught with a prostitute. He said he was researching a story, invoking the power of his professional position to escape a personal consequence. When the officer informed the reporter he witnessed the sexual act, the reporter tried to leave in his vehicle, causing the officer to jump onto the hood of his car to avoid being hit.

Clearly, the reporter should not have threatened a police officer that way. Additionally, the reporter was not exempt from the law, and soliciting a prostitute is illegal in the state in which the reporter is employed. Finally, the reporter harmed the journalism profession by lying about writing a prostitution story.

Another abuse of power occurred when the police fed the story to the police reporter at the competing newspaper. Two weeks after the incident, the story of the arrest had lost much of its news value, but the competing paper ran the story anyway. The police rarely feed stories to the press, except in self-serving circumstances; this was once such circumstance, since some officers believed they were harmed by the reporter's racial profiling stories and wanted him to experience what it was like to be discredited by negative publicity.

In doing his job, the minority reporter caused distress to police and occasionally to the competing newspaper. Now the reporter has created news with his own arrest. As a result, the reporter may gain a better understanding of what it is like to be the focus of a negative news story. Perhaps the newspaper for which the minority reporter writes should have run the news story as well; the editors there, however, opted not to do so. In the end, the reporter retained his job but was placed on probation for driving his car at a police officer, violating anti-solicitation laws, and lying.

The Cyber-Information Age

The technology explosion of the past 15 years is sending professional communicators back to their drawing boards, seeking answers to the moral complexities posed by the cyber revolution.

On the one hand, new technology is making far more information available to each of us through vastly expanded information networks. To the traditional forms of mass media (newspapers, television, radio, magazines, etc.) have been added the Internet and satellite and cable technology, which are making available many information channels that both compete for audience and add to the volume and scope of information available to that audience.

As one example, the nonprofit Public Broadcasting Service (PBS), generally viewed as owning the cultural and educational airwaves, has been challenged by other commercial cable and satellite channels, such as A&E, Bravo, the History Channel, the Discovery Channel, and the National Geographic Channel, all of which transmit material similar to that on PBS and thereby lure audiences away from PBS. Consequently, PBS has been forced to reexamine itself and determine not only how it will become competitive but also how that competition will affect (or possibly "dilute") the quality of their programming and affect the ethical structure of its system.

The PBS dilemma, the severity of which is measured by declining audiences and waning influence, is a microcosm of the problem facing the entire media industry. Broadcasting networks that can securely chart and safely follow their own moral pathway without interference from competition are increasingly rare. Competition stresses the moral resolve of many well-intentioned organizations; competition tempts or even forces them to cut moral corners to survive. And, of course, on the Internet lurk those ghostly sources that attract large audiences by distributing information without concern for whether it is true. Their anonymity allows them to circumvent the accountability to which most credible information resources are subjected. The new technology also allows special-interest demagogues to rant to those who want to hear only that which reinforces their views.

Another complication brought about by the cyber-information age is the conglomerating of media units under broad-based corporate umbrellas—the National Broadcasting Corporation (NBC) is owned by General Electric, for example. Such unions create massive possibilities for conflict of interest and deteriorating credibility as reporters at local broadcast stations find themselves covering stories that further the interests of the parent corporation for which they work.

On the other side of the coin is the breaking down of media monopolies. If you search the Internet, you can find stories on nearly any topic, a far cry from reliance on information provided by one daily newspaper and three local network television channels. This expands the ability of the individual to make decisions based on a broad base of information, which surely must be viewed as a positive development. With the emergence of "insider" newsletters on the Web, details about the inner workings of organizations are now available to investors, competitors, and interested observers. Inside.com is one such newsletter. Geared toward the media and entertainment industries, it provides statistics, databases, and detailed information that make it essential reading for virtually every media professional.

Thus, the cyber-information age, as with most new technologies in an open society, has brought about some harm and some good. While the cyber revolution makes vast amounts of information more readily available, it poses problems for the communicator scrambling to meet the challenge of informing the audience while contending with competitive forces. One beneficial effect has been to raise questions about corporate conflict of interest that have traditionally not been a part of media ethics discussions. Such questions arise as media companies scramble to position themselves favorably in a global economy rocked by collapsing dotcom stocks and a queasy stock market at the dawn of the 21st century.

While most public discussions about the media have concentrated on the ethical agency of individual journalists, broadcasters, public relations practitioners, or advertising professionals, little has been mentioned about conflicts such as the one that arose when ABC's *Good Morning America* weekday morning news show featured a guest puppet that insisted it be called the "Pets.com sock puppet." The puppet was making the rounds of ABC news shows, which would have been a cute and harmless novelty were it not for the fact that Pets.com was partly owned by a subsidiary of Disney, the parent company of ABC.

The hosts of such shows, the people the audience sees and to whom considerable credibility is assigned, normally are expected to bear individual responsibility for their ethical behavior. Yet the hosts of *Good Morning America* were largely powerless to determine whether the Pets.com sock puppet would appear and may not even have known of the connection among the companies.

In the Internet and satellite information world, meanwhile, virtually anyone can have access to vast audiences merely by creating a World Wide Web home page, which can be accessed and viewed by an almost limitless number of viewers. As other forms of media did in their exuberant youth, outrageous excesses can be expected as Webmasters test their powers and public protests multiply. Nevertheless, these resources may also publish legitimate news, news that would not be covered by the more traditional media. Early stories about former President Clinton's sexual escapades were published by online newsletters before being picked up by the standard media. Some argue that these were trivial stories the traditional media was forced to cover in order to compete with the online media. Others argue that legitimate stories are only covered by self-serving media once they are shaken from their comfortable roosts. A basic expectation of a free-speech society is that gluts of irresponsibility will subside as audiences tire of extremism or turn to other sources for new information. Whether this happens or not, moral obligations remain clear, mandating that new and merged media deal fairly with their audiences, tell the truth, and empower their audiences to make informed decisions.

ESTABLISHING BOUNDARIES FOR DISTRIBUTING INFORMATION

Boundaries of activity will often be determined by an individual's attitude and belief systems and how that individual views the role of information in his or her life and in society. In a thoughtful approach to decision making, a media professional evaluates a number of elements in his or her existing value system, using the Beacon on the Hill discussed earlier as a benchmark. Because the distribution of information is the central function of a media professional, consideration must be given to one's attitude toward the concept of *informationalism*. Information is the currency of the media professional in that the relative value given the distribution of information by a media professional is central to the decisions that person will make.

The media professional's attitude regarding the distribution of information will then affect all other values, as well as all other elements of his or her personal moral theory. A strong informationalist will see the distribution of information as a top priority, an attitude that will enable him or her to overcome reservations about harms and accept the maxim that the distribution of information, whatever the consequences, is good. For example, an informationalist would tend to disclose the results of medical disciplinary hearings, assuming that service to the many supersedes consideration of harm to the physician's reputation. An informationalist's reasoning, of course, would be that the value to society at large (help to individuals in society) of specific information about this practice (even the smaller community of the media being used) so outweighs the harm to individuals involved that the story should be made public. The information may be empowering in that previously powerless patients may now have the ability to make informed decisions.

Is Failure to Distribute Information a Greater Harm?

A basic premise made by the informationalist is that the harm caused by the failure to distribute information will generally be greater than harm caused by its distribution. The threat of physical harm or a life-or-death situation may be reason for pause. If a child is kidnapped and his or her life threatened if the kidnapping becomes public knowledge, an informationalist may see the potential harm of distributing that information as greater than the benefit and withhold the story until the threat of harm no longer exists. This simple reasoning, however, does not take into account other kinds of threats that create more serious dilemmas for editors.

Classic Case in Journalism: Juvenile Court Judge

A juvenile court judge who had been molesting children in his charge for a number of years threatened to commit suicide if newspapers published the details of this story. The story was published, and the judge killed himself.

The informationalist would say society deserved, for its own protection, to have access to this information in order to flesh out its view of the way the world is. The judge should not be allowed to hold the information system hostage with threats. Therefore, even though life (the judge's) as a value would normally take precedence over the distribution of information (as in the case of the kidnapped child), in this case withholding the information would endanger the entire information system, and victimization of the powerless would continue, fostered by journalists whose job it is to inform people.

Broadly applied, being deprived of information, no matter what harm results, limits the ability of citizens to make decisions that would help them flourish. Also, by implication, a participatory society is endangered when deprived of information because its members are not able to participate meaningfully with informed decisions.

CLASSIC CASE IN PUBLIC RELATIONS: JUVENILE COURT JUDGE, PART II

Others in the system had differing views. The judge's colleagues and others knew of the abuses but were concerned about the damage that disclosure would do to the entire juvenile justice system. For example, release of the information could result in that community's loss of faith. That faith, however, was built on the ability of the schools and other institutions to persuade the community that the system functioned well and that the community could be confident that the system was capably dispensing justice to juveniles.

Using Communication Skills to Advocate a Product or Idea

The professional persuader uses information and communication skills to be an advocate for a product or idea and, if successful, wins customers or adherents. The professional persuader's basic loyalty differs in comparison to the media professional's basic loyalty. Whereas an informationalist, or media professional, has an assumed basic loyalty to an audience (an audience is that which the journalist seeks to attract and hold), an obligation that may transcend loyalty to an employer, the professional persuader's basic loyalty is to his or her client and to the client's cause or product, with a secondary, but still important, loyalty to audience.

This loyalty to society, although secondary, sometimes forces professional persuaders to identify a threshold beyond which loyalty to a client will not take them—usually when his or her actions on behalf of a client would likely result in damage to society. A professional persuader usually makes two basic moral presumptions: first, that he or she may use information selectively, as long as it is truthful; and second, that he or she may choose not to keep secret severely harmful information (i.e., awareness that silicone breast implants may burst and cause severe health problems). Since laws generally do not specify the correct course of action regarding the distribution of information, it is up to the moral judgment of individuals to decide whether that information ought to be made public.

DEFINING HARMLESS DISTRIBUTION OF INFORMATION

The principle is that professional persuaders may deceive with the truth if the deception is relatively harmless, or "acceptable truth" as one marketer characterizes it. Since harm is a natural product of all communication as the power to distribute information shifts, so *harmless* becomes a relative term, implying that harm resulting from deception in the name of legitimate competition and persuasion is acceptable, but that fatal results are usually unacceptable.

Arguably, both professional persuaders and information providers should commit to the expanded distribution of information as a moral mandate. Such a mandate, however, would be difficult to accept by those who have been conditioned to accept restraints on the distribution of information. In a sense, both professional groups look to being informationalists, the journalist for quantity of information and the persuader for the quality of information. In both cases, the priority placed on the value of distributing information in the interest of advancing the social good ought to be a substantial determiner of a personal moral theory.

REGULATING INFORMATION: ABSOLUTISM

One who believes that people need to be directed in their decision making will be more inclined to regulate the information dispensed so that it will have a higher probability of producing the correct response. This attitude may have an inherently religious origin. In particular, the Christian doctrine of original sin tends to give us a somewhat dim view of the nature of humans in that it assumes humans need to be controlled. Thus, religious doctrine and secular doctrine (individualism) are at odds in a society that assumes the overriding validity of public opinion when it springs from an informed populace.

It seems fairly obvious that the Bill of Rights assumes the rationality of the citizens it protects. Therefore, whether it is correct or makes a disastrously bad assumption, it nevertheless is the system to which this country has committed itself and it tends to drive our laws and judicial decisions. Communicators who choose to adopt other assumptions must recognize that they are at odds with the system and should deliberate carefully on the effects of their decisions.

Court decisions based on the First Amendment discourage **absolutism**, complete and unrestricted power in government, and instead give preference to the dynamism of pluralism. As a consequence, communication industry personnel are not required to be licensed, nor may their ability to practice be held hostage by a code of ethics. This refusal to embrace absolutism inspires the absence of pedagogy in this book, which attempts to suggest principles that may influence the decision-making process rather than dictating which decisions should be made; this antidogmatic approach to the study of media and ethics, in turn, permits us to make troubling, yet thought-provoking statements, such as that made previously that fatal consequences are *usually* unacceptable as opposed to *always* unacceptable in cases of deception in the name of legitimate competition and persuasion.

How Does Information Affect Society?

Some Prefer Social Order

The professional communicator's central position in society as distributor of information (and thereby facilitator of informed decision making) suggests that professional communicators as a group greatly influence the way society functions. In light of this influence, professional communicators need to formulate a fairly sophisticated map outlining the roads they feel society should travel.

Discomfort with conflict and uncertainty, on the one hand, motivates media professionals to strive to reduce **social conflict** and competition. Such efforts are commonly referred to as *community building*. Media professionals who engage in community building actively seek to bring about social accord and harmony in that they provide information that is more likely to build a consensus than it is to pit community factions against one another.

Some Prefer Conflict and Competition

On the other hand, a media professional's appetite for conflict often leads to the promotion of competition and a degree of disharmony in the community, which is why it is often said that media professionals comfort the afflicted and afflict the comfortable. While a professional persuader may feel comfortable with either course of action, a community-oriented public relations person may see himself or herself as an arbiter of competing interests; conversely, the advertising executive most often thrives on vigorous competition. The prevailing social system, of course, suggests the primacy of competition and the general acceptance of inevitable social conflict in a pluralistic culture. It anticipates that progress and development (of both self and society) are likely to thrive in an adversary climate, rather than a climate of accord. General social conditioning, however, encourages individuals to moderate conflict and foster collegiality and harmony.

SOCIAL ORDER OR CONFLICT: WHICH IS MORE BENEFICIAL?

Much of the instructional influence in our lives may tend to favor the communal, conflict-free approach as a way of moderating the free-flying individualistic influence. This type of influence may predispose many to become consensus builders and even rule followers.

The challenge faced by media professionals in an adversarial social system is to develop their own moral reasoning mechanisms, apply principles derived from those mechanisms, and carefully prioritize their values. The moral obligation of media professionals, in return for constitutional protection, may consist of serving the public by assuring the continuance of a pluralism in the distribution of information (journalists) and assuring that the power of communication is not used to victimize (professional persuaders). For all media professionals, individual autonomy and systematic thought (i.e., a Beacon on the Hill) are required to provide these types of public service.

Certainly, one who values community and consensus may argue persuasively that because conflict drains a society's energies, reduced conflict and greater social order are needed. This argument, if successful, could bring about a fundamental change in our **social philosophy**—a change that would require serious advance thought instead of merely accepting it for the sake of comfort and convenience.

Few would argue that conflict and pluralism are comfortable or convenient; their value lies in long-term social benefits and social dynamism. For many, however, the visceral emotional response to pluralism includes striving for its reduction, seeking an increase in consensus, and bringing about a greater social order. Therefore, it is necessary that a considered attitude toward social order stand as another primary determinant of a person's moral theory.

WHEN NEW RULES COME ALONG: GENDER ISSUES

New rules are always being proposed by many who, uncomfortable with individual freedom, mistrust a human being's ability to handle it. Unless strong opposition deters the acceptance of such rules, authoritarianism rises. Throughout history, periods of expanded individual rights have alternated with periods of constricted individual rights, swinging like a pendulum from one extreme to the other. The speed and frequency of these pendulum swings depends on citizen activism. Women, for example, have until fairly recently been denied many rights, including the rights of inheritance, the right to vote, or even the right to wear "men's" clothing. The pendulum has swung in the other direction in the past century as women have exercised those rights formerly denied them.

Mass media professionals are purposely positioned by the First Amendment to exercise substantial power in the shaping of public opinion and therefore must be careful about how they go about it. The power of distributing information is one of the most profound an individual possesses. Information is the taproot of informed decision making and key to participation in a democratic society. Therefore, media professionals are the first line of defense in a society in which decision making is an individual right.

PUBLIC PRESSURE AND LONG-TERM CONSEQUENCES

CONTEMPORARY CASE IN JOURNALISM: THE INCENTIVE

A news story is publicly criticized because it details the actions of local officials in procuring prostitutes for visiting executives of a major corporation that is exploring the possibility of building a factory in the community and bringing with it 500 new jobs. The writer of the story is accused of sensationalism and is told that the story is not worthy of publication. The short-term effect may be embarrassment and some uncertainty about whether the potential employer of 500 local workers has been scared off by the publicity. Over the long-term, disclosure of misdeeds, such as the solicitation of prostitutes, should stimulate public discussion and result in greater community consensus about appropriate behavior for its public officials. In the short-term, by writing the story, the professional communicator has used her individualism to resist community pressures in order to serve long-term interests despite short-term concerns.

In this case, the individualistic media professional is an invaluable communitarian asset (see the discussion of *communitarian individual* in Chapter 4). Being ethical is often difficult in an individualistic society because the more pressing ethical questions require acts of sacrifice. It may be easy to sell a product or service (diet program, emergency unclogging of a sink drain, new engine, etc.) to naive or desperate people for twice its value, but perhaps one should refrain from doing so, refusing to victimize others merely for financial gain.

CONSIDERATION FOR THE WEAK

Differences in the requirements of the law as they relate to ethics will be discussed in later chapters. It is important at this point to recognize that ethics are necessary in those arenas in which one is not required by law to be considerate of the naive or powerless. Ethics causes one to be concerned about others and suggests that we treat them as one would want to be treated if in similar circumstances. A sense of morality and ethics requires people to look outside themselves to the welfare of others over whom they have some dominion.

SELF-INTEREST AND EMOTION

It is because the concept of morality has been construed differently by so many people in their formative years that we will return frequently to this topic for careful examination. People faced with decisions that affect others are very likely to react reflexively in ways that are both emotional and selfish. The term *uninformed* may also be appropriate in this context because there is some evidence that we often avoid knowledge that would change our reactions and make us less selfish.

You may, either consciously or subconsciously, avoid considering the consequences of your decisions in order to avoid being aware of the harm you may do. You may also purposely avoid knowing about something before you make a decision for fear that that knowledge would make the decision more difficult, troublesome, or possibly cause you to consider some sacrifice. Certainly, selfish, emotional, and uninformed reactions are not valid for everyone, nor are they valid in all situations.

We can all point to circumstances in which we have acted well on the spur of the moment. However, it is likely that we can also all point to moments when we have misled someone in our own interest; for example,

"The car was running well when I sold it to you," "I mailed the check three days ago," "I don't remember you telling me that," "I have tried several times to call you," "My computer crashed," "The specialist who handled your repairs is not here today," "Tell him I am not in," and so forth. All of these self-serving deceptions and their hundreds of variations are excuses that all but the most conscientious of us tend to use to avoid trouble with others or to explain away our shortcomings.

IS DECEPTIVE INFORMATION HARMFUL?

CONTEMPORARY CASE IN JOURNALISM: WIN AT ALL COSTS

Betty wants to be an anchorperson for a national broadcasting organization. She wants this position so badly that she is deliberately spreading "half-truths" about her competitors, such as "he is always late," "he doesn't check his facts," "she misses deadlines," and "political leaders just won't give him stories." The half-truths are intended to undermine the credibility of her competition.

Immediately, we recognize that Betty's actions are unacceptable. Spreading false and malicious **rumor**s about others is often a harm that cannot be corrected. Betty can pursue her own dreams to be a broadcast anchorperson, but society has moral restraints against this type of fraudulent activity. The entire concept of free speech is damaged by Betty's actions. Betty has a right to exercise free speech, but she does not have a moral right to tell untruths about professional colleagues. Betty has a right to pursue a media career, but she should advance in her career based on her own merits, not by planting damaging information that cannot be confirmed. If Betty is willing to cheat to get this job, will she also be willing to perform dishonest acts once in the anchorperson slot? As a media professional, Betty needs to take full responsibility for her utterances and choices.

Harmless Deceptions

Our "minor" deceptions may seem to be harmless ways of buying time or avoiding other problems, but their primary effect is still deception, causing others to make decisions based on information that we know is not true. However we may choose to look at these behaviors, we cannot escape the conclusion that in such instances we are deceiving for our own benefit. The concept of truth, which is an essential element in the life of any media professional, is discussed often in this book. "Minor" deceptions raise questions as to whether an absolute standard can be applied to truth telling.

If we all must tell the truth all the time, would society be a better place? Would we be better off as individuals? Is it clear that truth telling is an absolute ethic for all times and places? Most of us probably do not have to think back very far to identify occasions when we have not told the truth, occasions when it was not only convenient but useful and even beneficial to others to lie. Although truth telling is a basic element of any moral society, it should be quickly recognized that deception, by individuals and institutions, is an intrinsic element with which we must come to grips if we are to survive and flourish as individuals and as a society. This is particularly important, of course, for advertising and public relations professionals who are often accused of deception.

Common Deceptions

In society at large, police in unmarked patrol cars catch unwary speeders; football and basketball players "fake" one way and run the other; and you, by the way you dress, by the smile you put on despite your sadness, and by saying things you think people want you to say rather than what you think, show the world a "you" that you want it to see, rather than the real "you." It is generally that which is learned at home, in church, on the streets, and in school that provides individuals with the broad strokes of expected behavior.

Such teachings generally are aimed at helping you treat others well. Yet these teachings often may not take into account the kinds of behaviors needed to succeed in a competitive society like the United States, a society that embraces free enterprise, individualism, and capitalism.

Competition sheds new light on the question of how we treat others. What we find in the real world, particularly as media professionals, may be very different from what we were taught to expect, calling for different behaviors, perhaps even for behaviors we have been taught to avoid.

USING INFORMATION TO IMPROVE DEMOCRACY

It has been mentioned that to act ethically is to refrain from victimizing others, often making ethical behavior an act of sacrifice. Yet a democratic society seems to require that someone be inconvenienced or even be victimized in order that the rest may benefit from such sacrifice. That, in part, is the nature of competition. In addition to producing winners and the inevitable losers, competition causes all parties to improve themselves in preparation for the next competitive encounter.

It is this that may be the essence of a democratic, competitive society. Professional communicators are in the thick of it, providing the information necessary for competitive improvement. And, of course, it is important to recognize that, because of the very nature of our society, we are all in competition virtually all the time.

We compete for jobs, for space on the highway, and even with merchants as we seek the best product for the most reasonable price—an inherent competition between seller and buyer. Thus, ethics for media professionals (remember that distribution of information is an exercise of power) is not solely concerned with avoiding the victimization of others—that would oversimplify matters. Ethics for media professionals is really more about using moral principles and reason to decide when some victimization will result in benefits to many others in a manner that outweighs the undoubted harm.

THE REPORTING OF SUICIDE

Suicide, for example, is a tragic event that brings pain and suffering to family and friends. Because of this, and in order to spare grieving families, media professionals are pressed to omit the identification of victims and certain details. The usual claim made is that "publishing the names, or even the fact, of the suicide would do no good."

This illustrates a fundamental problem in moral reasoning—how does one go about making an uninformed judgment, one which, in this case, is emotional and selfish? When reporting a suicide, the decision to withhold information is emotional because the thought of causing pain to others is repugnant to most and we intuitively avoid it whenever we can. Seldom in this circumstance do we consider that a greater good is not without some pain. Wars to maintain freedom, for example, result in much pain and destruction. Similarly, surgeons inflict harm in order to assure a patient's healthier future (even a badly set bone is painfully rebroken in order to return the limb to its functional state).

In many cases, the infliction of pain may be the unavoidable outcome when information is dispersed. A loved one must be informed about the details of an unexpected death in the family. But what are the consequences of never telling others something that will bring them anguish? Selfishly, we make rash decisions about reporting suicide, knowing only what we know, without taking the trouble to consider that there may be good reasons for publishing names and details. To act in ignorance is a selfish act, for it assumes one knows all one needs to know in order to make a decision.

Such decisions are more easily made when complicating details are unknown, details that would make the decision to publish such information more difficult. Reporters and editors, while fully aware of the anguish they will cause with the publication of such information, need to identify the greater goods that may result from such publication, that is, identify the benefits that may more than offset the harm. The basic good, of course, is that to gather and distribute information is good—the journalist's basic function, and it is to preserve that good that the journalist is protected by law from government interference. The decision to withhold information should not be taken lightly; certainly, the routine withholding of information should be avoided.

RESPONSIBILITY TO BE INFORMED

As we previously noted, an individualistic society requires that each individual make his or her own decisions; those decisions, for the good of the community, need to be informed decisions, rather than decisions made in ignorance. Should a media professional withhold information when reporting a suicide? The primary function of a media professional is to distribute information that will help individuals to make informed decisions. Generally, a journalist will be keenly aware of the harm that will result from the publication of names and details in cases of suicide but will be unaware of any benefits that may result. Therefore, communicators must construct a philosophically thoughtful justification for such publication, one that is consistent with reasons for guaranteeing a free press in this country. Conversely, communicators have a moral obligation to thoughtfully justify withholding information about the suicides—an argument that goes beyond the emotional rationale discussed previously.

A media professional may rationalize that if the media fails to publish details of such incidents, then consumers of information begin to live in a world of false expectations. In this case, parents, in particular, may be unaware of the incidence of suicide in their community and therefore may not be sensitive to the warning signals of suicide in their own children, information that may help prevent a family tragedy. Alternatively, they may believe that suicide only happens to those in other socio-economic circumstances or to those who are "not as happy as we are." Therefore, a journalistic obligation might be to create as realistic an image as possible of the community in which readers or viewers live, one that will adequately prepare them for the decisions they must make. Knowledge of suicides, or even of the incidence of AIDS in the community, may be critical to an audience member faced with having to make a painful decision.

INFORMATION IS A COMMODITY

Two points are essential in this discussion. First, important information does not come easily in a democratic society. Second, the distribution of virtually any useful information will be harmful to someone. Central to these two points, of course, is the notion that information is an extremely valuable commodity that people guard or use to their advantage—one of the realistic consequences of living in an information society flooded with new electronic information resources.

Returning to the question of whether to publish a suicide story, one editor may decide that it is important to run the story, while another will kill the story, depending on the philosophy each has developed in his or her years of experience. If the editor decides that it is preferable not to cause pain, then he or she will not publish the story. If the editor decides that the information contained in the story is important and may affect people's abilities to make informed decisions, then he or she will run the story.

The first editor, of course, will feel that the information in the story is not as important as avoidance of pain. The second will recognize that causing someone pain will be an inevitable outcome and yet still run the story. These different decisions result from the different orientation of values of the two editors. Either decision can be justified, and it would be difficult to declare that one or the other editor is correct, which aptly illustrates the essence of media ethics in the United States. The least justifiable decision, perhaps, is to run the story simply "because it happened," suggesting a decision made in blind adherence to rules.

Information as Socially Acceptable Harm

The publication of damaging stories is not the only socially acceptable harm, for there are many reasons why it is not only socially acceptable but socially desirable to treat others badly, most of which can be attributed to the characteristics of a competitive society. For example, despite sanctions against inflicting bodily harm to others, a football player, when assigned to do so, is committed to the acceptable harm of temporarily disabling an opponent. Continued presence on the team is frequently dependent on how well that act is performed.

While causing harm on the football field is strictly regulated, the harm caused by distributing information is free from restrictions, perhaps because society recognizes that psychic or emotional harm is a price all must pay for the benefits of an open society, while physical harm is something to be avoided unless we put on protective padding and get on the field.

Accumulation of Behaviors Affects Quality of Life

If professional media ethics demands restraint in an unregulated environment to serve the community while striving to avoid causing unnecessary harm, then it is not the harm that the distribution of information will cause but the intent or motivation behind the dissemination of the message that is the key to this restraint. Moreover, it is the accumulation of these intents or motivations that determines the shape society takes. Unethical acts need not be of great significance, but may be relatively minor; nevertheless, others are needlessly and frequently inconvenienced (victimized) by such thoughtless acts.

Minor unethical acts, such as going down a stairway on the wrong side (most of us are accustomed to walking on the right) and requiring someone else to move, are victimizing acts—acts generally performed out of thoughtlessness or for our own convenience. Similarly, when friends gather in a narrow passageway to talk and impede others who want to pass by, they have victimized others—probably thoughtlessly—for their own comfort and convenience.

The cumulative effect of such behavior, which proves so frustrating for the victims, adversely affects the quality of life. These behaviors are exhibited by a variety of people in a variety of places—indifferent sales clerks, terse auto repair service managers, drivers hurrying to zip through a yellow light before it turns red, drivers who leave others stranded at a stoplight because they delay their own passage, and many others. Common in all of these readily recognizable examples is an inconsiderate attitude by which we all victimize others and by which we are all victimized.

On an everyday basis, the quality of life in any culture is improved by thoughtful people who make the slight extra effort needed to avoid creating unnecessary stumbling blocks for others. These stumbling blocks may be significant acts, such as lying about another person, or the relatively insignificant act of blocking a hallway when someone else is trying to pass.

THE RIGHT THING TO DO

It should be noted that, generally, neither lying about another person nor standing in the hallway violates laws; therefore, individuals engaging in these behaviors are not subject to any sanctions beyond one's own conscience and good will. Good ethical behavior results in an action that is motivated not by the sanctions of law, but in an action that is performed simply because it is the right thing to do. A moral culture is one in which a people engage in good ethical behavior because they recognize that it benefits not only others but themselves as well.

The communication industry has a special stake in ethics because of the American social system, a system that generally removes legal pressures from the practice of communications, leaving professionals to largely determine their own ethic. Absence of legal restraint similarly removes protection from audiences, allowing the victimization and manipulation previously described and making it very important that communication professionals "act well." Acting well recognizes that virtually all information pumped into the system causes harm because it empowers the receiver at the expense of the subject. In the face of unavoidable harm, the professional communicator must use principle and reason to identify the fine line between doing good and doing unjustifiable injury for selfish reasons and/or to little beneficial effect.

POWER

Power—particularly personal power—and its use are central to ethical decision making. Ethics regulates how individuals use the power they possess in relation to those with less power. Everyone has some power, that is, the ability to victimize one who has less power. Even those who are apparently the most powerless can destroy property, inflict mayhem on unsuspecting others, and organize and act in ways that disrupt the social fabric. Therefore, it is important to examine in some depth the concept of power, personal power and group power, in order to better understand the critical ethical demands that are made on the professional communicator, who both wields power and distributes power to (or withholds it from) the powerless.

It is axiomatic that a free flow of information has the ability to empower individuals in ways that generally distribute power—more or less evenly— over the entire society, rather than allowing it to accumulate to corrupting levels in "power centers" (individuals or groups). This is a process that requires a combination of conscientious communicators, individual citizens who will not allow power to accumulate, and power brokers (including professional persuaders, such as advertising and public relations workers) who use their power well. This concept of power will be discussed further in the text.

RACE AND GENDER

CONTEMPORARY CASE IN PUBLIC RELATIONS: GORE AND CAMPAIGN WORKERS

Columnist Susan Estrich explains in Sex and Power *that Vice President Al Gore did not have any women or minorities as part of his early presidential campaign team. It was not until she threatened to publish this information in a column that Vice President Gore hired an African American woman, Donna Brazille. Additionally, a Hispanic woman was initially selected to manage the National Democratic Convention based in Los Angeles. According to Estrich, that woman had little experience and was overpowered by the white men running the Gore campaign (p. 227).*

As this case demonstrates, power can be centered in positions as well as in individuals. If Al Gore's campaign staff was not representing and listening to the entire Democratic Party, it was abusing power. The hiring of two racially diverse women makes little difference unless they are allowed to fully make choices and contribute to the overall campaign. The conferring of power is an important ritual, but in such instances power generally must be earned rather than gifted. When women or persons of race are missing from positions in which powerful decisions are made, it is important that the media point this out. Those in power sometimes forget or neglect to include those who do not resemble them.

Additionally, as a practical matter, the system anticipates that individuals, such as Estrich and other professional communicators, may be moderating influences on the powerful, since professional communicators have historically empowered powerless individuals via the distribution of information. While journalists have the power to distribute or withhold information, advertising and public relations specialists have a disproportionate power springing from their enviably rare skills in communicating effectively and understanding the media systems through which they work. That they rent these powers out to clients or employers places a special moral obligation on them to act carefully in the open marketplace.

POWER OF GROUPS

Information filtered through the mass media is not the only way power is moderated, of course. Individuals or groups also stimulate activities that affect decision making.

CLASSIC CASE IN MEDIA: VIETNAM AND THE PRESIDENT

Public protests by groups opposed to the U.S. involvement in Vietnam in the late 1960s pressured the media (a power center) into providing coverage they were at first reluctant to provide. Adding to the protests was an evolving American skepticism in a war that was costly in terms of lives and money. The media coverage of the Vietnam War that was finally provided resulted in President Lyndon Johnson deciding not to run for reelection and President Nixon eventually seeking ways out of the involvement.

While we may see power as something exercised on a large scale by corporate executives or political leaders, the vast majority of power related to ethics lies in the daily behavior of hundreds of millions of individuals. A president, no matter what the popularity ratings are going into office, cannot ignore the public's displeasure with an unpopular war. Such a power shift makes the re-election of a president virtually impossible. The power of individuals makes reelection possible. President Bill Clinton made decisions based on weekly public opinion polls and his approval ratings when leaving office were still above 65 percent. His power remained intact because he understood the importance of responding to the views of the public.

The reporter who invades privacy and destroys lives with a story that is merely interesting rather than important to the audience has used professional power badly. The reporter, on the other hand, who invades privacy to gather and distribute important information that will greatly influence public opinion, even though such information may be devastating to the source, uses power well. Both actions are permitted by law and morally defensible but still presuppose some sensitivity to the use of personal power. The public relations counselor who publicly defends a client's position while knowing that the client engages in catastrophically destructive behavior uses professional skills to persuade a public that is dependent on that information for its decision making in the matter.

Considerate Use of Power

In an ethical society, individuals exercise personal power wisely and considerately, and the distribution of power to those who wish to accumulate it is carefully measured out. It should be clear from this discussion that power is an important element in a participatory society. Power distribution in authoritarian societies is very one-sided; in a democratic society the distribution of power should be much more equitable. This is certainly not to suggest that power should not be accumulated, but it does argue that power, no matter where or in whom it accumulates, be it the president of the United States, a corporate chief executive officer, or a physically abusive spouse, should be challenged by constant public scrutiny and discussion.

Ethical Judgments of a Community

Power should be subject to intense and continuing self-scrutiny by communication professionals. The quality of a society is determined by the collective ethical judgments of its citizenry. In an authoritarian society, morality tends to be shaped by rules designed to promote stability and social order. The profusion of rules required for the desired stability may produce so much social order that creative expression is very difficult, if not impossible. In a pluralistic society, rules should be limited to those that provide the stability and social order that restrains individuals from needlessly harming others, while giving their creativity wide room to flourish. It should be clear that a democratic society entails more risk because the widespread trust among its participants can easily be violated.

Those who are uncomfortable with such a society are often willing to trade individual agency for the security granted by a more restricted society, one in which they are certain that violators of that narrower trust will be punished. Nourishment for a democratic society, because of its individualistic nature, lies in expectations that citizens will be more productive as free individuals than they would living under restrictive regulations. If individual power is used well, the accumulated fruits of individual creativity will produce a superior society—a society that produces everything from higher life expectancy to individualized transportation to central heating and air conditioning and bigger and faster personal computers. Each of these improvements enhances the ability of its members to work out their own definitions of personal satisfaction or of a satisfying life.

INDIVIDUAL CREATIVITY

A democratic society gambles that individual industry and creativity will be more valid and productive than will the products of central planning and the conditioned cooperation typical of more authoritarian cultures. For these reasons, individual behavior and the parameters of group/cultural behavior will be very different in the United States than it is in those countries governed by authoritarian rule. Certainly, many behavioral conventions will be the same across most cultures, but there will be significant differences in details.

Young people treat their elders quite differently in the United States than in China, for example. While the loss of respect for the elderly may be deplored by many in this country, that very loss of respect (and its implied obedience) encourages young people to try new ideas, thereby feeding society's creative, entrepreneurial spirit. Although not readily acknowledged as such, declining respect for elders is an act of independence, freeing the younger individual to invent or err on his or her own.

In China, in contrast, young scientists returning from overseas with graduate degrees often find themselves working under the stifling control of a largely uneducated older supervisor who provides little latitude for experimentation and innovation. The privilege of seniority, or respect for the elderly, while valuable in many respects, can also produce a crippling waste of valuable resources. The young, educated worker finds his or her education largely ignored while work patterns are shaped by precedent and tradition. The very fact of expanded individual freedom, however, suggests the need for free people to behave well.

Individual competition among ethical people can produce both the dynamic, progressive society of individual enterprise (often termed *cutthroat*) and the gentler, considerate society of ethical behavior. When ethical behavior, the glue that holds a democratic society together, gives way, legislation and popular acceptance of rules move us closer to the authoritarian, divine right cultures of the past.

SUMMARY

This chapter examined the fundamental basis for learning ethics, primarily media ethics, and outlined the social system professional communicators must confront in their work. It explored some of the misleading social myths that drive ethical behavior, suggesting that individuals in the communication field must develop their own autonomous moral behavioral patterns if they are to fulfill their First Amendment obligations to society. The use of power is an integral part of the communicator's profession, with ethical deliberations expected to modify that use away from selfish purposes to some social benefit in a competitive society. Professional communicators are encouraged to recognize the social "game" of competition and to pick their way through the moral pitfalls of a largely unregulated culture.

MORAL REASONING QUESTIONS

1. Why is it problematic to tell a caller that your roommate is not at home when he or she is? What possible greater harm could result from the harmless fib than a roommate's anger at being forced to talk to someone he or she wishes to avoid? Why?
2. How can information possibly be viewed as socially helpful when it brings deep anguish to the subject of the information? Give an example.
3. What is meant by "When I follow the rules, it's not my fault when things go wrong"? What moral principles are involved in rule following?

4. What are the connections among standard of living, creativity, and free expression?
5. If information does not come easily in a democratic society, why is freedom of speech so important?

Contemporary Case in Journalism: Internet News

The editor of a new online newsletter purporting to be "the insider" in the political community of a medium-sized metropolitan area knows that she must make an impact on the area (and especially on her target audience) in order to establish the newsletter's presence and help make it commercially viable (with both advertising and subscriptions).

A friend who has been active in Democratic Party politics tells her that two contenders for the chairmanship of the County Republican Party Central Committee got into a fist fight over the party's future course near the end of the committee's meeting yesterday. The Republican Party dominates politics in the area but lost substantial support in two large minorities in the last election, so its future course is critical.

Neither the television stations nor the newspapers mention the alleged incident. The editor calls the only four members of the central committee she could reach to try to verify the story, but one says that she left before any such thing happened, one says that nothing happened, and the other two say that they do not want to talk about it. Calls to the two men involved go unanswered.

The editor is unsure whether either newspaper knows of the incident, but feels that because of the dominance and power of the Republican Party, none of the traditional media will mention an alleged incident that would be very embarrassing to the Republican Party. Moreover, this is exactly the kind of story she began her online newsletter to cover—stories that establishment media will not touch.

If you were the editor, would you put the story on your Web page, hoping to force the other media to pick it up and give you needed publicity, even if they just pass on denials by Republican Party leaders?

1. *You have read that 97 percent of rumors have some degree of truth. Is that, coupled with the fact that two committee members who were contacted did not want to talk about it, enough to justify publishing the story? Why?*

2. Is the publication of such a story about the most powerful political party in the region justified, since it might be true and thus be valuable information? (If it is not true, it will not likely hurt the party.)
3. What moral principles would justify printing something you think may be the truth but cannot be verified?
4. Should there be different rules for an underground publication with a small audience than for a major newspaper or television station? Why?
5. Even if the story turns out to be false but its publication assures your survival as another voice in the community because of the publicity, can your publication of it be justified? How? Does the benefit of having more voices in what appears to be a fairly closed community outweigh the harm of a false rumor?
6. Is it adequate to label an unverified story as a rumor and still publish it to inform your audience? Why?

Contemporary Case in Journalism: The Lie and the Consequence

A broadcast news reporter, leaving the secure area of the station by opening the door leading into the open public lobby, found herself confronted by an unkempt woman holding an automatic pistol who asked if that was the door to the newsroom. When the reporter hesitated, the woman fired one shot into the floor near the reporter's feet. The reporter quickly replied, "No, the newsroom is that way," indicating the door from the lobby into the area of the building's elevator doors, and quickly stepped back into the newsroom, slamming the door.

The woman with the gun went into an elevator, rode up a few floors, and began shooting into another office (a business unrelated to the broadcast station). A receptionist was shot to death before the woman was subdued.

1. Given the stress of the moment, could the reporter have done anything else other than what she did?
2. Is there persuasive moral justification for having sent a dangerous person away from her target area when she goes to offices close by and kills someone who is not the primary target of her wrath?

3. Is there a difference between lying to and withholding information from someone who is not entitled to that information? Was the "strange" woman entitled to any information?
4. How should a broadcast news station protect its employees? Is it a moral obligation to do so? Explain and defend your answer.

CONTEMPORARY CASE IN MEDIA BUSINESS: SELLING TO THE ELDERLY

As a way of earning money for college expenses, you take a job with a marketing service selling products over the telephone. You are specifically ordered to ask the age of whoever answers the phone and break off if the person is not over 60 years of age because, as you are told, older people have less sales resistance and are often lonely, wanting to keep sales people on the line for the conversation. Therefore, they are easily persuaded to buy products and amenable to installment programs that ultimately triple the product's price. Studies show the return to telemarketers for time spent on the phone is by far the highest for sales to those aged 60 and above. As a telemarketer, you can expect to sell products ranging from portrait photograph services and commemorative plates (e.g., those portraying Princess Diana that were marketed after her death) to flatware sets and herbal remedy products. There is no law prohibiting or seriously regulating this sales activity.

1. Since this activity is not prohibited by law, is it morally acceptable for you to earn your college expenses as a telemarketer for this firm? Why?
2. Can these sales be justified as improving the quality of life of the customers? Should that be a criterion? Why?
3. Can it be said that you are victimizing a powerless person when you make one of these sales? How?
4. Based on material in this chapter, what would be a sound moral justification for this activity?
5. Should customers, even those over 60, be assumed to be fully competent to play the game you involve them in, that is, your sales skills versus their good sense and possession of their reasoning faculties?

SELECTED SOURCES

Anderson, J. A. & Englehardt, E. E. (2001). *The organizational self and ethical conduct: Sunlit virtue and shadowed resistance.* Forth Worth, TX: Harcourt College Publishers.

Black, J., Steele, B., & Barney, R. (1995). *Doing ethics in journalism.* (2nd ed.). Boston, MA: Allyn and Bacon.

Englehardt, E. E. & Schmeltekopf, D. (1992). *Ethics and life.* Dubuque, Iowa: William C. Brown.

Englehardt, E. E. (2001). *Ethical issues in interpersonal communication.* Fort Worth, TX: Harcourt College Publishers.

Estrich, S. (2000). *Sex and power.* New York: Riverhead Books.

Jamieson, K. H. (2000). *Everything you think you know about politics . . . and why you're wrong.* New York: Basic Books.

Solomon, R. C. (1996). *A handbook for ethics.* Fort Worth, TX: Harcourt Brace Publishers.

4

THE POLITICS OF MEDIA DECISIONS: WHO WINS—THE INDIVIDUAL OR THE COMMUNITY?

CONTEMPORARY CASE IN JOURNALISM: FREEBIES

The Associated Press Sports Writers often pick ethics as a topic for conversation at their annual gatherings. The field of sports writing has been filled with problems involving gratuities. Some gifts are small, such as a golf glove or a baseball, while other gifts are large, such as free trips and jewelry. At a gathering, a discussion item was a contest sponsored by Nabisco/RJR called "Pick-The-Winners," which awarded a prize for two on a cruise with Royal Caribbean. Apparently, golf writers and others who covered for the media were awarded points based on picking winners on the PGA or Senior PGA golf tour. The sports writer accumulating the most points would receive the vacation at the expense of Nabisco/RJR. "It's outrageous. I didn't know about it and will see that it stops," said one sports editor representing his paper (Warren, p. 24).

For most media professionals, accepting gratuities is not ethical or acceptable. Such behavior creates conflicts of interest, thereby potentially allowing preferential treatment in coverage. Yet in the field of sports, there are still questions on some publications about the wisdom of turning down gifts. Sports writers seem to observe a professional community notion that it is acceptable to accept gratuities because sports are not "news" to be affected by gifts.

Depending on the publication, perhaps small gratuities, such as hot dogs and snack items, may be accepted. Other publications may allow free trips to sporting events or demonstration shows. Most other areas of publication and broadcast media shun gratuities. Sometimes we accept a practice without giving it much thought. It even becomes our outlook, independent of our own thinking on the matter. For example, if all the other sports writers are accepting gratuities, then it must be an acceptable practice.

THE INDIVIDUAL AND THE COMMUNITY

This chapter compares and contrasts two ethical and philosophical points of view that consider the good of the community versus the importance of individual choice, i.e., *communitarianism* and *liberalism*. These two systems fall within the rubric of **political philosophy** and are the center of many important media discussions. The liberal argument assumes autonomy in a society that is necessarily made up of communities. Individuals comprise the communities, and individual and autonomous rights are necessary, as is support to the community. Sometimes within a community the group in power is the one most often heard and given privilege. Both majority and minority must be heard, according to liberal philosophy. Part of the enterprise of political philosophy is to find neutral approaches in which both groups agree. Within this chapter, it is important to locate similarities in spite of the differences between the theories.

WHAT ARE LIBERALISM AND COMMUNITARIANISM?

This chapter combines duty, rights, and utilitarian notions of ethics, often called *liberalism*, and compares those philosophies with a combination of virtue and relationship ethics, often called *communitarianism*. As a political philosophy, **liberalism** refers to individual decision making. **Communitarianism** refers to decisions made by a group. These terms should not be confused with notions of the Republican or Democrat or even of political conservatism and liberalism.

The two dominant ideological positions in a liberal democracy are liberalism and communitarianism. When a question arises—for example, about whether an advertising agency should accept an account requiring it to promote a particular brand of cigarette or other tobacco product—an ideological conflict may be triggered. Some may accept the account, arguing that it is a legal product and therefore its promotion should be encouraged under freedom of expression provisions, giving targeted individuals the right to make decisions on the product for themselves.

Others may reject the entire concept of tobacco promotion—whatever its legality—as harmful in numerous ways to the entire community. Generally, those responding with arguments of freedom and individual rights are termed *liberals*. Those with responses designed to protect the overall community are likely to be called *communitarians*.

LIBERALISM

Liberalism argues that each person's rights must be protected in a democratic society. Liberty, the root of liberalism, hinges on the availability of options and freedom of expression, which includes artistic freedom, freedom of the press, and freedom of speech. Options and the ability to freely express views allow a person to make decisions and to pursue creative goals. Among communication professions, and central to a liberal democracy, fidelity to "truth" is vital for individuals who make up a society. When there is an absence of a clear truth, which occurs more often than not, the truth of a matter is most likely found through a process of debate and sorting through the range of information displayed in the marketplace of ideas.

Checklist for Ethical Decision Making: Liberalism/Individualism

According to Enlightenment and contemporary philosophers, there are some common traits of the liberal ethic. The following list is by no means complete, nor is it a comprehensive checklist. It will assist as you attempt to pull together the concepts of liberalism and individualism in this chapter.

1. The individual is a necessary base of liberalism. An individual's rights exist prior to a society's formation or its rules.
2. Within the individual are the resources necessary for moral judgment and right action. The individual is the best judge of his or her own interests.
3. The individual should be able to establish interests, preferences, and choices rather than relinquishing this duty to the community.

4. Groups, communities, or social institutions do not define the individual, but are merely instruments to help the individual attain goals or to allow for expression.
5. Individual rights must be protected in a democratic society. Any action, including law, that compromises individual rights would be logically and morally incorrect.
6. Personal liberty, the root of liberalism, is freedom of expression for the individual. This includes artistic, press, and speech freedoms that enable a person to make decisions and to pursue inclinations.
7. Fidelity to the "truth" is vital for a liberal. Truth is identified through a process of debate and acquiring disparate information from the marketplace of ideas.
8. Liberalism is criticized as being concerned about selfish pursuits that may not contribute to social good.
9. The liberal approach allows for moral autonomy; therefore, moral development is achievable and encouraged.
10. It is important to have a morally autonomous individual in any group. The individual must be allowed to examine the group critically and can withdraw if the group's actions are no longer compatible with the established goals that justified its original organization.
11. Liberals must advocate moral sensitivity, as the individual is largely a free agent capable of reasonable thinking, but also capable of unregulated, destructive behavior.
12. Breadth and depth of information are necessary in the liberal system. The extensive scope of media professions must ensure an open channel for the diverse information needed for the individual's decisions. Media networks are a powerful way of informing the public.
13. Truth receives the highest rank for a liberal. Sometimes truth is nothing more than adding information to the knowledge base. The liberal theory requires autonomy in making decisions from a broad base of information, a foundation for individual autonomy.

COMMUNITARIANISM: VIRTUE AND RELATIONSHIP ETHICS

Communitarianism centers on the welfare of the overall community as more basic, and ultimately more satisfying, than the rights of the community's individual members. Community members should be able to discuss problems and concerns as equals, and come to a consensus that would support community stability. In its applications to media professionals, the individual should actively understand, reinforce, and support community norms and values through speech, the press, and artistic expression. Information, therefore, is selected for its contribution to community solidarity rather than for its contributions to individual decisions.

Checklist for Ethical Decision Making: Communitarianism

There are common communitarian ethical tenets of ancient and contemporary philosophers. This checklist is not comprehensive but is intended to guide you in understanding the major concepts of communitarianism in this chapter.

1. Communitarians focus on common goods, social practices and traditions, character solidarity, and social responsibility.
2. Resources for moral judgment and action are found in the established mores of the family, the workplace, and the like, rather than within the individual.
3. The individual cannot survive without the collective; therefore, a major purpose of individual lives should be to serve institutional needs and goals rather than vice versa.
4. Community views should not be challenged without good reason. It is important that community leadership reinforce and strengthen community morality. For the media practitioner, this may include reinforcing community values.
5. Individual members of a community gain self-confidence and pride in membership. There is shared pride in the successes of individual members and of the group as a whole. There is also shared disappointment in community failures.
6. Frequently, the community remains together even after the goals of forming the community are met.
7. The community is more basic than the rights of individual members, as such concepts as loyalty, justice, or fairness are defined for community rather than individual benefit.
8. Members of a community should be able to discuss problems and concerns as equals and come to a consensus that would support community stability.

9. In regard to freedoms of speech, the press, artistic expression, and religion, the individual is not to remain a powerless pawn for a conglomerate (media owner). The individual is to actively understand and support the community norms and values.
10. The leadership of the community should disseminate information that will safeguard and enhance the future of the community. Therefore, some truths are less important than community solidarity.
11. Some information released through the mass media could damage the community or hurt the effectiveness of individuals in the community. Community leadership must question how the information might harm the community or individuals within the community and then judge whether it will be disseminated.
12. Members within a community must develop some sense of mutual responsibility toward each other in order for the community to flourish.
13. The mass media cannot be neutral because economic gain is the defining purpose of its activity. The press must balance self-interest with community interest to advance an ideological position that supports community stability.

HISTORY OF THE INDIVIDUAL VS. THE COMMUNITY

These discussions are not new for the media. Debates focusing specifically on the issue of the media and their duties to society were common in the 1920s, as academics and their writings exerted increasing influence on the media professions.

In books and journal writings of the early twentieth century, authors often mulled the conflict between individual liberty and community well being on several issues, including the following:

- ♦ Media duties to society
- ♦ Binding codes of ethics
- ♦ Licensing and professional requirements
- ♦ Crusading and editorializing
- ♦ Expressing opinion within the newspaper
- ♦ Suppression of news
- ♦ Conflicts in reporting crime

Additionally, the coverage of sporting events was often criticized by academics and media professionals as being free advertising for teams, colleges, and race tracks.

DOES CRIME COVERAGE PROMOTE CRIME?

Not surprisingly, the most frequent theme and most prominently covered subject in early journalism academic works was the ethics of printing crime news. Some authors argued that detailed crime stories are best avoided because their publication breeds more crime, instructing those with a criminal bent on criminal techniques. Other authors believed crime stories should be printed but, as with other news stories, the amount of coverage should remain in proportion to their news value. Some large city tabloid newspapers, in contrast, built their street sales on graphic front page headlines and photographs trumpeting the latest street crimes or sex scandal.

Political leaders and community members were often critical of newspapers, asserting that they were responsible for crime because of publicity given to crime and criminals. They claimed such coverage turned gullible citizens to a life of crime and asked the media, instead, to help in the fight against crime. In 1929, President Herbert Hoover listed problems caused by the printing of crime news at an Associated Press luncheon in New York. He asked newspapers for more support for the law, with less attention paid to the criminal.

> I wonder sometimes, if perhaps a little more support to our laws could not be given in one direction. If, instead of the glamour of romance and heroism, which our American imaginative minds too frequently throw around those who break the law, we would invest with a little romance and heroism those thousands of our officers who are endeavoring to enforce the laws would help. Perhaps a little better proportioned balance of news concerning those criminals who are convicted and punished would serve to instill the fear of the law.
>
> I need not repeat that absolute freedom of the press to discuss public questions is a foundation stone of American liberty. I put the question, however, to every individual conscience, whether flippancy is a useful or even legitimate device in such discussions.
>
> I do not believe it is. Its effect is as misleading and as distorting of public conscience as deliberate misrepresentation. Not clarification, but confusion of issues in the public mind arises from it. . . .
>
> Possibly the time is at hand for the press systematically to demand and support the reorganization of our law-enforcement machinery—Federal, State, and local—so that crime may be reduced, and on the other hand to

demand that our citizens shall awake to the fundamental consciousness of democracy which is that the laws are theirs and that every responsible member of a democracy has the primary duty to obey the law.

REDUCING CRIME COVERAGE

An example of the type of assistance President Hoover was looking for was written into the *Production Code of the Motion Pictures Producers and Distributors* in 1934, a movie self-censorship document, which required that all criminals be brought to justice by movie's end and that there be limited intimate contact between the sexes. Both provisions were premised on the assumption that criminals would be dissuaded from a life of crime if they learned through the movies that they had no chance of escaping the law and that intimate sexual interactions would be reduced if the movies did not give people ideas.

Hoover's plea and the *Production Code* were communitarian in their appeals to the media. He would have liked media to only report on events that would support and knit the community together and to avoid reports that would divide and create dissension or upset the order of the community.

The Liberal Approach to Crime Coverage

In many and perhaps most countries, the communitarian perspective inherent in President Hoover's plea fits comfortably with both the prevailing social philosophy and with the views of media operators to support that philosophy. A liberal democracy, however, at least tolerates a differing view and suggests that media ought be free to be adversaries of the civic forces for which President Hoover sought media cooperation and be free to challenge community norms. The underlying principle is that the long-term benefits of robust discussion and adversarial relationships more than offset the short-term inconvenience and inefficiencies of full discussion that inevitably slow the processes of government and place cherished norms at risk.

President Hoover's concerns about media are reflected today in similar suggestions to editors and news directors in most every corner of the country. Community leaders globally are frustrated by what they view as media intransigence over goals common to the entire community. Virtually all these feelings of frustration bear weight on the nature of a liberal democracy and the dynamics of group relationships. They ask who should assume the various roles necessary for a liberal democracy to function.

CONTEMPORARY CASE IN ADVERTISING: JASON AND NIKE

In the midst of the opening ceremonies for the Australia 2000 Olympics, a horror advertisement is run. The advertisement features a woman in a remote cabin. As she is getting ready for a bath, a chain-saw wielding "Jason" figure appears in her mirror. Jason, in full slasher character, chases her through the woods. Suddenly, the audience understands that this is not a movie advertisement—it is a Nike advertisement, and that this is not any woman running—it is Suzy Favor Hamilton, a favored Olympic runner. Suzy gets away because she is in better shape than Jason. Then the following logo pops up: "Why Sport? You'll live longer." Thousands of protests came into NBC over the advertisement, and they pulled it off the network as well as from MSNBC and CNBC. Nike stood behind the advertisement and continued running it on ESPN.

This case aptly demonstrates the differences between a communitarian and a liberal reaction to a public outcry. Out of viewer concern, NBC pulled the advertisement even though it meant a great loss of money to them. Nike continued to run the advertisement. They thought it was humorous, witty, and appealing to millions of youngsters.

SHOULD MEDIA USE THE POWER OF PERSUASION?

Perhaps the unspoken question most often hanging over the communitarian discussion is whether the media should not assume a role as community leader by pressing and persuading for a better living environment. Alternatively, should the media stand apart from the fray without taking positions in their news columns and allowing all views to be heard, particularly the acidic minority views that so frustrate community leaders and dilute momentum for improvement? At an extreme, of course, is the moral question whether a civic-minded publisher or station owner should serve on civic campaign committees, throwing the resources of the medium behind the campaign for a new library, a new gymnasium, or a new paved road that will serve neighbors and also the media owner.

Should the media be fully supportive of new and improved schools, more recreation areas, new stadia for professional sports, better highways, and so forth? Additionally, should the media be satisfied that leaders are doing their best to remedy such endemic problems as poverty, substandard housing, high rents for low-income families, deteriorating schools, and other mundane community problems without calling them to the attention of audiences so often? Finally, should the media weaken community confidence in the power structure by publicizing reports of suicide attempts, drunk driving arrests, or adulteries committed by civic figures?

These questions, posed here with answers from both camps, are indicative of fundamental differences between the two groups, resulting in very different responses to questions as to how the media should fulfill its functions:

CRITICAL QUESTIONS FOR LIBERALS AND COMMUNITARIANS

Who Determines What is Best for the Community?

COMMUNITARIAN: *Leaders, both formal and informal, emerge with community support; therefore, they are empowered to make decisions for the community.* Leaders, by virtue of their positions, are better informed than other community members, thereby *qualifying* them to make decisions for their fellows. Therefore, leaders are in the best position to determine community needs.

LIBERAL: *Communities tend not to be homogenous, and individuals should be free and sufficiently informed to make their own decisions and contribute to community decisions, even after leaders are selected.* Through activism, individuals in the community serve as a check on leaders. Those who attain leadership positions should not be assumed to have the best interest of the community in mind over the special interests that tend to intervene and divert leader loyalty from group welfare. Leaders are not necessarily representative of the entire community but are more likely to be from a smaller, elitist group of active community members. Leaders tend to come from within that group, consolidating over time the power of the smaller group. Community activity ought not lead to the claiming of such substantial rewards as domination of the community.

What are the Ethical Implications?

COMMUNITARIAN: *The community is the primary unit, superseding the individual, and the best interests of the community lie in cooperative efforts in which decisions are reached by the active majority.* This active majority generally has the community interest at heart and is likely to be best informed because of its interests and positions. Often, with a substantial investment in the community, the active majority has a greater economic stake in the community than most citizens, i.e., business owners. Such activity will produce the greatest good for the greatest number, with the well-informed making decisions to benefit the entire community and securing for the community the stability necessary for the general well being. Cooperative effort toward common goals is a virtue. These goals are achieved with relative efficiency and pursuing them consumes fewer community resources. The press cooperates with community leaders in supporting community projects, thereby reducing or eliminating public discussion of alternatives or criticism. Individuals are at their best when they are aligned in cooperative efforts.

LIBERAL: *The individual and individual rights predate the community; thus, the rights of individuals, at the expense of collective goals, are critical elements of community morality.* The media, as a matter of course, are morally obligated to challenge community leaders in their projects, presenting discussions of alternatives and seeking weakness in proposals. It is especially important that the media identify and discuss victims of the projects. Individuals are at their best when they critically evaluate proposals for community development, stimulate full public discussion before such proposals are approved, and refuse to cooperate in the advancement of flawed projects. A communitarian press, in its cooperative mode, fails to find and articulate the concerns of powerless minorities. Minorities and those outside community-leader ranks with differing views tend to be disenfranchised by the cooperative efforts of others, who close ranks to maintain stability and efficiency. The community's dominant value systems tend to prevail, submerging desires and even needs of minority members. Individual freedom to make decisions is often limited to retain community stability. Individualists cooperate in community efforts when they are persuaded, after critical evaluation, as to the validity of the project rather than automatically deferring to leadership. The continued existence of a liberal democracy demands active, critical individualists.

What are the Sources of Ethical Instruction?

COMMUNITARIAN: *Authority granted by a powerful, active minority to determine community direction.* This group may decide the quantity and

quality of information to be distributed in the community through local media. This information often both reinforces community values
and provides confirming support for the direction taken by leaders.
The community and its members benefit from such a system. The protective value system of the community instructs media as to what constitutes appropriate content.

LIBERAL: *The individual in the community is an end rather than a means to an
end.* The individual should have available through the media all significant views and relatively full information on an issue. With this knowledge, the individual is empowered to choose whether to intervene in
community affairs. Information from conflicting but informed sources
on a given community topic is important, even though it may slow
progress. Providing full information is an indication of respect for the
individual and the ability of the individual to reason and make rational
decisions. This notion also requires individuals to submit to inconvenience in order that full information can be provided for basic decisions. As a practical matter, not all individuals can be accommodated in
community matters, but information mechanisms should be in place
so all individuals are empowered by information to protect themselves
to minimize harms to individuals from community projects. Perhaps a
community needs relatively detailed information on a rape victim, a
suicide victim, or an AIDS victim to be able to make realistic decisions
about a community problem.

*Should Ethics be an Individual Duty with Full Responsibility and Liberty for
Performance?*

COMMUNITARIAN: *Individuals are often ill-informed and act out of self-
interest, or selfishly obstruct progress and the well being of the group.*
Adherence to community norms that have stood the test of time and
are considerate of the needs and wishes of the community and its
members assures behavior that is consistent with the needs and
wishes of the community.

LIBERAL: *The community retains its dynamism when it tolerates and allows
participation by eccentric individuals in its affairs.* Activism by individuals, often acting with self-interest in mind, is frequently critical of community justice. Their vigorous participation in public discussion helps
the community avoid denying rights to certain of its citizens, while also
causing the community to frequently reevaluate its norms and values.

The individual may demonstrate self-interest publicly, thereby allowing the community to evaluate and act.

Are Media Ethics More Appropriately Directed by the Church, Business Leaders, or Community Groups?

COMMUNITARIAN: *A more happy, secure, and satisfying lifestyle results when the community is united in its values and all agree on appropriate behavior.* Media messages that reinforce and support that lifestyle reduce conflict and produce a community in which everyone can take pride—a community in which parents wish to raise their children and that attracts business for its stable and productive work force. Such stability is achieved when the community accepts norms that will govern the public behavior of all. It is reasonable to expect members of a community to accept and live by certain behaviors. These norms are established both by tradition and by community leaders by virtue of their superior leadership positions. These positions may be secured by assertion of divine rights through clergy, accumulation of economic power by business people, by election or appointment through political leaders, or by vigorous civic activity. The durable pillars of any community, best suited to determine community standards, are its churches, business leaders, and civic groups.

LIBERAL: *Individuals need full agency for decision making.* A liberal democracy risks losing its character and its capacity for change when its individuals are forced to endorse the actions of community leaders with little information about those actions. Individuals lose their agency and moral autonomy to the wishes of the group and important elements of a progressive society are lost. A communitarian society is only as progressive as its leaders. Perhaps leaders ultimately tend to settle for stability over the risk of change. An individualistic, liberal society taps the creativity and progressive drive of all its citizens and is able to act somewhat independently. Autonomy is denied by media that do not identify alternatives for discussion but pursue the single-minded objectives of the community.

Is Community Interest Sometimes Streamlined to Further the Interests of the More Numerous or Influential Groups in the Church and Society?

COMMUNITARIAN: *Certainly, the wise are likely to be the most successful members of the community.* They achieved such success through hard work and intelligent adaptation to the demands of their work. This successful group is most likely to be able to produce decisions that will favor the entire community with the least discomfort to the community. All who wish to participate in the discussion may do so, but community leaders are by far in the best position to make the final decisions, and they deserve unanimous support once those decisions are made. Decisions made by the wisest in the community are in the best interests of the community.

LIBERAL: *Individuals, particularly minorities and the underprivileged, can be easily marginalized by the majority.* Communitarian decision makers are likely to arrive at their decisions on the basis of what they know, and what they know best is their own experience, with its inherent bias toward their own interests; therefore, their decisions are naturally inclined toward the convenience of the decision makers. This tends to disenfranchise, marginalize, and isolate those not represented in the process, however few they may be. What had passed for comfortable community consensus for decades before the tumultuous 1960s was merely agreement reached among like-minded leaders who successfully denied participation to such powerless groups as women and racial minorities. These were exclusions in which the media participated, ranging from completely ignoring significant racial groups in news coverage to movies and television entertainment that idealized or trivialized women and minorities with stereotyping roles, such as obedient housewife/super mother (June Cleaver) or buffoonish racial characters. The growing pluralism of the latter third of the twentieth century was also a call for the recognition of individuals as participants in community processes.

Certainly, many individuals belong to community groups and religious organizations and are able to perform many important functions within these groups; however, they also live a separate and autonomous existence apart from the groups. This seems to be the important middle ground for both points of view.

MORE ABOUT EACH APPROACH

LIBERALISM

The roots of liberalism are deep and distinguished. Philosophers such as John Locke, Jean-Jacques Rousseau, Adam Smith, Immanuel Kant, and John Stuart Mill created a rich tradition of rights, liberty, and notions of social contract that have shaped Western social thought. These Enlightenment theorists are often cited as having established the foundations of liberalism.

Although there are major differences among these thinkers, the concepts of equality, neutrality, and government preservation of equality and neutrality are essential to all their theories.

The works of John Locke and Jean-Jacques Rousseau posit the fundamental commonality of human beings with the social contract. This contract, as defined by these philosophers, is an agreement by which society is founded by rational, autonomous human beings who compromise self-interests to establish a society in which self-interests are maximized. Through this contract, individuals are equal in both society and in basic rights. Individuals may define through the contract the conventions they will support in society.

Today's Liberal

Basic to today's approach to liberalism is the premise that individuals are to be treated as equals. Liberalism, through the theories of these foundational philosophers, centers on conceptions of the "right" in society. Notions of the right refer to the entitlement to the basic means of life in a society, such as rights of life, liberty, the pursuit of happiness, and to the right to free, open religious worship. The basic duty of government is to maximize the autonomy of individuals in a society, thus enabling them to satisfy their needs and pursue their self-determined interests to the greatest possible extent. Notions of the "right" are contrasted and compared with communitarian notions of the "good." Conceptions of the "good" are generally moral choices made for a community by individuals in leadership roles. Conceptions of the good inevitably posit the stability of the community itself as the highest good.

Today's most prominent proponent of liberal theory is John Rawls. In *A Theory of Justice* (1971), Rawls attempts to find a proper ordering between equality and liberty, with particular concern for the needs of the "least advantaged" in society. Concerns that plague philosophers such as John Rawls, Ronald Dworkin, John Locke, and Jean-Jacques Rousseau involve where rights end and when the good should limit individual autonomy. From the liberal viewpoint, these rights include artistic freedom, freedom to worship, and freedom to speak and write openly.

COMMUNITARIANISM

The Athenian Oath is an excellent example of communitarian **idealism.** In ancient Athens, when a young man turned 17, he showed his loyalty to the state by taking the following oath:

We will never bring disgrace on this our City by an act of dishonesty or cowardice. We will fight for the ideals and Sacred Things of the City both alone and with many. We will revere and obey the City's laws, and will do our best to incite a like reverence and respect in those above us who are prone to annul them or set them at naught. We will strive increasingly to quicken the public's sense of civic duty. Thus in all these ways we will transmit this City, not only not less, but greater and more beautiful than it was transmitted to us.

Socrates, Plato, and Aristotle believed the most virtuous society would be one based on communitarian ideals. The individual, in living a virtuous life, would form part of an overall virtuous community. Decisions were not to be determined by rights of the individual but by how the decision would affect the overall good of the community.

Today's Communitarian

We find some philosophers today encouraging the youth of America to take a similar oath when reaching voting age. Some noted communitarians theorize that societies such as the United States suffer from a loss of moral and civic orientation caused by excessive liberalism—specifically individualism. Philosophers such as Robert Spaemann and Allan Bloom surmise that "political liberalism and moral pluralism" are the chief causes of this situation. Other thinkers who write on the decline of moral and political communities in contemporary societies include Michael Sandel, Charles Taylor, Michael Walzer, Ametai Etzioni, and Alasdair MacIntyre.

These communitarians consider that the liberalism legacies of Enlightenment thinking have been, as MacIntyre said, "historically implicated in developments that have led to the decline of community as a way of life." They believe that the Enlightenment legacy "constricts our imagination and impoverishes our moral vocabulary so that we cannot even conceptualize solutions to problems such as poverty."(Benhabib, p. 131).

Communication scholars who specialize in communitarian ethics include Clifford Christians, Kim B. Rotzoll, John P. Ferre, P. Mark Fackler, and Tom Cooper. Christians explains the communitarian position in his article, "Fifty Years of Scholarship in Media Ethics."

> It seems obvious that we need renewed emphasis on ethics as a discipline, as a normative science of conduct. While avoiding inflexible rules, we can formulate meaningful ethical guidelines, meticulously derived and capable of adequate defense. The educators' task certainly involves aiding journalists in

determining what is right to do, and what moral norms are appropriate (Christians, p. 27).

The communitarian philosophy in communication asks for a **normative** ethic in which the media has a moral duty to society to preserve the values of the community.

BLENDING THE PHILOSOPHIES

Liberalism and communitarianism each have outstanding philosophical roots and tenets. However, it is often difficult to blend these two political philosophies together into cooperative action. How does one determine when it is appropriate to be part of a group and allow the group's decision to be one's final decision? When does one separate from the group and insist that the moral choice is the individual decision? These considerations are particularly important when the development of moral autonomy is a goal of the individual and when it is mandated by the First Amendment for those in the media.

Practical Uses for These Theories

Working for a media agency presents some strong ethical problems. Imagine that you are asked to report an extremely negative story about your alma mater. Out of loyalty, you want to report only positive, nice things about your favorite university. As a reporter or editor, however, there is no choice—if negative acts were committed by the university, it is your job to fairly and professionally report the events so that individuals in your community can make better informed decisions about the university. As a public relations specialist, your choices are not much better, as strong loyalty is often expected by an employer. But if your employer is involved in wrongdoing, is it your job to stay loyal or to make public the problem? Furthermore, if the problem is exposed to the media by others, you must truthfully, carefully respond to questions from the media. You are part of this business community, but the career of a public relations specialist is founded on a social system grounded in freedom of speech, autonomy, and accountability.

In the case of Gerald Ford and Jerry terHorst, Gerald Ford probably expected that his press secretary would report the pardon of President Nixon as a matter of course. terHorst, however, made the decision not to stay with the "firm." He was so opposed to the decision to pardon President Nixon that he resigned. Part of ethical training in media professions is to understand when personal ethics come in conflict with a decision an employer has made. At what point does a media professional leave a firm? Perhaps an employee will be able to influence an employer before a particularly harmful decision is put forward. Alternatively, perhaps an employee can change a procedure or policy that brought about an unethical action on the part of the firm.

While liberal theory encourages full liberty of the media, it particularly stresses that the news media are to be neutral in society. An example of a liberalism choice is the decision to state on the air or to print the names of individuals caught in a prostitution sting, even though several are high-level politicians and clergy. A communitarian may argue that too much damage would be done to the individuals and overall community in the printing of such delicate, destructive information. A communitarian might argue that printing the names of those arrested is an unnecessary punishment inflicted by press. The liberal would need to broadcast or print the story in the interest of full disclosure if it were fair, accurate, and of importance to the community.

Contemporary Case: The Sorority Sister

Shelly, a broadcast major at a Midwestern university, was duty news director for the campus radio station when a female student in the closing minutes of a sorority party fell headfirst from a second-story balcony onto a concrete driveway below. The student who fell had been drinking heavily, and the partygoers had been warned by police earlier in the evening to make less noise.

In her responsibility to determine what the station's news coverage would be that night, Shelly refused to air the story. As a member of a sorority herself, she explained that she had a greater responsibility to help the Greek chapters avoid bad publicity than she had to her position at the radio station. "One must not hurt one's brothers and sisters in fraternities and sororities," she said.

Shelly made her decision partly as a communitarian. She believes in the sorority society and would like to see it continue to thrive. She knows the accident would bring more negative publicity to the system. She also understands that the event is a news story. Should she turn her back on what she knows to be a valid and important story? Why?

Media professionals find many stories that should be written but that are personally painful to others around them. In a communitarian system, it is hard to determine whether professionalism or the group to which you belong should come first.

ANALYZING A CASE: CAMPAIGN SABOTAGE

As a part of media neutrality, club memberships sometimes cause a **conflict of interest**; therefore, they are a luxury generally to be avoided by media professionals. The need for independence and autonomy leads editorial, broadcast, and journalism codes of ethics to discourage membership in most organizations as a potential conflict of interest. When a reporter is a group member, pressures may be applied to the reporter for special favors. Other media practitioners may decide to join an organization. As a member of the organization, some autonomy is lost. The individual can voice objections to what the group decides, but the group will act as a group. The individual has the autonomy to leave the group or remain.

CONTEMPORARY CASE IN ADVERTISING:
CAMPAIGN SABOTAGE

David, a junior member of an advertising firm, is a member of an executive team assigned to a political campaign. David likes what he knows about the candidate so far. She is a member of David's political party, and she seems to follow party lines on most issues. There is an issue, however, on which they disagree. The candidate, Mary Jo Killpack, is opposed to the establishment of national wilderness areas, particularly new national monuments in the West.

David is to do a background search on Mary Jo because the advertising firm wants to cover any surprises that may come up during the campaign. David learns that Mary Jo, as a corporate executive, had several dicey international business interests, including a very expensive water plant that was never functional in West Africa. She was also part of a highly profitable mining project with another African government. The project involves major environmental problems, including severe destruction of natural resources and wildlife. There has also been a significant rise in the incidence of asthma and other lung problems since the mine opened in the area.

David is now disgusted with Mary Jo. He is a member of a conservation group and is particularly opposed to any environmental destruction. David's information on Mary Jo belongs to his company. However, he believes he owes a greater commitment to the conservation group and the voters in the state than he does to his firm. Consequently, he leaks the information to his group.

Some Communitarian Choices

As a communitarian, David is pleased with his choice to leak the information on Mary Jo. He has acted in the best interests of the conservation organization. David and the group reasoned that they had to look out for the greater good for the community and had a duty to protect the environment. With Mary Jo's business record, they did not believe that she would support any environmental issues. Not all members of the group needed to be informed, since the leadership of the group can make decisions for all. David is just an individual who does not believe he can change the campaign through his position at the company. However, he knows that public pressure, particularly when coming from a group, can hamper the candidate's campaign, especially if the truth about Mary Jo is released. He believes that working through the group, the necessary power sources needed to defeat the candidate will be found. As a group, they believe they are doing what is in the best interests of the majority and that the defeat of one objectionable candidate is an important benefit for all.

In this case study, we cannot be sure what will happen to David's job. Certainly, he was not loyal to the company. He did not work within the rubric of the company by declaring a conflict of interest and requesting to be taken off the campaign. David did not want the ad campaign to succeed and worked outside the ad agency to bring about the change. Nevertheless, if David had left enough clues regarding his actions, he would most likely have been fired for lack of confidentiality and loyalty.

Liberal Analysis

A liberal may or may not agree with the candidate, and the individual may also be repulsed both by the candidate's background and her campaign. Liberal theory is based on full disclosure of information, but it also would allow the candidate to run her own campaign. Therefore, a liberal David would have a conflict between the need for the community to have full information on which to make a decision (and his obligation to supply what he knows) and Ms. Killpack's right to direct her campaign. He may accept a professional responsibility to advance her cause, while perhaps asking her to withdraw because he was personally uncomfortable with her background. He may also do as terHorst did and withdraw, disclosing the information he had gathered.

In either case, his problem would lie in resolving the conflict between his concern that voters would have full information about the candidate and his recognition that Ms. Killpack had a right to direct her campaign and be selective in disclosing her background.

Paradoxically, a communitarian David would have roughly the same options, but would bring different reasoning to the decision. He may work vigorously on the campaign in order to advance the interest of his immediate professional community, a community obligation he would feel for any candidate represented by his agency. He may also support the campaign if the candidate is endorsed by the community's leadership. Or, for the good of the community, particularly if the candidate is not from the mainstream party, he may choose to disclose (either covertly or overtly) the candidate's background.

Given the nature of the two philosophies, the communitarian David is likely the more predictable of the two: He would probably accept the direction of the agency and try to get Ms. Killpack elected, whatever his personal feelings. The liberal David has more of a dilemma and would likely be more difficult to predict. Certainly, either the liberal or communitarian could ask to be excused from working on the campaign, even if it does cause problems for his/her career.

NO EASY ANSWERS

Whether liberal or communitarian, within the field of ethics there are no easy or clear-cut answers. We will not be handed a pretty box with a bow on top with a note that says, "Here is the answer to your problem." It is important that an ethical analysis survey numerous rational, workable approaches to the problem. Perhaps the events of another historical era can illuminate the issues.

CONTROVERSY OVER NEWSPAPER EDITORIALS

Editorial writing was another topic of sharp debate in the early 1920's when liberals and communitarians discussed ethics. Neither the communitarian nor the liberal position discourages editorial writing, and neither position allows for the expressing of opinion in news columns. The scholarly communitarian perspective on editorial writing advocates that the editorial should be a means of strengthening the community. Because communitarians are primarily interested in community welfare, they worry about the harmful effects of an antisocial newspaper editorial on the community.

Some journal and textbook authors of the 1920s proposed that reporters and editors should publish editorials that would strengthen community stability rather than detract from it. Their reasoning was that individuals in the community were influenced by the newspaper editorials. As such, it was felt that the editorials that were published should be those that would enhance public opinion as well as educate the community in a wholesome way. These authors also assumed that the editor would only publish editorials that promote community stability.

For example, author Leon Flint advanced the idea that "the editor who wants to print the whole truth is an extremist" (p. 376). He theorized that for the good of the community it is important that the editor determine which information the community should receive and also provide an understanding of the context and importance of the information through the editorial. He felt that complete editorial independence for a newspaper is not a desirable thing, any more than absolute truthfulness is always desirable and that any newspaper, by printing the whole truth about people and events for a single day, could become an antisocial influence (p. 377).

Flint also argued that newspaper crusades are necessary for the community, as they bring about improvements. He believed that through crusading, newspapers could help communities to develop a greater tolerance for social and industrial well being and arouse community pride. Because of this, he states that the reader "should look upon a newspaper as a friend" (p. 365).

The early media ethicists from the liberal camp were Nelson Crawford and Albert F. Henning. These ethicists did not place the editor in a position of promoting the values of the community. Rather, the liberal ethicists expected the editor to provide newsworthy information, thereby strengthening the reader's ability to develop opinions and ethical priorities critically. By only printing a majority opinion, the liberal ethicists stated that citizens were being denied rights to make informed decisions. Information important to the public should not be restricted merely because the reporter or newspaper administration may not agree with the topic.

Nelson Crawford advocated the belief that readers understood when they were reading opinion and bias (p. 120). He declared that editorials must be marked as such, as there should be no manipulation or deception when information is presented to the public. Crawford believed that the newspaper could provide information and the editorial interpretation; however, the individual should be responsible for personal actions and attitudes.

Crawford, as an early media liberal author, believed it was important that Americans be exposed to diverse views from which they could make independent decisions. He felt an editorial writer must use good logic and avoid specious arguments (p. 124). "The editorial writer on whatever paper should have as his primary function clarifying facts and helping readers to draw dependable conclusions from the facts. More and more it is being recognized that the editorial is an interpreter more than an advocate. . . . It combines in one the parts of public prosecutor, public defender, and judge" (p. 126).

Crawford further theorized that all newspaper opinion must be on the editorial page and that editorials must be carefully, critically, and ethically analyzed before they are printed. In today's media, there appears to be more sophistication in the decisions regarding editorials. After decades of debate, most news organizations produce editorials that give opposing views on an issue. On the other hand, some political and business publications print only a single point of view. Most airline passengers understand that when they pick up a Delta Airlines magazine from the seat pocket in front of them they will be looking at a publication that is very favorable to Delta Airlines and Delta Airlines customers. When that same passenger reads a copy of the *New York Times*, there will be expectations of fairness, balance, and an abundance of information on news topics.

SUMMARY

In this chapter, we explored differences between two systems of thinking in ethics, both of which are political. Liberalism and communitarianism, however, also necessarily overlap. The liberal argument assumes autonomy in a society that is necessarily made up of communities. Individuals comprise the communities, and individual and autonomous rights are necessary, as is support of the community. Part of the enterprise of political philosophy is to find neutral approaches in which both groups agree. It is important to locate similarities in spite of the differences within the theories. The two systems contribute to a necessary dynamic. The dynamic inspires improvement, controversy, and change. However, we theorize that the dynamic would not work nearly as well if liberalism were not the prevailing norm. Communitarian notions beg the question of how an individual or body could responsibly decide which single system of ethical behavior is acceptable for the American media. The battle to undo closed information systems is more futile and damaging than the ability to work within an open system that allows the weaving of a dynamic social fabric on many levels.

Chapter 5 focuses on the valuable currency in a democratic society that makes media and the media professions critically important—power. The chapter proposes the theory that power is dependent on information; in a culture in which public opinion is stronger than the law, information drives the acquisition and use of power, making the distribution of information a redistribution of power.

MORAL REASONING QUESTIONS

1. How have you maintained the benefits of a liberalism system in your life? What are some of the expectations that you have for individualism?
2. How are you protected by communitarianism in your life? What are some of the benefits that you most respect in communitarianism?
3. How are the systems of communitarianism and liberalism combined in society? How are the systems combined in the place where you work or go to school?
4. Using an argument from John Stuart Mill, detail the importance of liberalism in the communication industry.
5. Using an argument from Aristotle, explain the importance of the community when using the media.
6. What is your personal moral theory on accepting gratuities? Is it acceptable under some circumstances? Explain your position.

CLASSIC CASE IN PUBLIC RELATIONS: THE EXXON VALDEZ

On March 24, 1989, at four minutes after midnight, one of the largest environmental, corporate, state, and public relations disasters occurred as a supertanker carrying 1,250,000 barrels of crude oil, the Exxon Valdez, ran aground on a reef in Prince William Sound, Alaska. About 11 million gallons of crude oil gushed into the pristine waters. Captain Joseph Hazlewood and his crew had put in a long, tiring day and had gone drinking prior to departure. The third mate was on the bridge and was not qualified to navigate the waterway. By 4:30 A.M. Alaska time, Lawrence Rawl, chairman of Exxon, received the news and knew he had a major problem. He set up an emergency communication center at his home in New York state and began assessing the situation. His concerns were as follows:

1. Who was responsible for the accident?
2. Should he immediately go to Alaska?
3. How should information about the spill be disseminated?

He responded as follows:

1. Exxon took responsibility for the spill, and 18 hours after the accident, took over control of the crisis from Alyeska (a consortium of seven oil companies that runs the Alaska pipeline).
2. Even though Exxon took responsibility for the accident, Rawl did not travel to Alaska.
3. Rawl and Exxon decided to let all communication come directly from the Alaska site in Valdez.

From an ethics and communication perspective, there were several major problems.

1. Exxon responded slowly to the crisis. It may have hoped that Alyeska would help with the cleanup, but the only oil spill emergency barge belonging to Alyeska was in dry dock for repairs. After 18 hours, little had been done to stop the flow of oil from the massive tanker.
2. Rawl was often criticized for not going to the site of the spill and recently stated that "I wake up in the night questioning the decision to stay home."
3. Exxon decided to release all news about the spill from the site in Valdez. This just did not work because phone lines to Alaska could not contain the heavy demands placed on them and were constantly busy. Also, reports on the disaster and cleanup were issued at inconvenient times for media networks and newspapers.

Questions:

1. Is poor communication a moral problem? What were the true moral problems? You may use sources other than this case to answer this question. How should the oil community respond to this crisis? Why should the individual CEO of Exxon respond? Explain.

2. *The spill was allowed to spread and eventually foul 1200 miles of shoreline in Prince William Sound and kill 980 otters, 138 eagles, and 33,126 other birds. From a communitarian point of view, who is most harmed by the environmental damage? From a liberal point of view, what should be done for environmental restitution?*

3. *Even though Exxon paid out between $1 and $3 billion and employed approximately 11,500 people in the cleanup effort, most critics state that the cleanup served no other purpose than to bolster public relations. Explain the implications of a major profit-making corporation causing a major environmental catastrophe. What is owed to the state of Alaska? What are you owed? Why is this disaster and the response more than a public relations problem for Exxon?*

4. *At the time of the accident, Captain Joseph Hazelwood was not on deck. He and his crew had worked hard all day. Exhausted, they had gone to a bar for a few hours before the departure. Hazelwood was legally drunk at the time of the accident and his third mate was piloting the supertanker. Explain how Hazelwood's individual choices have affected the community. What does Hazelwood owe the corporation and the community?*

CLASSIC CASE IN JOURNALISM: LEON FLINT
AND EDITORIAL PRIVILEGE

Early media author Leon Flint advocated the idea that "the editor who wants to print the whole truth is an extremist." He theorized that for the good of the community, it is important that the editor determine which information the community should receive and also provide an understanding of the context and importance of the information through the editorial. For Flint, complete independence for a newspaper is not a desirable thing, no more than absolute truthfulness is always desirable. Flint, as an ethics scholar, further stated that any newspaper, by printing the whole truth about people and events for a single day, could become an antisocial influence. He concluded that the reader should look upon a newspaper as a friend.

Questions:

1. *Should the media only release information that would be helpful to the community? Explain why it should or should not.*

2. *Should a reader expect a newspaper to be a friend? Explain the implications of this theory.*

3. *Is it appropriate for a media ethicist to state that the truth is not always desirable? Is it important to refrain from printing information in the hope of building a strong community?*
4. *How is the media an antisocial influence? Is it a community decision or an individual decision to participate in media? Explain.*

Selected Sources

Baker, L. W. (1993). *The credibility factor: Putting ethics to work in public relations.* Homewood, IL: Business One Irwin.

Barney, R. (1997). *A dangerous drift? The sirens' call to collectivism.* In Mixed News: The Public/Civic/Communitarian Debate, Jay Black (Ed.). (pp. 72–93). Mahwah, NJ: Erlbaum.

Barney, R. (1986). The journalist and a pluralistic society: An ethical approach. In D. Elliott (Ed.), *Responsible journalism.* Beverly Hills, CA: Sage Publications, Inc.

Barney, R. (1975). The ways of the world. In J. C. Merrill & R. Barney (Eds.), *Ethics and the press.* New York: Hastings House.

Benhabib, S. & Dallmayr, F. (1990). *The communicative ethics controversy.* Cambridge, MA: MIT Press.

Black, J. & Barney, R. (1985). The case against mass media codes of ethics. *Journal of Mass Media Ethics, 1,* 27–36.

Carey, J. W. (1960). Advertising: An institutional approach. In C. H. Sandage & V. Fryberger (Eds.), *The role of advertising.* Homewood, IL: Richard D. Irwin.

Carey, J. W. (1987 March/April). The press and public discourse. *The Center Magazine,* pp. 4–16.

Chenery, W. L. (1955). *Freedom of the press.* New York: Harcourt, Brace, Jovanovitch.

Christians, C. G. (1988). Can the public be held accountable? *Journal of Mass Media Ethics, 3,* 50–58.

Christians, C. G. (1977). Fifty years of scholarship in media ethics. *Journal of Communication, 27,* 9–29.

Christians, C. G., Ferre, J. P., & Fackler, P. M. (1993). *Good news: Social ethics and the press.* New York: Oxford University Press.

Crawford, N. A. (1924). Do newspapers thwart criminal justice? *The Journalism Bulletin, 1,* 19.

Crawford, N. A. (1924). *The ethics of journalism.* New York: Alfred A. Knopf.

Daly, M. (1994). *Communitarianism: A new public ethics.* Belmont, CA: Wadsworth Publishing Company.

Douglas, P. F. (1929). *The newspaper and responsibility.* Cincinnati, Ohio: The Caxton Press.

Elliott, D. (1988). All is not relative: Essential shared values and the press. *Journal of Mass Media Ethics, 3*, 128–132.

Englehardt, E. (1994). *An interpretation of academic discourse in journalism ethics in the early twentieth century: A liberal and communitarian framework in ethics,* Salt Lake City: University of Utah Press.

Etzioni, A. (1993). *The spirit of community: Rights, responsibilities and the communitarian agenda.* New York: Crown Publishers.

Flint, L. N. (1925). *The conscience of the newspaper.* New York: D. Appleton.

Gibbons, W. F. (1926). *Newspaper ethics: A discussion of good practice for journalists.* Ann Arbor, MI: Edwards Brothers.

Glasser, T. L. & Ettema, J. S. (1989). Investigative journalism and the moral order. *Critical Studies in Mass Communication, 6,* 1–20.

Habermas, J. (1990). Discourse ethics: Notes on philosophical justification. In S. Benhabib & F. Dallmyr (Eds.), *The communicative ethics controversy.* Cambridge, MA: MIT Press.

Henning, A. F. (1932). *Ethics and practices in journalism.* New York: Long and Smith.

Hestevold, S., Black, J. & Barney, R. (1991). Mass media morality: An introduction to philosophical ethics. In R. Barney (Ed.), *Ethics and problems in mass communication.* Provo, Utah: Brigham Young University Press.

Lahey, T. (1924). *The morals of newspaper making.* Notre Dame, IN: Notre Dame University Press.

Locke, J. (1983). *The second treatise on government.* Indianapolis, IN: Hackett.

McIntyre, A. (1981). *After virtue.* Notre Dame, IN: University of Notre Dame Press.

Tamer, Y. (1993). *Liberal Nationalism.* Princeton, NJ: Princeton University Press.

5

PUBLIC PERCEPTION OF MEDIA DECISIONS

CONTEMPORARY CASE IN CYBERSPACE: NAPSTER

Marcy loves music and is able to get her favorite artists' songs free through the Internet and free computer software from Napster. The music is available in the MP3 computer file format, which she downloads and plays on her stereo through her laptop. Marcy can do this with any entertainment medium that can be converted to a digital file, including movies, books, and pictures. There are other search engines, such as Gnutella, Scour, and Wrapster, that allow computer users such as Marcy to locate free downloads. These engines create networks of users, all of whom have hard drives filled with MP3 music files, movies, or software programs. Once the user finds the gold mine of products desired, he or she simply downloads. Some users call it swapping, while others call it theft; some artists and courts, however, are calling it copyright violation.

Recording artists sued Napster, claiming copyright infringement. Even though the courts upheld the recording artists' rights, this case is still being considered in appeals courts. As a countermove, Napster now requires artists who do not want their songs to be available for download from their Web site to show proof of copyright. Where is the ethical violation? Is it ethical to download music through the Internet and bypass paying an artist's royalties? Is the recording of movies from a television set just an earlier rendition of the same case? Is the fact that Napster makes money through advertising on their site one of the ethical problems? Has the technology moved faster than ethics or the law?

What Causes Tense Social Relationships With Media?

We already know that many Napster users are angry with government officials, recording moguls, and communication executives for trying to take away their newfound source of free media. What are the social forces within a media system? Where does power reside in the Napster case—the courts, the public, or the corporation?

The previous chapter examined the political philosophies and power that govern many decisions made by media professionals in a variety of communities and organizations. Discussion centered on First Amendment rights and responsibilities attached to individual freedom rather than to various leaders who might make decisions for groups or communities. This chapter will further examine power beginning with the power of information. Also detailed is a **"green-light/red-light"** model of information distribution balanced against power. The American system gives inherent power through rights to each individual, expecting that the power will be used well. This system places the professional communicator in a unique position to help empower many individuals to act well by providing them with the information they need to contribute to the great social decisions of the day.

In return for First Amendment protections, a professional communicator has a moral obligation to act well in ways that will strengthen society as well as the profession. Individual thought and application of ethical principles are needed by all of us. Opinions differ drastically in our society over what it means to be ethical. For the professional communicator, the feat of acting well revolves around practices involved in the distribution of information. It is information that makes possible our viable, dynamic individualistic society.

Many, if not most, Americans have an uneasy relationship with mass media, one that produces widespread suspicion and criticism. That the traditional forms of media (i.e., newspapers, television, radio, and magazines) have until recently been most Americans' sole sources of information adds another dimension to this love-hate relationship of dependence on and suspicion of the media by the American people. One reason for the deep suspicion may be self-preservation; audience members are uncomfortable with having to be dependent on media for their information. Some leaders claim the media run rampant, with no controls, creating the impression that the media are not responsive to public interests.

The explosive emergence of cyber media is changing this relationship; Internet surfers are better able to control their own media and still generate a broad range of information for themselves. Nevertheless, the traditional forms of media still are the major, unregulated source of information for most Americans.

DEPENDENCE ON MEDIA

Americans' dislike of their dependence on media extends from the limited number of ultimate media sources that are available. Television newscasts and front pages of newspapers across the nation tend to be very much the same, no matter which region of the country the audience member is in. There is also a public perception that the media are pursuing their own agendas. Suspected agendas vary from one of profitability and **sensationalism** designed to attract larger audiences to one of ideology—that of a "liberal media" in a conservative setting.

Implicit in the concerns of those who feel media-dependent is the belief there is no controlling authority to assure this dependence will not produce harmful effects. Governments regulate everything from food labels to plumbers to the medical doctors who treat life-threatening illnesses. The media, on the other hand, are largely untouched by regulation, courtesy of the First Amendment, which prevents formal, legal controls over media and their content. Such independence creates anxiety about the way media power is being used and, subsequently, a wary public hostility toward the media. Such concerns lead, in turn, to questions about whether the media are indeed pursuing their own agendas or whether they are acting in the interests of their audiences. These concerns are magnified by recognition that most of us not only should but do accept at face value the vast majority of information presented by the media. This information ranges, of course, from the price reliability of a $.79 can of peas advertised by the local supermarket to the time and place of tonight's city council meeting or high school football game.

SELF-SERVING ACTIONS AND SUSPICIONS ABOUT THE MEDIA

CONTEMPORARY CASE IN MEDIA: PRESIDENTIAL ELECTION 2000

On November 7, 2000, at 7:40 P.M. (EST), George W. Bush was declared president-elect of the United States by all the major media. Almost four hours later, this announcement was retracted. The state of Florida had serious problems in fairly declaring a winner of the state's 25 Electoral College votes.

The news media were criticized for making this and several other announcements too early in the evening, only to retract their statements shortly thereafter. Did the media act irresponsibly in their early announcements? Did the release of information further complicate a very complicated election?

This example illustrates the extremely clouded relationship our society has with an entity it cannot control but nevertheless relies on to supply the vast majority of the information it receives. The public's relationship with the media produces a number of self-serving actions that range from the guarded skepticism of the average reader or viewer to the venomous accusations by leaders whose power depends on the media.

In this environment has grown the ridicule and derision that place the mass media at the top of the list of targets to blame when things go wrong. Consider the following:

- Many in government and the U.S. military blamed the media for loss of public support for the Vietnam War and even loss of the war itself.
- The advertising industry has been accused of popularizing footwear and clothing styles ghetto youth sometimes kill for.
- "Slick public relations" has been blamed for everything from whipping up support for the Gulf War to creating favorable public opinion for questionable causes.
- Television programs and movies contain story lines that validate sexual promiscuity.
- The media have been accused of purposely targeting political leaders and interest groups in smear campaigns.
- The entertainment media have been accused of marketing extreme violence to children to swell their own coffers.
- Virtually every public official or celebrity caught in wrongdoing or an indiscretion blames the media for blowing the incident out of proportion.

These accusations and suspicions all imply unethical conduct on the part of the media and may be followed by open or veiled threats that the media must be restrained—by law, if necessary. This is the downside of the American social system, a system that finds it convenient to batter a very visible media industry for society's failures and shortcomings. The upside, of course, is that Americans are among the most well-informed people in the world thanks to the media industry, and that information contributes to the United States having one of the most dynamic and progressive social systems in the world—a system committed to innovation and change.

A DEMOCRATIC MEDIA SYSTEM IS NOT COMFORTABLE

Innovation and change are products of open information systems. In order to understand the role one may play in society as a media professional, one must understand some of the subtle forces of the system in which one works. First, a democratic system is not meant to be a comfortable system for its participants, although most strive for comfortable lives. Therefore, there exists, if the system is to function properly, a constant turmoil that is unsettling to many.

Tolerance of others is essential, since all participants must, in order to enjoy a measure of freedom themselves, tolerate others who exercise their freedoms. Yet it is the need for tolerance of others whose behavior and utterances border on the extreme that is often found wanting as some find the actions of others threatening to a would-be well-ordered world. The media are often accused, by providing attention to those extremists, of encouraging antisocial behaviors and groups.

The valuable currency in a democratic society that makes media critically important is power, and power is dependent on information. In a culture in which public opinion is stronger than the law, it is information distributed by the suspect media discussed above that drives the acquisition and use of power.

MEDIA AFFECTS DISTRIBUTION AND ACQUISITION OF POWER AND INFORMATION

Power may lie in the ability of the individual to determine his or her own destiny to a large degree, or it may rest in the accumulation of political power with life-and-death influence over millions of people. As mentioned in Chapter 3, the distribution of information in this context redistributes power. Picture the individual who has advance information regarding the location of a new highway that is to be built through an undeveloped section of the community. With that information land can be purchased for a relatively low price and later sold at a substantial profit for the highway right of way or as business property along the highway for construction of gas stations, motels, restaurants, and other conveniences necessary for highway travel.

The individual who regularly receives such advance information has the power to amass a huge fortune by acting before anyone else knows action is necessary. The deadly enemy of this powerful person is the mass media system, for it has the power to inform everybody at the same time, thus leveling the playing field so no one gains the advantage formerly bestowed by the distribution of exclusive information to a select few in a closed information society. The distribution of information to a select few is one of the forms of extreme corruption prevalent in closed cultures in which those in the inner circles with advance information can exploit that information to their own ends. It is one reason why media are rigidly controlled in closed cultures.

THOSE WITH POWER, THOSE WITHOUT POWER

Given these circumstances, it is no wonder those who wish to accumulate disproportionate power become the chief accusers and adamant enemies of the media. If the media can be muzzled by law or forced into a humble position by public opinion emerging from the accusations, they are less able to provide the information needed to diffuse power. In the same vein, those who have power often recognize that media may threaten that power at any time through disclosure or by turning a public spotlight on the powerful. It is not surprising, then, that those with power or those who hope to accumulate power have a strong interest in discrediting the media so they may later point to, should the need arise, the poor reputation the media have for distributing half-truths and for victimizing the innocent in order to build audiences.

Those without power, by the same token, are subject to the concerns listed above about how much they should trust an uncontrolled and powerful entity in their lives. The media must function within this social system (described in admittedly extreme terms). Often the media are pressured from all sides by those with an interest in either controlling or discrediting the media. In this environment, media professionals must keep in mind that if information is power and the open flow of information discourages its accumulation, then it must be recognized that media are in the business of redistributing power. Information control should not be accumulated and centralized, thereby creating inequities among people.

WHICH SOCIAL GROUPS ARE IN CONFLICT WITH MEDIA?

The conflict is not only intense, but everybody participates in it, often moving among the groups listed below. It is intense because in the absence of formal controls—the laws and regulations that govern media in other countries—informal pressures are brought to bear on the media as the various forces fight to gain advantage. One might say it is a war out there, with three roughly defined groups at work in the battleground to define the terms and scope of media activity. The groups are as follows:

1. Those who would control information by bringing what pressures they can (economic, public opinion, personal, etc.) on the media to withhold or weigh with great caution the information they distribute.
2. The media professionals who operate under a national philosophy that argues a "green-light" approach to publication.
3. Audiences made up of citizens who must make the collective decisions that shape our society.

The media occupy a central position in the conflict, and many find themselves in the other two camps at one time or another in their lives, as they stand between would-be power centers bent on shaping society according to their interests and the people whose actions determine who has power and who does not. Political leaders try to defuse media power by discrediting the media and courting public opinion in order to more easily advance their agendas; parents try to disenfranchise the media in order to gain more control over their children and thereby make them more amenable to a parental value system. Both are in the final analysis trying to consolidate their power—politicians over their constituencies and parents over their children. These attempts to consolidate power are not necessarily bad; they are merely elements in the democratic society that tend to assure us that issues and instructions are appropriately examined and not arbitrary and punitive. It has the practical impact, however, of making both politicians and parents (and other power brokers) work harder to regulate their own environment.

MEDIA'S RESPONSE TO THE CONFLICT: GREEN-LIGHT JOURNALISM

This conflict places a moral obligation on media professionals to work their way through these strong pressures to perform their functions; it also explains the further obligation, advanced by the Poynter Institute for Media Studies in Florida, to be green-light communicators, distributing more information rather than being persuaded either to distribute less or to filter what they do distribute through power-oriented filters. Green-light communications is informationalist and a source of discomfort to many, if not most, of us. It advises publication of material that, in professional judgment, is accurate and important. Such publication, the argument goes, treats audiences with respect, assuming they will find the information of value. Such information may also generate additional information that would never have come to light had the original story not been published.

For journalists the "green light" involves finding and writing stories that describe an environment many would prefer to ignore; for the advertiser it may be advising clients to put more information into commercial messages than the clients would wish in order to better and more completely inform customers and audiences; and for public relations practitioners it means advising clients to disclose more and offer more truthful information about their client's business than many clients feel comfortable with.

PUBLISHING INFORMATION REDISTRIBUTES POWER

Examples of both green-light and red-light publishing are in evidence in related incidents that took place in 1992. The following classic case will be referred to in several chapters of this book. While illustrating the effects of both green-light and red-light journalism, it also illustrates the interplay of power dynamics.

CLASSIC CASE IN JOURNALISM: RED-LIGHT CONCERNS, PUBLISHING CLAIMS OF SEXUAL HARASSMENT

The Seattle Times *published the story of eight women who claimed separately to have been sexually harassed and assaulted by a U.S. Senator from the state of Washington. The women asked not to be identified, though they agreed to testify in the event of libel action against the* Seattle Times. *The senator, Brock*

Adams, denied the allegations of harassment but announced he would not seek reelection that year. The story destroyed his political career. Some 200 miles to the south, in Oregon, the Portland Oregonian *received similar information about one of its U.S. Senators and chose not to run the story because sexual coercion could not be confirmed from sources other than the women making the allegations. In the wake of media silence, Sen. Robert Packwood was reelected. The story, however, was published soon after the elections—2,000 miles away by the* Washington Post. *For nearly two years, the senator was virtually defending himself full-time, denying Oregon the effective services of its senator. Ultimately Sen. Packwood resigned after the Senate Ethics Committee recommended his expulsion on the basis not only of the original story but also in light of additional information that surfaced as a result of the story and subsequent public discussion.*

RED LIGHT OR GREEN LIGHT?

It is important to note in these cases, as in most others involving allegations of sexual harassment, that even today few know whether the accusations were true. Evidence suggests they might be true, but only the accusers and the accused know for certain. The important moral principle illustrated in this case is that the *Seattle Times* opted to assist powerless women who claimed to have been victimized by a powerful senator. The story certainly redistributed power by diminishing Senator Adams's ability to chart the course he laid out for himself. The *Seattle Times* chose to green light the story; that is, it followed the green-light path of bringing the accusations into the sunlight of public discussion so all sides could discuss and defend their positions publicly.

Public criticism of the story was immediate and strong, centering on the *Seattle Times'* willingness to quote anonymous sources and its failure to provide corroborating evidence. The senator named in the story chose not to participate in a public discussion, instead withdrawing from public life. Such an action indicates neither guilt nor innocence, but it did mean the full story would not be told in public discussion.

The *Portland Oregonian* opted to red light the story, thereby protecting the power of a senator at the expense of the women until more complete evidence could be presented. That decision allowed power to perpetuate itself through reelection. Had the *Washington Post* not published the story in the nation's capital, the women's case might never have been made public, and additional information about Sen. Packwood and his behavior that eventually led to the ethics committee action may never have been disclosed. Public silence would have continued to protect his power. The women would have been powerless to advance their allegations.

Some believe strongly that power should be allowed to prevail undisturbed until definitive evidence is found to justify public accusations—generally a communitarian argument. Arguably, the Constitution and succeeding legal decisions encourage verbal assault on power, even though the information underlying that assault may not be complete. The basic premise, of course, is that the nation can better afford to lose a few from leadership positions (even unjustly) as a result of open discussion than it can to suppress discussion and consolidate power by withholding information media professionals reasonably believe to be true.

When in Doubt, Publish Information or Withhold Information?

This is the essence of a "free and open marketplace" of discussion in which all ideas are introduced and the operant truth is determined by public opinion. The green-light ethic argues that, when in doubt, publish, as opposed to the red-light ethic, perhaps more likely to be the emotional favorite, that argues when in doubt, withhold and leave the status quo intact.

Under the green-light ethic, the moral obligation still mandates media professionals to ensure as much as humanly possible that the truth is being told, but it encourages informed public opinion rather than maintenance of traditional power. The two harassment cases illustrate the immense pressures on journalists. Either course of action in each case would have met with strong criticism. Importantly, the conditioned reflex about protecting power placed public opinion initially on the side of the senators. That reflexive response is indicative of the public responses professional communicators must consider virtually every day.

WHAT AFFECTS SOCIETY'S ATTITUDES TOWARD COMMUNICATORS?

ATTITUDES ABOUT INFORMATION FLOW

Professional communicators recognize that society must be both courted and resisted. All media people and professional communicators face the task of reaching audiences as a matter of survival, so media content must be audience-friendly, providing what people want as well as what they need. On the other hand, many outside the media with a vested interest in affecting media content for their own purposes form formidable groups to bring constant and often fierce pressure to deter media from their primary responsibility of serving audiences.

These groups often use the media to enlist audiences to pressure the media or to discredit the media with those audiences. Paradoxically, much distrust of the media springs from media stories quoting leaders and surveys that declare the media cannot be trusted. The exclamation that "the media are attacking me, an innocent person, for their own purposes" is a recruitment call to audiences to side with the accused. Sen. Adams made the accusation against the *Seattle Times*. The call takes advantage of public anxiety about the power of the media and concerns about whether they can be trusted to keep us appropriately informed.

Potential rewards of being empowered by media attention (or of being a professional communicator able to use the media to help clients accumulate power) are enough to make the media and those who contribute to them the center of intense, high-stakes attention. The potential social power of an information disseminator (in distributing power to some while taking it from others) combined with that of those who exercise power, produces strong social pressures on all handlers of mass information. Many pressures on the media are well founded, of course, but others also have the practical effect of crippling the important information-gathering and distribution process, both for individuals and for society. All are society's way of responding to a perception of the power of both media and information (even in interpersonal situations).

CHILDREN'S ATTITUDES ABOUT MEDIA

In the absence of formal controls over the media, extraordinary instructional devices are used to assure that social pressures are exerted to moderate media behavior. The devices, recognizing the social power of a professional communicator, encourage children to be suspicious of media. In addition to reinforcing suspicions about the media, early socialization of a child by parents, churches, and at school is often designed to affect the child's attitude toward information and, not incidentally, favors the power status quo, whether it be parent, teacher, church leader, business leader, or political leader. Widespread attitudes produced by this process resulted in public outrage over the publication of the Brock Adams's story and confirmed the rightness of with-holding the Packwood story.

RUMORS

It is for good reason that a child's significant tutors favor a power status quo. The status quo, at any level, makes it easier for a leader to control and direct followers, giving a child's overseers, whether at church, home, or in the classroom, a vested interest in passing on behavior rules that may discourage the seeking of alternative information or of using the media as trustworthy and valuable information sources. The spread of rules is not bad unless creativity is effectively discouraged in favor of social order and relative ease—or maintenance of excess power—for leaders.

Youngsters are invited through repetition to accept some rules reflecting conventional wisdom without discussion, which shapes young attitudes toward information and later views on media content. As an example, children hear of the false and destructive nature of rumors and are warned to avoid rumors. They are taught to place confidence only in authoritative sources (i.e., teachers, parents, and church and civic leaders). The convention is that rumors are destructive and that the wise avoid both trading in rumors and listening to them. This form of communication is often called *gossip*, a negative term that strengthens the admonition.

At best, cautioning children about the destructive power of rumors is an intuitive attempt to promote social harmony and encourage children not to engage in behaviors that may be damaging to others. At worst, it is a control device used by those in authority to encourage others to voluntarily restrict information intake to that which comes from authority (therefore, it is not rumor); in addition, it instructs children not to redistribute information that does not issue from authoritative sources. In this way, each becomes a self-censor who voluntarily controls information flow so a minimum of pluralism enters public discussion. Nonauthoritative (often powerless) people are barred from public discussion by the very nature of their low standing in the community and because they are persuaded as to the pernicious power of the media.

As a matter of fact, rumor is an extremely important part of life. Through rumor is learned the informal information that provides alternatives to instructions from authority or even alternatives to tradition. Contrary to conventional wisdom, rumors tend to have a high degree of accuracy and are useful to thoughtful people trying to find their way in life.

Both rumors and media are threatening to powerholders and are therefore often condemned.

SOCIAL BELIEFS ABOUT MEDIA

There are other devices that affect attitudes toward information flow, all of which have intuitive validity and deserve attention for their tendency to increase pressures on the media. In addition to do no harm, these admonitions include the following:

- Shield the innocent from harmful influences.
- Authority is beyond criticism.
- Do not intrude on the privacy of others.
- Concerted effort produces the best results.
- Be morally superior by giving people what they need rather than pandering to their wants and discounting the validity of public opinion.
- Advocacy (persuasion), deception, and greed (profit motive) are undesirable.
- Personal values should prevail over professional values.
- Despised or "destructive" causes have no right to public representation or defense.
- Media should take a limited, submissive (subordinate) social role (bulletin board function).
- Media are monolithic as they exercise conscious, overwhelming power to control thoughts and follow their own agendas.

Many of these notions are discussed in theory in Chapter 4. From a more practical position, we will now discuss a few of these beliefs.

Protect the Innocent Who Cannot Handle Information Well

Controllers protect the innocent by keeping information from them. Every reporter is familiar with the source who says, "but they [your audience] don't need to know that." The implication, of course, is that many are unable to process complex information and the media would do more harm than good by disclosure. The social premise driving free expression is that individuals can handle information and need to be well informed in order to make valid decisions, whether for buying, voting, or expressing opinions on issues of the day.

Reverence for Authority

Respect for leaders and holding them above criticism is viewed by many as important to the maintenance of an orderly society. Certainly, that view has some validity, but at an extreme, it violates the basic premises of a pluralistic society. A recent case that illustrates this point is the 1998 scandal surrounding the 2002 Olympic Winter games scheduled to be held in Salt Lake City, Utah.

CONTEMPORARY CASE OF OLYMPIC PROPORTIONS: CORPORATE PUBLIC RELATIONS AND BRIBERY

After nearly $500,000 in gifts, money, and other rewards was used to "encourage" International Olympic Committee members to vote for Salt Lake City as the Olympic Winter Games site, it soon became apparent that the opaque nature of the activities of Salt Lake City's bid committee was largely responsible for the corruption. The community, including political and business leaders, was so concerned about bringing the Olympics to the state that it allowed bid committee executives free and largely unsupervised rein to win the bid. In the process, bid executives committed acts that, when discovered, the community found reprehensible.

A more transparent operation, one in which actions would be visible to public reaction and criticism, would arguably have avoided subsequent community embarrassment over the antics of the leaders. Reluctance to criticize and efforts to entice the Olympics went beyond ignorance when a state government audit in 1988, ten years before the public scandal, warned that funds were being mishandled and that bid committee actions were highly irregular. To their ultimate shame, media and state officials, with their eyes on the big prize of an Olympics in their community, turned a blind eye to the warnings.

Protect Children from Destructive Messages

While children do need to be protected from some media messages, such protection often masks efforts to discourage media from distributing legitimate and vital information. Media need to establish their own policies, taking into consideration community information needs as well as the protection of children. If all community discourse were to be conducted at a childlike level, complex solutions to complex problems could not be sought through public discussion. The philosophy of restricting information unless it is safe for children would tend not only to leave power undisturbed, but would also add immeasurably to the power of those in positions to make public policy decisions. For a policymaker, power and influence are increased if there is no need to submit results of work to public scrutiny and open discussion. Therefore, professional communicators need to be judicious in deciding whether to withhold information because of its presumed effects on children. Some would even argue that the green-light decision ought to apply when in doubt.

ADDITIONAL SOCIAL MESSAGES

Other messages that discourage or affect media performance are as follows:

- Shame for intruding on privacy rights.
- Community effort (i.e., don't dilute the community spirit). More is to be gained by cooperation than by individual effort.
- Moral superiority discounts the validity of public opinion (i.e., give people what they need rather than pandering to their wants).
- Advocacy (persuasion), deception, and greed are unethical (i.e., suspect the profit motive under First Amendment protection).
- Personal values should prevail over professional values.
- "Destructive" causes have no right to public representation or defense.
- Media should be objective (bulletin board function) with a limited, submissive (subordinate) social role.
- Monolithic media can exercise a conscious, overwhelming power to control.

These devices are variously used to discourage the distribution of information and to warn audiences about the damaging intent and behaviors of the mass media. They are not necessarily malevolent conventions, but they are social responses to widespread fears about the uncontrollable power of media and of information generally. Nevertheless, powerbrokers (political leaders and others with a vested interest in having their messages reach audiences with a minimum of mediation) do use these devices to damage media credibility and to bring public pressure on media professionals to restrain themselves and be less independent. And media professionals pass the accusations/warnings along—as they should, thereby fulfilling a difficult ethical obligation by contributing to their own declining credibility.

Persuaders: Finding Common Ground Between Clients and Audience

Few critical leaders can claim that media professionals do not air their comments that criticize the media. Persuasion professionals feel similar pressures, accused as they are of controlling minds and decisions through what are often called the "unholy" skills of persuasion and manipulation. The information they distribute is often determined by their clients, but they should recognize that their clients have the same interest in manipulating audiences as other powerbrokers. They should find some common ground between the needs of audiences to know about the client or product and the intent of clients to control information. This becomes particularly important when vital information exists that would prevent consumers from being needlessly victimized.

Contemporary Case in Public Relations: Sport Utility Vehicles and Tire Safety

The Firestone tires installed on Ford Explorers had a fatal flaw. The tread on these tires peeled off causing fatal accidents. It has been charged that both Firestone and Ford were aware of a problem but that they decided not to make the information public. By not making the information public, they allowed accidents to occur that may have been avoided. To prevent tire-related accidents, the companies could have issued an announcement warning drivers to increase tire pressure on Ford Explorers with Firestone tires.

The Firestone tire case has raised public concern over the safety of sport utility vehicles, with the Ford Explorer and Ford Explorer Sport still implicated in the controversy because of their proclivity to roll under freeway conditions involving a swerve. Because of the gravity center of sport utility vehicles, a swerve can often cause the vehicle to go out of control and roll. Passengers who are not in seat belts will most likely be the fatal victims of these rolls. Sport utility vehicle manufacturers are still not releasing information about the propensity of these vehicles to roll in a swerve; however, after ten years of requests, the National Highway Traffic and Safety Administration (NHTSA) in 2001 released star ratings on all sport utility vehicles. For years, the information was contested by lobbyists for the automobile industry who argued that the ratings would be misunderstood by the public.

In this instance, persuasion specialists might have foreseen that meeting audience needs for more information would have saved lives and prevented disastrous consequences for both the auto maker and the tire company. These are circumstances in which professional persuaders must be persuasive to their clients as well as to the public.

INFORMAL WAYS TO TAME THE MEDIA

The First Amendment prohibits regulation of media and speech, narrowing the options for controlling media content and maintaining power. Legal regulation of speech and the press is the way many societies force media industries to be submissive and guarantee power centers will not be threatened. Because formal regulation is prohibited, more informal ways of taming media and information professionals must be used in America. Methods by which these control devices are put in place vary, but they seem to be reliable in inducing socially approved behavior in large segments of society. Examples include families, schools, religions, and corporate acculturation. A novelist, recognizing the problem, declared several years ago that "public schools have become boot camps for conformity."

SOCIAL CONDITIONING PROGRAMS

Indeed, the Vietnam War of the 1960s and early 1970s may provide a look at both the success and failure of social conditioning programs. On the one hand, hundreds of thousands of young men accepted the call of their country to serve and possibly die in the military without understanding what they were fighting for beyond the generalizations they were "making the world safe for the American Way." Thousands of others refused to serve in and even demonstrated against what they viewed to be a very bad war. It was observed at the time and reinforced later that schools, in the wake of World War II and the Korean War, had relaxed efforts to instill patriotism in their students. For example, the daily Pledge of Allegiance to the flag had fallen into disuse in many schools. It was generally reinstated in the 1970s and is used universally today. One result, presumably, will be more patriotic young people who are willing to serve their country and fewer who will question their leaders.

The social conditioning process instills attitudes about both information and the mass media. The primary effects, not altogether unhealthy, include the media being discredited in the public eye and casual attitudes being cultivated about the importance of having information available for decision making. Both effects reduce the power of unregulated social entities in favor of approved authority. A disbelieving public reduces its exposure to media, particularly to news, and individuals without extensive personal information systems are vulnerable to their limited sources, opinion leaders, telemarketers, public figures, and public officials.

CONSOLIDATION AND AUDIENCE SHIFTS

More pernicious than social conditioning, however, may be two dramatic events of the final quarter of the twentieth century: the rise of media conglomerates and the drift of audiences away from traditional news media. Both trends have had and are continuing to have a devastating effect on media ethics. The implications of the rise of media conglomerates were summed up in the journalism criticism magazine *Brill's Content* in August 2000, which declared that "anyone with a monopoly or near monopoly on distributing content has tremendous leverage over the content providers." Here *Brill's Content* laments the fact that journalists who provide news, rather than placing emphasis on informing the public, are instead being swayed to emphasize profit by the influence of those with control over distributing content. *Brill's Content* suggests, of course, that owners of media conglomerates ought not have control over content, but should instead settle for providing information access to all audiences.

The incident triggering this statement occurred when American Broadcasting Company (ABC) network stations, which provide news, were bumped from the cable channels of Time-Warner (a huge media conglomerate) in a dispute with the Walt Disney Company over inclusion and payment for Disney entertainment channels on Time-Warner cable. This dispute between giants (ABC is owned by Disney and was a pawn in the conflict) caught a news medium in its vortex, illustrating the vulnerability of news to the tussles of giants. This situation was further complicated and the distribution of news inherently imperiled by the merger of Time-Warner and America Online (AOL), placing a major online news service under the same umbrella as *Time* magazine, Cable News Network (CNN), and a variety of other media outlets.

Disney, on the other hand, owns a variety of cable channels as well as the Entertainment and Sports Network (ESPN) channels on cable and satellite. Thus, consolidation and conglomeration has moved from a drastic reduction in the number of independent daily metropolitan newspapers in the United States over the past 50 years, with its dramatic impact on journalism and individual journalistic autonomy, to the combining of companies into not only mega-media giants, but also mega-corporate giants involved in both media and nonmedia interests.

As discussed previously in this book, power is routinely used reflexively to promote self-interest, as occurred in the Time-Warner and Disney case. Also in an economic vein, audiences first shifted dramatically from relying on print media for information (particularly newspapers) during the mid-twentieth century to relying on television and other electronic media in the late twentieth century and now to Internet media, drastically reducing audiences for both newspapers and television. In such desperate circumstances, both newspapers and television stations have shifted to audience-catching techniques that are deplored as destructive to journalism. A recent technique used by newspapers is to interview focus groups of citizens to see what they want and do not want to see in their newspapers.

A local election in a California community was influenced a few years ago as a result of focus groups decrying negative political campaign stories. In this case, the newspaper decided not to run a story regarding conflict of interest. The story involved a county supervisor's spouse receiving a large amount of money from a contractor who had a matter pending before the supervisor, several months previously. Although reporters discovered the details of the story some weeks before the election, the story was killed because of focus group feelings about negative stories. The woman was reelected by voters whose newspaper did not provide them with critical information about the candidate.

Fleeing audiences are creating great anxiety in the counting rooms of media, anxiety stemming from news operations with mandates to provide coverage that attracts and holds audiences (to stimulate ad and commercial sales). This results in clear conflicts of interest in which reporters are ordered to consider the interests of advertisers and station or newspaper ahead of the interests of audiences.

The serious moral question that arises is to what extent media ought to alter their coverage out of commercial considerations, which raises the argument that no news at all would be distributed if there were no media; therefore, media professionals have a responsibility to see to the survival of the outlet through which information is distributed. Journalists' problems multiply, however, as they try to assert their autonomy in gathering, writing, and distributing stories but find themselves having to argue the merits of good stories with their supervisors. Those supervisors may not have audience interests in mind, so reporters have to make cases for good stories that audiences need rather than want.

Complex stories, such as the beginnings of the collapse of the savings and loan industry in the United States in the late 1980s, are the kind of stories that go uncovered because they do not have the same sex appeal to audiences as a story on a Hollywood star's sex or drugs misdeeds.

Presumably, early media coverage of the savings and loan scandal could have put the matter on the national agenda and forestalled the disastrous collapse of the industry, with its billions of dollars in bailouts paid with taxpayer money. At the very least, business writers should have more forcefully pushed the story until mainstream journalists were covering these important events as well. In this case the autonomy of journalists may have harmed others.

MINIMIZING THE HARM OF MEDIA INFORMATION

As described in previous chapters, one of the chief arguments used against the media is that the media cause harm when distributing information. Publicize the protests, and it will only spawn more protests, the argument goes—take note of a suicide, and "copycats" will follow suit; describe in detail a horrendous crime, and the incidence of similar crimes will surge; disclose a congressman's sexual strayings, and his family is devastated; and expose a juvenile court judge's sexual misconduct, and it harms the entire justice system.

The moral mandate to do no harm is logical in any moral code and an intuitive, emotional favorite. Yet it is impossible to distribute information without doing some harm. In the process of empowering one, the power of another is reduced. The free flow of information is society's nonviolent way of redistributing power. Ideally, power, through information, will be equitably redistributed. A professional communicator must recognize that the harm resulting from redistributing power through information is inevitable and concentrate on minimizing harm or on avoiding causing unnecessary harm. Sensitive communicators who vow to do no harm must come to terms with this aspect of their profession.

EXAMINE THE POWERFUL BUT DO NOT VICTIMIZE THE POWERLESS

One way journalists minimize unnecessary harm is to follow the rule-of-thumb principle of publicly examining the powerful while vowing not to victimize the powerless. When deciding whether to publish a credible accusation against a powerful figure made by one with little power, a journalist might favor publication in this case more than if the roles were reversed.

Of particular public concern is the inevitable invasion of privacy resulting from the media finding and publicly distributing information that the public has no right to know (the paparazzi and Princess Diana, for example), thereby damaging reputations and credibility, and the distribution of the kinds of information that have no beneficial effects, but which titillate the voyeuristic tendencies of audiences, harm readers and viewers, and lead them into socially destructive mischief. Such declarations tend to frame the discussion in ways that put media professionals on the defensive and may incline them to *do no harm*. Yet systematic, professional, socially approved, and even unique harm is not foreign to society.

CONTEMPORARY CASE IN JOURNALISM: EXPOSING DISCRIMINATION

ABC News *recently aired stories on the discrimination against minority women by Immigration Services. The stories featured two female victims, both of whom were black and both of whom were stopped by Immigration Services (at different sites) and detained for over 24 hours. Both women were forced to take laxatives, which caused severe diarrhea and cramping. When no problems were found with the feces, the women were allowed to go on their way, but no apologies were given. One of the women was eight months pregnant and delivered her child early. She claims the abuse caused by Immigration Services forced the delivery of her child just days after the detainment.*

Why is it important that news organizations expose abuses such as those described here? Both women have sued Immigration Services, with the first woman winning her suit. The second suit is still pending. Is the media exposure merely to help the women prevail with their lawsuits, or does the exposure help the public to understand larger problems within an organization or society? *ABC News'* investigation of Immigration Services also found that black women were discriminated against more frequently than any other ethnic group.

SOCIETY APPROVES HARM IN SOME CASES

It is not difficult to identify exclusive, unanimously acceptable roles that allow professionals to engage in behavior prohibited to the rest of us. A layman who carves on another person with a sharp knife, for example, is universally condemned. On the other hand, a surgeon does this routinely, and society sees it not only as acceptable but as highly beneficial behavior. It is ethically permissible for a surgeon to inflict trauma to relieve a deeper suffering, to cause pain for a greater good. Similarly, a military commander can cause the deaths of thousands in wartime, including his own troops, and be hailed a hero, provided a greater benefit to the military commander's nation accrues. However, it is not socially acceptable for the average citizen to order even one person's death; in such instances, the offender's sense of right and wrong will certainly be questioned. The distinction here is that the surgeon and the military commander each have a social role that justifies behavior that is clearly unacceptable in the rest of us. Certain role-based behaviors become morally acceptable only when occurring within their narrow professional context.

Admonitions to communicators to *do no harm* are further invalidated by recognition that communication cannot be conducted without harm. To provide information to one person broadens that person's ability to function while inevitably weakening another person's ability to exercise power. To distribute information is to shift power by taking it from one entity and giving it (in the form of information) to another. For example, children learn early the power of information. In threatening to tell a parent of the transgressions of a sibling, a child is threatening to take power from the sibling (the power that comes from secrecy, which prevents punishment) and transfer it to the parent who, with the power of knowledge, brings the transgressor to justice with punishment. Without knowledge of who broke the window or ate the strawberries, the parent is powerless. Yet with the knowledge, the transgressing child loses the power that comes from having the parent uninformed. Similarly, the child who threatens to tell is using the threat of disclosure for his or her own purposes—another information power play.

Public Image and Power

On the broader public stage, disclosure of President Clinton's alleged sexual adventures drained him of power that previously was inherent in his position. Being forced to deal publicly with the allegations diluted his power in other areas because his time had to be reallocated to deal with the accusations. The allegations empowered many of his political enemies to an extent that exceeded the accumulation of power resulting from the sexually oriented allegations. Once impeachment proceedings were over, it was generally acknowledged that President Clinton's final two years in office were not nearly as effective as they could have been had there not been the ordeal.

Therefore, it is important to examine whether bystander condemnation of public relations or advertising persuasion may be akin to the *do-no-harm* advocate condemning the surgeon or the *thou-shalt-not-kill* zealot condemning the military commander who pursues "just" war objectives. Before making judgments, then, it is important to examine the socially contributive roles of those who gather and distribute information with the intent to persuade. The need to identify an ethic that allows for justification of legitimate professional behavior intensifies in the light of broad public suspicions, and fear-evoked tendencies to advocate control of professional persuaders. An ethical construct allows media professionals to justify behavior in forthright ways without having to avoid or trivialize the issue in the face of growing pressure on professional communicators.

RULES: HOW SOCIETY HANDLES MEDIA INFORMATION

One way to look at justification for the information and persuasion roles is to start with the structure we may detect in society by which individuals handle information. Society, particularly a pluralistic society, shapes itself in two ways. First, it encourages and/or compels its members to adapt; second, it uses both formal and informal information systems.

Formal and Informal Rules

Formal rules for information are created by legislative bodies (e.g., parents, commissioners, employers, teachers, and senators) with the power of enforcement (e.g., parental sanctions, courts, and firing and/or promotions).

Society, overall, also develops informal conventions that eclipse formal rules when they are not adequate. For example, it is a formal rule that one must generally be dressed when in public. Informal conventions, however, have emerged that prescribe certain kinds of dress for certain occasions. Informal and nonbinding as they are, informal conventions permeate our lives and often produce automatic behavior, determining how we will act. Freedom allows for new ideas (fashions) to be distributed through informal information systems so they can be either rejected or accepted. Society (more likely, certain age groups) tests the idea and decides whether it is to become an accepted convention (even a transitory convention, such as men's hair length). At its most fluid, an informal convention is called a *fad*. At its most stable, it becomes a powerful social mandate. Examples include eating certain types of food for breakfast, working flextime instead of the traditional nine-to-five schedule, and challenging the corporate culture of coats and ties in the workplace. Each instance is a challenge to the status quo and is likely to be resisted by more conservative elements of the community. Once accepted, however, even conservatives are likely to adopt the new idea as the status quo and, in turn, defend it against change. Resistance emerges from a desire for predictability in behavior—the right to have today's world conform to yesterday's comfortable conventions.

Formal rules are passed down to us through established, universal channels, such as schools, churches, corporate memos or examples, tradition, and bulletin boards. The informal rules are formulated through less formal systems, including rumor mills and examples set by innovators who try new things (i.e., the employee in the coat and tie corporate culture who shows up in khakis and a twill shirt and is not punished). Informal rules also occur in discussions with friends and observations in the mass media. Hair styles and new clothing fashions are often introduced on television shows. The media serve as both formal and informal channels—formal in the sense the media pass along new laws, proclamations, and admonitions of leaders and other rule makers and informal to the degree the media distribute information not generated by formal rule makers. Specifically, the media foster a pluralistic society by articulating alternative ways of living and of doing things.

As advertisers develop new products, they show audiences alternative ways of doing things, be it how to use a new toothbrush or why they should drive more environmentally friendly solar cars. The advertiser's primary task, in fact, is to promote pluralism by marketing one specific brand of a product. Both formal and informal sources are critically important to an open information system because among them they should lay out the range of alternatives available to us in a given circumstance. Because of the vested interest the formal information systems have in projecting their power, they often try to discredit the informal media (e.g., warning about the dangers of rumors, unsavory friends, and the media). At the same time, the chief function of the informal systems seems to be to generate information that conflicts with, or at least offers alternatives to, that distributed through the formal systems.

The Pluralistic Society

A pluralistic society needs both systems to be vigorous. The formal systems tell us what we must do in order to stay in the good graces of the community, and the informal system gives us clues about how we can challenge the status quo, providing us with alternatives and stimulating individualistic behavior and the changes needed for a dynamic, progressive society.

A courtroom pronouncement by a Texas bankruptcy judge provides an excellent example of the dynamic process by which such changes take place. Judge Massie Tillman declared women would no longer be allowed to wear pants or pantsuits in court and men would be required to wear a coat and tie. This is a good example of formal rule making; what followed provides an excellent example of a challenge to the rule-making process and to tradition. Of ninety messages reacting to the news story about the judge's edict on a news comment board, forty-two (47%) opposed the new rule and eighteen (20%) recognized the need for such a regulation but opposed the specific skirt requirement. Only nineteen (21%) supported the judge, often with ferocity, deploring the decline in civility that made the rule necessary. The opposition was also vigorous, with some calling for the judge to come into the 1990s.

Within a week, the order was rescinded. Important lessons lie in the process and the content of the discussion. Without mass media, it would have been impossible for such a discussion to take place because relatively few would have known about the edict; the only way information would have been distributed would have been by word of mouth. Those the rule affected would have been powerless under the judge's jurisdiction and therefore reluctant to protest for fear of future treatment at his hands. Publication of this story and the subsequent change in the judge's restrictions demonstrate the threat media represent to established power. The media acted as an informal information source by stimulating involvement of people outside the judge's sphere of influence who were willing to enter into the public discussion without fear of punishment; they involved themselves in an issue concerning gender equity, an issue on which they had strong feelings.

Responses that favored the judge's actions often lamented changing dress patterns and sought return to rules of the past. In such circumstances, it would not be unusual for the judge to blame the furor on the media for blowing the matter out of proportion.

Informal Rules: Conventions in Society

Media are viewed with suspicion and criticism by a society uneasy with an open information system entrusted to a media industry, including the new cyberspace media, which cannot be legally reined in when it commits excesses. Fueling the pressures are the socially active people who achieve power by controlling and manipulating information. They recognize, as their power grows, that uncontrollable media are a threat (*media* means in the middle—mediating between powerful and powerless.) A median position in society challenges power brokers to adopt stratagems for direct influence, bypassing or neutralizing the media.

Classic Case in Public Relations and Advertising: Billionaire Access

Ross Perot—with all his billions—found it necessary to go through the media to reach a national audience in his abortive campaign for the presidency of the United States. He was a master at acquiring power in his own business venue but had not developed a mechanism for the nationwide exercise of power. To maximize control of his presentation, Perot bought millions of dollars of network television time to explain his platforms.

Society is often uncomfortable with those who appear to exercise unlimited power, often applauding media efforts to redistribute power in those instances. As was demonstrated with Ross Perot, his message was presented to Americans, but the millions of dollars spent on advertising and public relations could not buy him the presidency. It is through the mass media that new conventions (challenges to the status quo) are presented for testing—and, in the end, either rejected or adopted.

SUMMARY

Virtually everyone has some fear of change and therefore is uncomfortable with the mass media as uncontrolled agents of change, leading to nearly universal suspicion and ambivalence toward the media. Yet vigorous media are the single most compelling sign of a dynamic, free society. Consequently, ethical behavior is important for professional communicators because they inevitably are going to cause harm and as a result outrage virtually every member of their audiences at one time or another, of which the premature announcement of the winner of the 2000 presidential election is another reminder. But what outrages one is helpful to another. If professional communicators can exercise care in causing only justifiable harm, justifying their actions based on principled rather than selfish or egoistic behavior, then the pressures will not cease but will instead assume a proportion that allows media professionals to realistically perform their functions.

This chapter examined the dependence of our society on the media and the fact most individuals have little control of the media. Power is an essential feature in many media professions. Media professionals have the power to present angles, to withhold information, or to publish information yet to be verified. The green-light/red-light model demonstrates how powerful individuals can influence the distribution of information. The professional communicator is in a unique position to help empower many individuals by providing them with information. Through First Amendment protections, a professional communicator has a moral obligation to act well in ways that will strengthen society as well as the profession. It is information that makes a viable, dynamic, individualistic society possible.

Chapter 6 will incorporate the theories, models, and notions of ethics contained in the previous chapters but also will offer a specific focus on journalism ethics. The chapter will feature the notion that ethical markers in journalism may be stricter than those in other media professions and can serve as signposts for all media practitioners.

Moral Reasoning Questions

1. Identify a news story that might "redistribute power." Explain how power may be redistributed if the news story were published.
2. How can a media professional justify to both audience and subject the publication of a story harmful to the subject of the story? Find an example in a newspaper.
3. What happens to the moral concept of truth when information is published that cannot be substantiated?
4. What are some current examples in your community of informal rules in the process of being rewritten through public discussion?
5. What are some conventions in your community that keep public discussion from occurring?

Contemporary Case in Journalism: Small Town, Small Crime?

As a reporter for a small community newspaper, you learn that the mayor (married) and the town's hospital administrator have been having a sexual affair, something the town council members have known of for several months. The council members recently discovered, however, that weekend trips for the affair have been financed by the hospital administrator taking money from the vending machines in hospital lounges. Council members you talk to tell you there is no need for a story to appear in the paper—most people already know something about it. Putting it in the paper would subject two good people to public humiliation when the matter could easily be handled by the council, which will punish the administrator and give the mayor a friendly warning.

1. *In a small town, wouldn't it be better to handle this problem involving two respected citizens in a quiet way, without stirring up a storm?*

2. Should the pilfering of vending machine money be treated by the police chief as a criminal offense, the likely outcome if a story appears? Alternatively, is it appropriate to discipline the administrator without public fanfare that would disrupt the community?

3. How important is it for a newspaper to provide information of which many of its readers already have some inkling? Is credibility lost when newspapers do not provide information that deals with rumors in the community? Why?

4. If council members argue that a competent replacement administrator at the hospital would be almost impossible to find, would you agree not to run the story?

5. What sound ethical reasons exist for running the story despite the problems it would create in the community?

CONTEMPORARY CASE IN ADVERTISING AND BUSINESS: THE SNOOPERS

Personal information is easily found in databases that were once only accessible by government agencies, private investigators, and reporters. Many new companies electronically collect information about consumers and sell it to clients through their Web-based systems. One such company is Acxiom Corporation, which has obtained over 350 trillion characters of personal information. Their service sells information on everything from magazine subscriptions to credit reports to social security numbers and a great deal more. Many methods of invading privacy are available on the Internet if a company would like to take advantage of the services offered by organizations like Acxiom Corporation. These invasions can be done for financial gain or to snoop into the lives of employees. Currently, many corporations consistently electronically snoop into the lives of their employees in an attempt to crack down on personal usage of company computers on company time.

1. Is it ethical for an advertising company to sell information about individuals? What if the individuals have no idea their personal information is being sold?

2. What are the long-term effects on media of selling personal information? What are the ultimate harms? What are the ultimate benefits?

3. *Is it acceptable for an employer to electronically snoop on employees, particularly in relation to company computers used on company time? How can this be seen as an abuse of power?*
4. *How are trust issues in cyberspace linked to various trust and social issues in media?*

SELECTED SOURCES

Altschull, J. H. (1990). *From Milton to McLuhan: The ideas behind American journalism.* New York, NY: Longman.

Altschull, J. H. (1995). *Agents of power: The media and public policy.* White Plains, NY: Longman.

de Tocqueville, Alexis. (1969). *Democracy in America.* Garden City, NY: Doubleday Anchor.

Fallows, J. (1996). *Breaking the news: How the media undermine American democracy.* New York: Pantheon.

Mill, J. S. (1956). *On liberty.* Indianapolis, IN: Bobbs Merrill.

6

JOURNALISM ETHICS

CONTEMPORARY CASE IN JOURNALISM: THE DRUDGE REPORT

The Drudge Report *is an Internet newsletter specializing in scooping traditional media, often with salacious gossip about celebrities and public officials. The author, Matt Drudge, was self-taught and says he gets his information by listening to police scanners, monitoring online services, accessing unpublished underground Web sites, and receiving tips from online users. The* Drudge Report *became famous when it broke the story of the sexual affair between President Bill Clinton and Monica Lewinsky. As a result of the story, this online "service" started getting about 200,000 hits per day. There have been numerous suggestions of control relating to services such as those offered by Matt Drudge. At present, full First Amendment rights are protecting most materials in cyberspace, including Drudge.*

THE JOURNALIST IN CYBERSPACE

Cyberspace adds a new dimension to journalism that is tantalizing and disruptive. Cyberspace ethics is another factor in the journalism ethics equation. As the previous chapter pointed out, the media are largely untouched by regulation, courtesy of the First Amendment. This is protection not changing with Internet journalism. The American Society of Newspaper Editors is concerned about problems in cyberspace. In some respects members say they believe that the Internet can enhance balance, fairness, and wholeness because access is available to unlimited information on a subject. But will accuracy and authenticity be compromised because the information is moving faster than the ability to check for accuracy? Are these new social responsibilities for the journalist? Will the poor and disadvantaged not receive the services provided by the Internet? Do minority interests have journals, magazines, books, and other culturally and racially specific materials for online use? More detail on cyberspace is found in Chapter 8.

The previous chapter emphasized the power of information and the ethical obligation of media professionals to respect society and themselves. Journalists and other media practitioners have extensive power through the First Amendment, and one task of media ethics is to theorize how that power will be used well. This chapter moves from the general media professional to the specific duties of a journalist and explores the moral obligations of the journalist to act well in ways that will strengthen not only the profession but society as well. It will further examine the delicate balance that must be maintained among business interests, the journalist, and the public.

Social Responsibility and the Journalist

Even without the added burden of cyberspace, the role of mass media in American society has never really been the center of a comprehensive, dispassionate public debate, so definitive answers are still a ghostly specter hovering over public affairs and public interest issues. Virtually everyone knows what he or she would like the media to do (or not do), but the media are fated to almost never make everyone happy. This makes the journalist's role a highly emotional topic because of wide-ranging feelings. As a result, journalists often have vague and general perceptions upon which to base their ideas of professional ethics, including social responsibility or serving as watchdogs.

Setting a Baseline of Media Expectations

This chapter focuses on a reasonable foundation upon which to build ideas of journalism and the fit of that foundation in American society in particular. Furthermore, this chapter proposes that journalism and the moral principles that guide the field may differ according to the society or social system being served.

This baseline, in whatever society, should be one that most reasonable people can recognize or upon which they can agree. Yet once it is established, diverse interests may still have differing views of journalistic shortcomings; however, those views will be within a narrower field imposed by requirements of the baseline. Such a baseline is fairly unyielding, since it is established by law and has universal application throughout the United States and, in the final analysis, cannot be varied for local conditions or attitudes. Those principles must be based largely on the social system the media are serving.

Using a Baseline as a Point of Reference

Media have a far different role in an authoritarian or totalitarian social system than they do in a democratic system in which citizens participate in the decision-making process. In a totalitarian system, media function mainly to instruct citizens in their duties and assure they receive a list of behaviors expected of them. Media in these countries are often mere bulletin boards providing marching orders or motivating citizens. These instructional media serve a function far removed from the information function of media in a democracy.

Therefore, if the United States expects its citizens to play active roles in national and local discussions and to affect decisions, media must be free to provide the information that will produce informed decisions. The word *free* is important here because the media cannot, under the Constitution, be required to furnish such information. Whether they do so is a matter of their own ethical sensitivities and civic consciousness. The information the media do provide, however, should range from high politics of national and international import to everyday economic information about products, their prices, and their availability.

This expectation might almost be classified as morally obligatory. Any baseline of media expectations should take into account the pluralistic nature of society and its need for vast quantities of information, even that which conflicts or contrasts with community desires. Such information provides the meat for discussion (and change) in a dynamic culture, even sometimes to the outrage of those who dislike having their comfort zones invaded by public dissent and discussion.

Journalists may gauge their own performances on this baseline of media expectations and use it as a reference point in establishing ethics criteria. Critics can also use the baseline as a point from which to base valid criticism of specific media practices. In both cases, the self-interest that often typifies such analyses resides in community leaders, advertisers, or others in positions of power who seek to shape stories of importance for audiences as well as typifying an illusory and destructive Beacon on the Hill.

Can the Profession Be Regulated?

The baseline journalists and other media professionals are in unique positions in the United States, and certainly in the world, because the Constitution and subsequent court opinions have given them protection, making them largely unregulatable. That is, there are almost no enforceable rules about what a newspaper ought to be, nor are there rules about who may be a journalist and what practices a journalist ought to follow. As a result, media and journalists may make their own rules, tempered by their community environment and moral suasion. Newspapers may choose to be sensationalistic tabloids emphasizing sex, crime, gossip, and tales of the unnatural, or they may be highly opinionated persuasive publications aimed at achieving specific ideological or social goals. Free from regulation, they may choose to be what their owners wish them to be.

Media critics who declare that newspapers and other media are obligated to provide truthful, fair, and complete accounts of the day's events are much like parents who tell their children what characteristics they are obligated to look for in a marital partner; it would certainly be nice, but you get what you get, both in media and in sons- or daughters-in-law. The underlying idealistic principles behind press freedoms guaranteed by the First Amendment of the Constitution (the first item in the Bill of Rights) is that good, conscientious, well-educated men and women will produce media (competition within a community would be most desirable) with a public interest in mind that contributes to well-informed, healthy, dynamic communities. Public decisions in these communities would be directed by the informed discussion and consent of the citizenry.

Choosing Between Imperfect Media and Media Regulations

A less idealistic but no less important principle is that even if the media do not perform a perfect function there must still be the possibility for them to do so. To that end, principles suggest, media that go astray cannot do as much social harm, whatever their evils, as would media whose nearly limitless freedom is proscribed by law or regulatory bodies.

In furthering this principle, courts have allowed "excesses" that appear outrageous: publication of the *Pentagon Papers* and of a recipe for the hydrogen bomb, invasions of privacy by photographers, as well as circus-like coverage of the O. J. Simpson trial and other apparent trials-by-media that appear to deny defendants' fair-trial rights. In other words, the law allows for the ideal in the distribution of information, but does not guarantee that it will happen. It also does not prohibit excesses.

This is a nation of people who are becoming increasingly accustomed to seeking guarantees. In this case, if a well-informed citizenry were to be guaranteed, questions would always be asked about who should assure these guarantees. As it is, a pluralistic press provides the greatest assurance of such a citizenry.

PROFITS AND ADVERTISING INFLUENCE NEWS COVERAGE

As a practical matter, news media tend to exercise First Amendment latitude by starting with such traditional news practices as those taught in journalism schools and often by following self-serving courses that increase income and profit. Such traditional practices tend to ensure similarities across media because of commonalities in views and attitudes (the "shared culture" of journalism) and some standards that permeate the news profession.

In seeking profit, however, media often do what will maximize audience size and attract advertisers. When this occurs, the information function implied for the media is likely to suffer. The shared culture, adapting to demands for larger audiences to finance the venture, often emphasizes the coverage of spectacular events, such as murder, catastrophe, scandal, personal conflicts, celebrity and politician sex lives, and other very visible events, all of which may not yield the information present-day readers and viewers need to make weighty decisions. A *Drudge Report*, for example, is more likely to glean stories of sexual misconduct from its list of sources than the more valuable story, such as information about a sharp decline in the economy.

This type of coverage tends to ignore the more subtle but significant happenings that require public understanding. School shootings, for example, have produced public discussions about the controlling of guns, with little more than superficial discussion of the underlying conditions in homes, playgrounds, and schools that produce the rage leading to shootings of schoolmates or parents by emotionally immature children. The operative principle here, of course, is that if both gun concerns and the rage problems were discussed thoroughly in public media, the nation could reach more reasoned decisions rather than being rushed to make superficial judgments forced by emotional hyperbole.

Such discussion needs substantial commitment of resources and well-educated media professionals to adequately explore the issues. Perhaps an inherent need to have some stable direction gave rise to the tradition that newspapers ought be "objective." Objectivity, which was equated in its original sense with neutrality, had a very practical origin as a product of newspaper dependence on advertising and the need to attract a broad base of readers in order to sell life-giving advertising (more than two thirds of a newspaper's revenue normally comes from advertising).

NEUTRALITY AND "OBJECTIVE" REPORTING

During the eighteenth and early nineteenth centuries, major newspapers tended to be vigorously partisan, supported by political parties and other ideological organizations. Late in the nineteenth century, an almost universal literacy saw an eruption in the number of newspapers and a shift from ideology to profit orientation.

Advertisers in this new age tended to discourage newspaper content that would drive readers (potential customers) away, even though it might attract a few others. Newspapers generally could not afford to express extreme views or support extreme positions, as their ideological forbears did, because advertisers usually were nonpolitical in seeking customers from all opinion ranges in order to boost their own incomes.

Thus was born the "objective" tradition of neutrally telling it like it is, which led to the current myth that newspapers are obliged to be objective. In such a climate, newspapers in smaller communities of necessity often became town boosters to increase community growth and accelerate economic activity that would result in more advertising and greater income. That practice, for all its benefits, is not objectivity in action.

BUSINESS NEEDS IN JOURNALISM

Advertisers in this context were often the primary concern of publishers and journalists. As communities grew into metropolises and media competition increased, it was important for newspapers to boost circulation by luring readers from competitors—again so they could attract more advertising.

This allowed newspapers to be more reader-oriented, and less dependent on advertiser attitudes.

Advertisers (for obvious business reasons) tend to follow the reader, viewer, or listener. This trend gave impetus to the perception that media have some public service obligations. The number of media outlets not only has multiplied but has exploded (even as the number of competitive newspapers decline) because of a wave of electronic developments that started with radio and has brought us to today's Internet.

RETAINING AUDIENCE

From this is arising somewhat of a return by media to the early days of display advertising; a combination of dependence on advertisers tempered by perceptions of prevailing community pressures that may threaten circulation or viewership. In monopoly communities, this often works in negative ways.

A newspaper that can retain audience, whether because of audience dependence on its retail advertising or because of habit, may feel less of an obligation to be sensitive to community attitudes. That works in two ways. Some may see the need for a higher quality product going into more depth and committed to explaining community issues. Or, more likely, a newspaper or radio or television station may feel the community seeks more entertaining news that lightens the day and deals less with heavy issues.

The newly competitive environment of exploding media outlets (e.g., Internet, direct mail, radio, television, and cable or satellite services) and declining reading skills and interests has shaped and altered attitudes between media managers and workers. Distant, corporate ownership increases emphasis on profits in a sharpened imperative to survive and produce economic return.

ECONOMIC DISCORD BETWEEN JOURNALISTS AND ADVERTISERS

Therefore, there appears to be increasing emphasis on the economics of desperation in many newspapers and television and radio stations at the expense of even the shared culture of journalism. The *Los Angeles Times* is probably one of the most dramatic public examples. Despite generations of shared values—journalists who were horrified at the thought of lowering barriers between the editorial and the advertising departments, the *Los Angeles Times* embarked on a "break-down-the-walls" program.

Journalists saw this as a near-fatal threat to news judgment, and advertising sales staffs saw it as a way to curb unruly journalists who inevitably made blocs of advertisers angry enough to cancel ads and campaigns. Independence of journalists from the newspaper's commercial functions had tended to insulate them from pressures that would moderate community coverage. The fundamental moral conflict in this new situation was that economic interests that buy advertising and otherwise support the newspaper are also the power centers. Loss of editorial/news independence in the newspaper or television or radio station also meant a further consolidation of power among the powerful to the inevitable detriment of and further problems for the community's powerless.

Media Power in the Automobile Industry

A simple but powerful example lies in the automotive industry. Newspapers derive a large portion of their revenue from new and used car advertising. A newspaper series, describing the many pitfalls of shopping for a used car, empowers auto buyers. Yet if auto dealers use their economic power to object to such a series, and the series does not appear, then they retain power over vulnerable buyers who would rely on the media for instruction in the simple art of successful auto buying.

Auto dealers essentially have the power to close the education system down in their community for auto buyers. Extend this to the influence of other powerful advertisers, and much information that consumers would find valuable in order to make reliable buying decisions is lost with the loss of journalistic independence.

A bright spot in this picture is the galaxy of Internet resources for information on used cars and virtually any other topic. In their early stages, these resources concentrated on attracting audiences (hits) so they could be more attractive to advertisers. Their effectiveness, of course, depends on the accuracy of their information, which subjects them to the same moral mandates of journalists and enshrines truth as a premier virtue in the operation.

Media Ethics in a Profit-Oriented Culture

The *Los Angeles Times* example above shows that although constitutional prohibitions effectively suppress overt government subsidization, requiring media to make their way economically in a free-enterprise society may drain their independence when moral priorities are jumbled. Perfect journalists of the constitutional ideal will resist pressures that deflect them from serving the best interests of the community, but various pressures, combined with remnants of the shared culture of journalists, often make it difficult.

The auto dealers discussed above, for example, may be able to bring pressures on journalists that dissuade them from their obligation to their readers in favor of enhancing the power of those who are already powerful enough to have their way with the media. As the number of media outlets grows, escalating competition both for advertising dollars and for audiences, media units are caught in battles for both audience and advertising sustenance. This battle, a desperate one for survival in many instances, may divert news media from their primary protected function of informing to one of entertaining, or even of pandering to audiences in order to be able to present to advertisers the attractive audience numbers that will lure the commercial dollar.

Television and radio stations, often in intense competition for audiences reduced by cable and satellite broadcasting, are especially accused of having reverted from the primacy of news to the primacy of entertaining delivery of entertaining news.

ATTRACTING READERS THROUGH CREATIVITY

The moral argument, of course, is that media, including the Internet and other cyberspace news sources, must be creative and inventive enough to attract readers, while at the same time providing the substantial information needed to feed the social requirement for informed decisions. This position condemns media outlets that take the easy or even lazy way out by pandering to audiences with cheap and spectacular entertainment that has high sensory appeal but little informational value. Professional journalists and others in the information business are enjoined to accept moral obligations to create informational media that will attract audiences rather than use the attraction of audiences as an end in itself.

The latter approach violates the obligation of the autonomous moral agent to treat audiences as ends (as informed decision makers) rather than as means to ends (the attracting of audience to better sell advertising). The idealistic notion—indeed, the prevailing social commitment—is that audiences will be attracted to carefully crafted information media and that the income will take care of itself.

Perhaps the most visible example of such a medium is the *Wall Street Journal*, whose success is based on its calculated approach to providing (through a deadly dull format) invaluable information to business and political audiences who live in a highly informational environment and dare not miss a day of the high information content contained in that newspaper.

The Shared Culture of the Journalist

The journalistic shared culture emerged from a time in which communities were in strong agreement within themselves about roles and customs. The entire community generally agreed, for example, on what was "good taste" and on such concepts as public discussions of mental illness, gender roles, as well as the values leaders should display.

The change, as differing groups began expressing themselves and demanding shares of the power structure, has often not been served well by journalists. The shared culture of news values, as well as pressures to capture audiences, often push journalists to deal with the superficial rather than confronting complex problems that require greater discussion.

Shared values, such as the need for dramatic visuals, drives television journalists to favor stories of burning structures or of spectacular accidents with their attention-getting graphics over much more significant, though detailed, reports explaining the implications to the viewer of tax legislation or the declining quality of public schools. Both latter topics have more effect on the changing shape of society than either of the highly visual stories.

This reflects, of course, a shared broadcast cultural convention that audiences have short attention spans and will drift away if stories run beyond the 30 second "sound bite," something that obviously precludes in-depth coverage of complex issues. Similarly, for newspapers, complex issues may be avoided because they are topics audiences "need" more than "want" in a competitive climate that leans toward pandering to the latter.

Journalists in all media may typically find two people speaking out on an issue to present their opposing views but ignore other sources with more moderate views and the thoughtful reasoning behind those views. Two views at polar ends of the discussion offer more conflict than does the reasoned discourse of the moderate. Yet the moderate is more likely to express views that may already nag at the reader's subconscious but that cannot yet be put into words, thereby serving a more valuable function than does the bombast at the poles. Opposing views on talk shows have become depressingly predictable and tend to preach to the converted, but moderate discourse on the pressing issues of the day has become something that is difficult to find, except in the more serious media, such as the *New York Times* or the *Wall Street Journal.*

ARE THERE MORAL OBLIGATIONS TO THE COMMUNITY?

In view of the constraints on journalistic regulation, it cannot be asked "what should one (a journalist) be required to do or prohibited from doing?" (legitimate questions for medical doctors, lawyers, plumbers, contractors, and many others whose rights to practice their professions are regulated by state authority). The questions posed to journalists must be about guiding principles that morally justify protections under the First Amendment and how those principles apply to the shared culture (dogma or orthodoxy, usually of the past) of journalism. Again, although the rationale for regulating such professionals as medical doctors and lawyers is that benefits of regulation far outweigh harm, the national rationale shielding journalists is that even extreme harm caused by journalists would not approach the harm that would result from regulation and the consequent reduced free flow of information.

The argument is that all citizens have a stake in the free speech of journalists (and in their own free speech, for that matter) and must suffer consequences of such freedom in order to reap the benefits of greater information availability. Journalists are pressed by their moral obligations to forgo personal gain and gratification and assist the community. To be sure, much that assists the community is gratifying and profitable.

For example, one may claim to provide an indispensable service to the community, such as being the only medical doctor in town. In this case, medical services may be available to all comers with the medical doctor receiving only enough in return to meet needs; alternatively, one may serve only people who are able to pay the fees, arguing that the right to profit from an investment in a medical education is expected to yield rich returns. The latter position, however, is difficult to defend morally if the powerless (those without resources) are victimized when denied available medical treatment because of economics.

THE ETHICAL JOURNALIST

The ethical journalist may be guided by a Beacon on the Hill that inclines him or her to sacrifice for the good of an informed community rather than sacrifice community knowledge for profit. In this context, of course, media owners and publishers are asked to invest their primary loyalty in the welfare of the community at the expense of some profits or at the expense of conventional journalistic wisdom that limits the information a community receives.

If the *Los Angeles Times* and other newspapers are typical examples, many have reversed the priorities and are placing profit over service. A competitive, free-enterprise society offers expansive leeway for selfish behavior and for behavior that victimizes others. Many argue that this is a characteristic that has made this nation great. Yet the greatness of the nation also relies on the good will of its citizens (both corporate and private) to be willing to be vigorously competitive, but to not victimize those who, realistically, are unable to compete.

Journalists find themselves occupying the central (median) position between society and the decision makers in that society. They must be selfish to a degree in that their economic survival may require certain expedient behavior. However, they must sometimes weigh whether they will flourish (not merely survive) or whether they will serve the community.

To flourish suggests accumulation of wealth and power or even of prizes and honors. To earn prizes at the needless expense of the community or some of its individuals may be difficult to defend in the shadow of an altruistic Beacon on the Hill. The moral individual is careful in making decisions, looking for a line that best serves both the interest of survival and the interest of the community in having enough broad information to make decisions.

A Journalistic Guideline for Developing a Personal Moral Theory

In the pluralistic society fostered by the Bill of Rights, journalists might well look to professional pluralism as a key element in the construction of their personal moral theories as described in Chapter 3. That pluralism carries them beyond merely observing and reporting the visible and into assuring them of dimensions that help audiences understand rather than merely know what is happening. A pluralistic society requires diverse views in order to function; since pluralism implies some individualism, individuals in the society also need more information than those in more communal societies in order to make personal decisions.

This, of course, provides a sharp distinction between media in communal, traditional cultures and media in individualistic cultures. Traditional culture information systems tend to be nondisruptive and instructional, providing marching orders for their members. Individualistic cultures assume their members will make their own decisions and need diverse information to allow the shaping of those decisions. Any moral position for journalists based on a pluralistic society needs to take into account more than the traditional interpretation of the First Amendment, which grants journalists freedom to provide political information that allows citizens to monitor their government. It suggests that journalists should be providing the broad scope of information that allows citizens to make not only political decisions but also the myriad of day-to-day decisions that affect the quality of their lives. It should be indisputable that newspapers or television stations that tell of health epidemics in the community or even of the availability of a new and useful product are doing at least as great a service to individuals and families as stories about activities in government that allow better public political decisions.

Similarly, ads that lay out the price range for an automobile make any medium a broader information system than merely a news provider, serving up an inclusive array of political, personal, and commercial information. Journalists in a rapidly changing world of mega-mergers that link many media outlets with a broad range of commercial ventures need a moral compass to guide their day-to-day activities as they compile the day's news for their audiences. An example are the two main adversaries in a recent merger action in which Time-Warner, which had already acquired the Cable News Network (CNN) channels, sought permission to merge with America Online (AOL), the largest Internet service. This merger, which was approved in early 2001, was disputed by, among others, the Walt Disney organization, which itself owns a wide range of media units. The new AOL/Time-Warner joined 27 million online subscribers to Warner Brothers movies, CNN, Home Box Office (HBO), *Time* magazine, *Sports Illustrated*, and others in what *Brill's Content* magazine calls a blending of huge audience access (AOL) with Time-Warner's existing "content factory."

That moral compass, which helps point to basic principles involving most stories, is one that should enfranchise all groups in the community and make them a part of the public debate. A pluralistic journalist should accept responsibility for keeping audience members informed across the broad dimensions of important topics rather than merely serving as a bulletin board for those who make the efforts to place their stories in the medium.

The pluralistic journalist has at least two critical functions in society. First, the pluralistic journalist should provide broad and in-depth coverage of issues that ensure that audiences are well informed on nuances rather than having them rely on two extreme views. Second, such coverage, using competent and credible sources, should reassure readers and viewers that the journalist is not an advocate for a particular view.

PROBLEMS WITH EMPHASIS ON INDIVIDUALISM

Society is in serious danger of being polarized because of the growing power of individual consumers in recent years to fashion their own media systems and thereby control almost absolutely what society will see and hear. This is possible because of the growing ease with which online publications are established and the increasing willingness of advertisers to seek narrow, specialized audiences, as traditional audiences (circulation and viewers) for established media shrink.

While expansion of media outlets is generally a positive development in a society that emphasizes individualism, it also tends to make it much easier for those comfortable in their belief systems to ignore alternative views. While it is the right of people to reject, ignore, or avoid views with which they disagree, the public debate suffers and polarization increases as more people feel threatened by views contrary to their own. Advocates such as Rush Limbaugh and many other talk show hosts attract like-minded individuals as audience members. Equally important, they repel those who know they will disagree with the views expressed on those shows. Neither the attractions nor the repulsions serve the national decision-making process well.

When one is determined only to absorb information from a single set of favored ideological sources or value systems, the net effect is often an unremitting and unhealthy reinforcement of views by advocates. Current trends tend toward hardened attitudes, leading to a social decision-making process based on untested ideas. Such a condition is seriously at odds with the premise of an individualistic, free-enterprise society as anticipated in the wake of the Bill of Rights.

CLASSIC CASE IN JOURNALISM: IMPEACHMENT HEARINGS

Polarization and its effect on rational public debate were clearly evident in the public discussion surrounding impeachment proceedings against President

Clinton in 1999. Ideologues on both sides were so committed to their views that little moderate dialogue was possible. On the one hand, President Clinton's ideological opponents were determined to drive him from office for whatever he did regardless of the facts. Conversely, of course, President Clinton's supporters were determined to keep him in office. One result of the polarized frenzy that surrounded the president's predicament was a strongly opinionated group that could not understand why up to 72% of Americans did not find President Clinton's transgressions serious enough to merit his removal from the White House. The public opinion figures emerged from opposing positions by media figures. In that climate, the minority could not understand, perhaps based on their singular and restricted sources of information, why the rest of the nation did not share their views.

Insular individuals who limit their information intake often are puzzled by the world around them, but they are also willing to make dogmatic statements in support of their singular views and even willing to force others to accept their untested belief systems. In the midst of this climate of change and polarization, the pluralistic journalist becomes increasingly important and must reject the temptation to become a social engineer, directing community decisions.

THE IDEAL PLURALIST

The number of advocates in the media willing to succumb to the temptation of being social engineers has grown astronomically as media proliferate. Instead, the journalist should accept a commitment to full discussion of issues and problems facing society as well as a commitment to provide the information needed for the public dialogue to regain a solid footing in society. Such pluralism requires not only finding and using information from traditional sources, such as public relations, government, business, and so forth, but also seeking hidden sources not normally appearing in media with their views.

The ideal pluralist is constantly seeking additional sources for every story. Time and deadline limitations may reduce the number of sources, but pluralist journalists should nevertheless be concerned about whether they have the significant aspects of their story covered. The pluralist will certainly cover both major sides of a story, but a major failing of today's journalism is that only the two polar sides (product of a black-and-white syndrome in the media) are covered, leaving little room for discussion of the complex center.

INCLUDE NUMEROUS PARTIES IN THE PUBLIC DIALOGUE

An operating credo for the pluralistic journalist might be, "I have covered both sides, but there is always another side, not yet found, for which I must search." Such an attitude will ensure that neglected elements of any community, whether economics, employment, technology, education, race, gender, or any of the other thousands of smaller colonies hidden in any community, will be invited to participate in the public dialogue.

Principals and parent-teacher leaders, for example, are not necessarily the only logical spokespersons on school and education issues. Single parents, ethnic minority parents, and even affluent individuals are only a few of the groups that have unique problems that may be seriously affected by virtually any decision made in a school. In their concern with the central problem at hand, neither parent-teacher association presidents nor school principals are likely to voice the reservations of all the significant groups affected by an issue.

Even when a variety of views are presented in a public hearing, there are almost always groups that for reasons other than apathy do not participate in such meetings. To accompany the bellows of accomplished public speakers, journalists should provide public "squeaks" from some members of those groups, always recognizing that there are more who were not contacted. If this occurs across the range of public issues, the public dialogue becomes much more meaningful and better informed.

ENCOURAGE INFORMED PARTICIPATION

Beyond pluralism, which encourages informed public opinion and public participation in the democratic process, journalists have many obligations to their readers, including the moral obligation to provide accurate information so the debate will be truly informed, to generally avoid deception and respect privacy (of sources and audiences) whenever possible, and to help ensure a steady flow of useful information by respecting the confidentiality of sources when appropriate.

Also, of course, journalists must recognize that their primary loyalty is to their audiences and avoid conflicts of interest that would compromise that loyalty. They should ensure that sources and audiences are treated fairly in circumstances in which either could be victimized by the journalist's actions, and journalists should promote public harmony and participation by ensuring that the "vanilla" society of the past continues to integrate all its members into full participation in the economic and social process.

Each of these areas is important and deserving of discussion because of its implications for and guidance of the journalist.

PROVIDE ACCURACY OF FACTS AND CONTENT

Once the rhetoric has been put behind us on the role of the journalist in a democratic society, one obligation still stands out, namely, the journalist is charged by society with the moral obligation to create images in the minds of audience members that will match the realities they will encounter. Such images are the subtext underlying the concept of objectivity—telling it like it is.

Armed with images in the mind that faithfully reflect the reality of the world, audience members are able to prepare for what lies ahead, increasing their chances of successfully negotiating the minefields of life. Ignorance, or the absence of those reliable images, requires one to formulate responses to situations in ignorance, reducing one's chances of successfully resolving problems. Once the image-matches-the-reality concept is spelled out, however, it must be recognized that this is an impossible task, that audiences must still confront many situations for which they have not been prepared by the media.

Nevertheless, the concept is an important one, for it requires the journalist to be consciously aware of the importance of not only accurate information (the facts), but also that the image requires enough context that the facts of the matter make sense for the situation. It also imposes a moral obligation on journalists to be constant learners and to know enough about their topics to have a sense that coverage is fairly complete. In this sense, journalists must always be more knowledgeable than their audiences so they know whether their audiences are well served by their sources. Journalists manipulated by sources break their faith with audiences by allowing the power of the source to override needs of readers or viewers.

DECEPTION

We deceive when we cause others to believe what we ourselves do not believe. Such an act, of course, suggests a willingness to build images in the minds of audiences that the journalist either does not believe are accurate or knows are not accurate. Alternatively, it causes journalists to dupe sources by causing them to believe what the journalist either knows or believes is not true. Deception is an insidious force in society, for it is designed, on the face of it, to cause people to act on false information.

In a culture in which accurate information is highly prized as the most effective way of producing reliable social decisions, deception by the journalist borders on the inexcusable. Successful deception denies victims the free agency to control their own actions by compelling them to act on false information and in ways they presumably would not act. This strikes at the heart of a society committed to the rights of individuals to control their own destinies. Yet for some greater causes, society tolerates deception. In wartime, to deceive the enemy is a tactic that may lead to victory and save lives.

In athletic contests, the well-timed fake or feint allows runners or dribblers to break free to gain yards or score goals. Allowing police to cruise in unmarked patrol cars to catch the speeder on the highway, to wear plainclothes in order to catch the unwary criminal, or to pose as a prostitute to deter prostitution have been time-honored traditions in law enforcement. However strongly journalists feel about avoiding deceptions and being honest and accurate in all instances, situations may arise in which it appears to be in the audience's best interest to engage in deception.

UTILITY AND DUTY

Utilitarian journalists might declare that deception (of sources) is often justifiable in the service of audiences' need for information, arguing that virtually any method of gathering information from those who would hoard it in order to protect their power is justifiable. Other journalists would prohibit deception entirely as destructive to the social contract journalists have with both sources and audiences.

Most ethicists would agree that deceiving audiences is rarely justified. A Kantian argument would hold it just is right to always tell the truth; that is, to construct the image that will match reality. The utilitarian would concur, declaring that truthful information to the audience results in more credibility for the media and more reliable information for audiences.

Kant would argue it just is right to avoid deceiving people. Utilitarians, on the other hand, might justify deceiving people when a greater public good is served by providing audiences with useful information. News generated by deceptive methods regarding corrupt automobile repair shops, police officers who steal and sell drugs taken in arrests, or defense contractors who plunder public treasuries might be justified as deception in the public interest. Generally, however, deception tends to be destructive in its effect on the credibility of the major players and should be avoided whenever possible.

CAN A JOURNALIST JUSTIFY DECEIVING AN AUDIENCE?

A test for whether deceiving a source is justified would include questioning whether the story is so critically important that damaging deception (with its inherent manipulation of the source) is justified and whether the deception is the only way the story can be gathered. Furthermore, those who deceive a source to obtain a story should be willing to describe later, to both audiences and sources, the deceptions that were used in preparing the story. This, of course, alerts both audiences and sources that the reporter is, indeed, one who should be viewed warily. Instances in which deception of audiences is justifiable are very rare. Of course, sources that provide journalists with information are often bent on deceiving audiences for their own purposes, but pluralistic journalists should be reluctant to accept self-serving messages at face value. They should seek other sources that will provide countering information.

Attorneys, for example, will nearly always declare their clients are innocent (or prosecutors will confidently declare the guilt of the accused); police will predict an early solution to a baffling crime or will name a suspect; celebrities will assert that "this is true love and this marriage is forever"; and presidents and governors are very likely to brand accusations of sexual misbehavior as lies. Nevertheless, journalists are obliged to seek the broader information that will prepare audiences for the realities. While attempts at deception by sources may be acceptable, deception of audience through the media is seldom an option in that equation. (More discussion on deception is found in Chapter 7.)

PRIVACY

The privacy issue is one of the great paradoxes of American media life. Personal privacy, the right to be left alone, has been called one of the great benefits of a democratic society, necessary to assure individual freedom. And although it is not protected by the Constitution, Americans have a strong emotional attachment to the concept and react vigorously to invasions of privacy by the media.

A frequent discussion concerns whether public officials and public figures lose their right to privacy by virtue of their high-visibility positions, but public criticism is immediate and strong when the media name names and show photos of the grief stricken, crime victims, or other private citizens who have been thrust into a public spotlight. The U.S. Supreme Court has established classes of people whose privacy is less secure than others, a division helpful to journalists as they ponder the morality of privacy invasion.

Privacy and Classes of Citizens

Classes of citizens have been specified for consideration in libel and privacy cases. The first two, public officials and public figures, are generally given few privacy rights by the courts, since these groups receive their support from the public (for political leaders it's votes and public money and for celebrities it's ticket and record sales) and therefore should be held accountable for that support through public scrutiny. Morally, journalists may also justify such privacy invasions as serving the needs of average individuals for role models in an increasingly complex world.

Public officials and public figures live public lives, which, if adequately chronicled, teach many lessons. That is, it is helpful to see examples of laudatory behavior in order to learn which actions to emulate. Seeing the results of scandalous behavior helps others avoid making those same errors. More importantly, to see the mixture of behaviors in others repeatedly demonstrates to us that everyone lives a life of mixed behavior and that no one is perfect. Darryl Strawberry, a superb baseball player, and Robert Downey, Jr., an acclaimed actor, both of whom are gripped by addictive drugs, are excellent examples.

Such an image is more in keeping with the realities we will encounter than are images of total virtue (created by press agents) or total depravity (created by gossip mongers). Therefore, media chronicles of the tragedies as well as triumphs of highly visible professional athletes or television or movie stars are, if they are relatively complete, instructional for onlookers who see a wide range of behaviors that comprise the human condition and may explain outcomes, as well as demonstrable rewards and consequences of these mixed behaviors.

A particularly pernicious form of privacy invasion is the manufacture of false celebrity behaviors or fictional elaborations of celebrity actions. Supermarket tabloid newspapers are particularly accused of pandering to shoppers by making graphic, exaggerated, and lurid descriptions their stock in trade. Yet professional athletes who excel on the playing fields but whose personal lives are in turmoil can provide observant young would-be athletes with valuable instruction about the competing forces a professional athlete faces.

The courts tend to protect private citizens from both libelous statements and from egregious privacy invasions by journalists and photographers. Yet it may sometimes appear that the activities of private individuals are, indeed, instructive to an audience and that privacy invasion is justified. Some of these areas include suicide, rape, tragic accidents, death from sexually transmitted diseases, and other incidents whose details would be instructive. Suppression of such incidents, sometimes to the extreme of refusing to mention them at all, leaves the impression in readers or viewers minds that such things do not occur in the community and are therefore of no danger or concern.

As agonizing as a story of a suicide is to the parents, family, and friends of a teenage victim, the benefits of a public discussion that may result from a fairly detailed story of the death may more than offset the anguish of those immediately affected by such a story. Journalists should consider in these cases that, as a principle, information is empowering. To withhold information, often of painful or embarrassing events, is to withhold power from someone. When a suicide occurs, it is often symptomatic of a community condition that may need public attention.

MORAL DILEMMA: REPORTING ON FAMILY DISTRESS

If the information is not distributed to the community, the community is not aware of the problem, nor does it give credence to efforts by teachers and social service workers to raise concern. For example, there are probably a large number of communities in the United States in which avid readers of the local newspaper would say "there are no AIDS cases in this town," or "people in _____ just don't commit suicide." Yet it is not necessarily true that those problems do not exist, but that the media, often in deference to the families of the victims, do not identify the single instances of death by AIDS or suicide that would, when all told, indicate the true scope of a problem. This occurs when media policies obstruct publication of suicides or identifying AIDS victims in deference to survivors.

CONTEMPORARY CASE IN JOURNALISM: COVERING FOR THE CHURCH

Mac is a lay or volunteer religious leader for the majority religion in a small town. A fifteen-year-old teenager has confessed to Mac, as his ecclesiastical leader, that he and two friends have had sexual relations with four adult women in the town within the last year.

Mac knows he should uphold the sanctity of the confession, but because of the teen's age, Mac knows these acts are criminal.

Mac contacts one of the women to discuss her sexual transgression. She immediately hires an attorney. The teenager's parents learn of their son's confession and contact the police. They charge that Mac should have contacted the police. Now the press is contacting the police and Mac. Should this information be released to the media?

It may not be appropriate that adult names and details in the above case be published until legal charges are filed. Yet it is important to recognize that systematic deletion of this information, for the sake of not causing distress to families or a religious organization, may create an information vacuum on an important topic in the community. One moral question raised is whether family distress should be spared at the expense of the community knowing details of a problem involving sexual misconduct as well as church confession.

COVERAGE OF PUBLIC FIGURES

A democratic society, it should be remembered, is an uncomfortable society to live in because it is demonstrable that public knowledge of intimate secrets is preferable to closely held knowledge by government agencies—often the secret police in more repressive cultures. Therefore, open discussion of embarrassing facts regarding private individuals is sometimes a burden those individuals must bear in a democratic society in order that the society may be better informed and better able to face its problems. Clearly, these disclosures should be sharply limited when they involve private individuals, but it would be folly to suggest that public knowledge always should submit to private comfort.

Some public figures and public officials are well rewarded, both financially and in terms of personal power. Should this offset the problems created for them by invasions of their privacy and make moral justifications of such invasions valid?

CLASSIC CASE IN JOURNALISM: PRINCESS DIANA

In the wake of the tragic crash that took Princess Diana's life in a French street tunnel, there was a general public outrage at the paparazzi photographers who dogged her from the time she became engaged to marry Prince Charles in 1971 and who appeared to redouble their efforts following her divorce in 1996 until her death in 1998. There were accusations that her fatal accident resulted from her driver's attempts to flee the photographers. The net result, of course, was outrage at the blatant invasions of her privacy, photographs, and disclosures making her private life very public.

Without justifying the actions of predatory photographers, it must be recognized in the wake of her passing that this very public woman did far more for groups and causes than would a reclusive person who successfully avoided the spotlight or in whom the media took no interest. Princess Diana became the poster woman for the anti–land mine movement in war-torn Eastern European and African countries, doing far more through publicity to advance that cause than most would have believed likely. The land mine issue largely dropped from the public agenda with Princess Diana's death, suggesting that public visibility (and loss of privacy) are important ingredients for a crusader. Arguably, the land mine issue would not have received the public attention it did had Princess Diana not taken on the cause. An individual living in obscurity, for example, who suddenly stepped into the public arena to plead the anti–land mine cause would not likely have attracted nearly as much worldwide attention as did continuing coverage of Princess Diana on both that issue and her private life.

Former French film star Brigitte Bardot's recent efforts on animal rights come to mind as a fizzled example of a private person trying to create public support for a cause. Similarly, a very visible Princess Diana gave effective public voice to a number of charitable and political causes in England while she was married to Prince Charles and after the divorce. Consider, too, that the British royal family, under media scrutiny of the marriage, found itself in an unprecedented humanizing era in which published information fed much more public discussion than was comfortable for the family. One result was hundreds of millions of dollars of donations to a Princess Diana fund for charitable causes after her death. While it might be argued she was beloved by the people, it should also be noted that she would not have had the opportunity to be beloved if traditional restrictions on media coverage of the royal family had been left in place.

Smothering Coverage of the Royals

Prince Charles, too, became a much more human entity in the eyes of the public, not always to the delight of the rest of the royal family. Conversely, consider the two teenage sons, Princes William and Harry, whom Prince Charles vowed to keep out of the limelight in reaction to the very public coverage and tragedy of Princess Diana. Can it be doubted the British people will know very little about the young men who one day may ascend to the throne of the United Kingdom? What will be known, generally, is what palace sources want known and may not be reflections of the individuals at all. Thus, Buckingham Palace has retrieved control over the public images of members of the royal family, images that traditionally have been very favorable, whatever the reality.

Given the graphic example of the royal family, it should be evident that the intensive coverage and privacy invasion that occurred in the case of Princess Diana had visibly distressing effects, but there are also benefits that must be considered from such invasions. For example, while the distress of smothering media coverage may be as inevitable as it is regrettable, it must also be recognized that such coverage granted Princess Diana considerable power (the power of public visibility), which she used to benefit causes of her choice. Princess Diana put that power to use, while others may not have done so. It cannot be denied that many benefitted from the way she used her power.

DOES INVASION OF PRIVACY SERVE THE PUBLIC?

Similarly, of course, the loss of privacy by Monica Lewinsky (of White House internship fame) gave her the power to at least try to launch an entertainment career. Journalists should certainly consider whether the information they are about to gather and publish is sufficiently valuable to the audience to justify the personal anxiety surely to be caused by the intrusion. The seamy side of journalism, of course, covers such events to feed a public appetite for intimate disclosures and for building circulation and audiences. That coverage most often exploits the vulnerability of public figures and public officials resulting from their lack of privacy.

Basic ethics suggest privacy is best invaded when the public will be served rather than when one's own purposes are paramount. The dilemma produces one maxim that would serve journalists well, based on the social premise that audiences should be well informed, namely, if journalists are in doubt, after all their deliberations, they should be moved to publish rather than to withhold from publication.

Reporters and editors will frequently have no idea of the value of the information to their audiences but are sensitive to the harm and may decide to decline publication on that basis. The "when in doubt, publish" admonition is based on the premise that journalists will virtually always know of the harm they do but will rarely know of the good of their stories. Therefore, on the assumption that "to publish is good" and that information just is good (for audiences) to have, journalists should err in favor of more public information rather than less, assuming that secrecy (withholding information from audiences) is inevitably more damaging than disclosure.

CONTEMPORARY CASE IN JOURNALISM:
PAULA JONES AND PENTHOUSE

Paula Jones disclosed that she needed to pose nude for Penthouse *magazine because the wealthy individuals who promised her money for charges against President Clinton just did not come through with the amounts she needed. Her situation has changed since she leveled her initial charges that President Clinton propositioned her while she was in a hotel room with him, thus damaging her self-concept. She is now a single mother of two who needs college fund money for her children. She promised the press that "This will be a one-time only event."*

Journalists already wary of "he said/she said" sexual disclosures are reconsidering and learning from their coverage of Paula Jones. Should media coverage be different based on whether her pronouncements came from politics, self-esteem, or monetary concerns?

Confidentiality

For both moral and practical reasons, journalists who promise to protect the sources of their information should accept the moral obligation to keep the promise. The practical reason, of course, is that subsequent sources will hesitate to provide information to someone who has not kept promises of confidentiality and valuable sources of information will dry up. In the ongoing battle for information between journalists and the subjects of their stories, those who hold information will use their power to maintain that hold, including visiting serious harm on those who disclose. Sources who have information that will be helpful in exposing corruption or public misdeeds often fear for their jobs or that they may lose the goodwill of their neighbors if they disclose the information. A promise to keep the source confidential eases some of those concerns. If the reporter does not keep the promise, however, sources will be hesitant to come forward.

There are two fundamental moral reasons for keeping sources confidential. First, in instances when promises are made, sources must be kept confidential out of regard for the damage breaking such promises may do to other reporters and to the public, thereby fostering a suspicion that reporters will not keep secrets. This suspicion is heightened when the public hears of other sources who have been burned by reporters. Second, as sources dry up for fear of being punished as a result of disclosure, the public suffers because information it should receive is not distributed.

Journalists are expected to accept a moral obligation to disclose information that will help audience members make informed decisions and to gather information to that end. As with other ethics questions, there are notable exceptions to the general policy of protecting sources.

CONTEMPORARY CASE IN JOURNALISM: ELECTION LEAK

Editors of a Minneapolis newspaper decided, just before election day several years ago, to disclose the source of a leaked story. Disclosures about one candidate by a supporter of the second candidate only one or two days before the election were made on the basis of a reporter's promise to keep the source confidential. Editors, in deciding to identify the source, felt readers had a right to know the disclosures came from an opponent's camp.

The moral principle operative in this case, of course, was that readers' rights to know in order to make more deliberate election choices outweighed even the reporter's integrity in making a promise that was not to be kept.

CONFLICT OF INTEREST

When a reporter and editor no longer have a primary obligation or loyalty to their audiences but instead to someone else, problems of conflict of interest emerge. A reporter who accepts gifts or favors from sources has a potential conflict of interest. When sources are viewed, even subconsciously, by the reporter as such "nice persons" that news coverage is skewed to favor them, the conflict of interest is apparent, and audiences pay the price. If a journalist's primary obligation is to create an image in the minds of audiences that will match the reality those in the audience will encounter, it is also important to recognize that most of the people the journalist encounters have a vested interest in influencing to their advantage the image the journalist projects. To do that, many are positioned to offer either inducements or threats designed to skew stories.

The journalist provides the doorway through which these sources must go to reach and influence audiences. Conflicts of interest may emerge gently and painlessly early on as sources enfold journalists into inner power circles by offering friendship and association with prominent figures. Alternatively, journalists may be offered gifts either out of gratitude or out of friendship, which, if accepted, place the journalist at risk for giving the gift-giver the special treatment that will skew the stories.

Serious problems for many journalists, as well as others who must deal with conflict of interest issues, is that the offering appears mostly made from "friendship" rather than ulterior motives, and the journalist inevitably claims the relationship makes no difference in coverage. Yet the journalist must consider two things in dealing with conflict of interest.

CONTEMPORARY CASE IN JOURNALISM: A MARRIED TELEVISION REPORTER

A television reporter covering the police beat marries the police department information officer and retains her police beat assignment. She sometimes arrives at late-night crime scenes with the information officer, meeting the station video cameraman there. She convinces her news director she can maintain her objectivity. The station does not disclose the relationship publicly, but reporters from the other major media know about it, and most police officers are aware of the situation.

This case illustrates the twin problems of conflict of interest faced by the media. The first problem, of course, is whether the reporter's conflict of interest (some suggest that marriage vows between a police reporter and her police officer spouse almost mandate a shift in her loyalties from the audience/station to her husband) would naturally lead to a distortion of coverage at critical times on the job. Although the reporter argued otherwise, her situation nevertheless typifies the first of two problems.

PERCEPTION AND REALITY

The second problem is whether the actuality of the stories this reporter writes affects the image created in people's minds; in other words, will people believe the journalist involved can be trusted to create the accurate image? Either way, the credibility of the journalist is suspect if the relationship becomes known. Consequently, journalists may want to accept an operating principle that they would be willing to have such relationships disclosed to their audiences, being willing themselves to do so in order that audiences may make the decisions about the journalist's credibility.

When Is a Gift Not a Gift?

It is not only important that journalists avoid skewing the message, but that they avoid giving the appearance they are likely to skew the message. This imperative leads many newspapers and other media outlets to draft strong statements on conflict of interest, defining carefully what constitutes a conflict. Their journalists may be prohibited from accepting anything valued at more than a few dollars or even a few cents.

Often, minor gifts, such as a cup of coffee from a source, are acceptable, but in some cases are not. An operating principle might be that journalists themselves may not know what affects, even subconsciously, their coverage of sources; therefore, they should be extra careful to distance themselves, both physically and psychologically, from sources.

Additional Perception Guides

Washington Post reporters, for example, are forbidden from joining political movements for fear the involvement will alter subsequent stories (not only about the movement but about others with even a distant relationship). Other editors disagree with the extremity of the *Washington Post's* injunction but accept the principle that distancing oneself from sources, even when coverage requires close proximity, is desirable.

At the same time, editors do recognize that a good reporter who gets very close to a source will often generate information valuable to audiences that would otherwise not be forthcoming, illustrating the difficulty of truly defining conflict of interest in journalism. In the final analysis, it requires reliance on the moral integrity of journalists to recognize and avoid conflict of interest situations. In order to do that, they must continually remind themselves of their basic responsibility: serve the audience with complete and reliable information. Thus, journalists and their superiors should recognize that a fine line exists between civic spirit that results in community involvement and an immersion that directs the content of the media.

COMMUNITY INVOLVEMENT AND CONFLICT

It should always be a matter of concern when an editor and sometimes even a publisher or station owner become heavily involved in a community project, such as construction of a new stadium, library, or a campaign for approval of a school bonding issue. Until recently, the dividing line was sharp in a media organization—publishers were expected to involve themselves in civic projects, but would, in turn, distance themselves from newsroom involvement.

Now, typified by the *Los Angeles Times*' disastrous efforts to topple the walls between the news and the commercial functions of the newspaper, publishers and owners are showing less restraint in setting news policies. That combination of community activity and involvement in news policies backfired when the *Los Angeles Times* combined promotion of a new professional sports facility in Los Angeles with profit making.

The newspaper published a special dedication advertising/editorial insert in the newspaper and shared the profits with the owners of the new Staples Center. This disclosure of the intimate relationship between the newspaper and sports facility promoters raises the question whether the newspaper could be an impartial observer (or an audiences' advocate) of the processes by which a facility receives government approval and funding or whether the newspaper became a cheerleader for the project with profitable alliances in mind.

THE IMPORTANCE OF DISCLOSURE

There is not, nor can there be, a law that prohibits the type of arrangement made between the *Los Angeles Times* and arena operators, but it certainly does not auger well for the likelihood of reasonable community decisions when promoters and media are bedmates on projects. No matter how desirable media executives feel a project is, they can only show respect for their audiences by providing audiences with full information about these matters and allowing collective decisions from the full community rather than attempting to direct those decisions by stories slanted toward a decision.

Still, a similar test of public disclosure may be as helpful here as it was in the previous discussion regarding disclosure (see PRIVACY section above). If the newspaper is willing to disclose its connections and its biases and let the audience decide, it mitigates some of the problem. If the *Los Angeles Times*, for example, sought to be seen as an independent newspaper with only audience interests in mind, it perhaps would have been reluctant to disclose its close ties to business and other interests for fear of negative community reaction. Because the social system has a commitment to the ability of audiences to decide, the principle of disclosure is an important one.

If audiences accept a medium's behaviors after full disclosure and discussion, editors can claim some ethical high ground. Yet in a society in which individual rights are important, media must still be sensitive to protection of those rights, whatever the community may think. This is an example of doing well for the community while not victimizing minorities. Both are ethical imperatives for journalists.

DIVERSITY: THE FAIRNESS OF REPRESENTING DIVERSE VIEWS

Many in any community who have activist inclinations as well as strong feelings about the way their community is functioning develop a sense of powerlessness and frustration in attempting to have some impact on shaping their environment. This drive toward involvement makes their cause neither good nor faulty, but suggests not only a disposition to take a hand in influencing events, but also a sense that some changes are needed. In any event, access to and attentive treatment by the mass media are very often critical elements in an activist's successful efforts to influence the course of public events.

There are also some who feel isolated because they are not represented in the public dialogue. Opinions expressed by traditional sources in the media do not represent their views, creating feelings of powerlessness that spring from a sense of futility, a sense that one is substantially alone in the world, that no one in the media speaks to their points of view.

One editor, new to his newspaper, lamented, for example, that photographers sent for weather shots invariably brought photos from "only one side of the tracks." Many in the media respond that those who work in the media are able to adequately represent all groups in their stories and presentations. Indeed, they claim to make special efforts to assure that a diversity of views is inclusive enough to represent all significant views.

INCLUDING MINORITIES

Yet newsroom discussions find that few reporters fill out their source lists with phone numbers of African American economists, Asian American political scientists, female e-commerce experts, or other minority groups who have a stake in the economy, the political system, or the new-technology world. An African American economist, for example, might have a far different take on the implications of rising housing or gasoline costs in the community than either a representative of African American community groups or white economists. The African American would be able to integrate minority experience with professional expertise to present important insights that might go missing if someone without experience in one or the other of the areas were interviewed.

The pressure is on the media, as it is in areas throughout society, to broaden the diversity of staff in order to broaden the diversity of views in stories as a service to audiences who need diverse views in order to make cogent social decisions. As the number of minorities grows, and as they become more active in civic matters, the need for them to be represented in media power positions grows. The facts that media may select their own course in these matters, are protected by the First Amendment from compulsion, and thus may be immune to entreaties, compounds the frustration for minorities.

ENTRENCHED POWER MAY SILENCE MINORITY VOICES

One problem is that of entrenched power and an accompanying arrogance, which asserts that "I know what is best for everyone." Yet a great deal of evidence suggests that power protects power, making it difficult for the powerless to crack the portals and take a place in the discussion.

In the Brock Adams/Bob Packwood cases mentioned previously, the effects of power are easily evident. A female staff member in Sen. Adams's Washington office had, several years earlier, complained that Sen. Adams had drugged and raped her in his office. An investigation, predictably, could find no corroborating evidence in the case, so the matter was dropped.

Similarly, though a number of women had complained about Sen. Packwood, the *Portland Oregonian* chose to leave power in place by not running the story, thereby keeping the matter out of the sunshine of public discussion, further entrenching power and ignoring the women who were powerless before his advances. It took another newspaper, after Sen. Packwood's reelection, to make the public disclosures.

EMPOWERING DIVERSE GROUPS

Perhaps it is coincidental, but both instances above protected men of power. It required two newspapers, doing what their moral obligations demanded, to make the disclosures in the face of very strong and instant public criticism. The practical moral argument for diversity, both in content and in staffing, sees empowerment of the powerless as important products of the natural power and protections granted to media. Moreover, pluralism and diversity in content are natural elements in the national redistribution of power, the leveler of the playing field of public policies. It would also be morally desirable if equity and justice considerations would lead the media establishment to seek expressive participation by diverse groups and also seek staff diversity through recruitment and training of minority members to become effective communicators.

JOURNALISM ETHICS AND THE LAW

Illustrating the conflict between ethics and the law, the U.S. Supreme Court ultimately punished the Minneapolis newspaper for violating the promise to keep a source confidential. This conflict, as in a clash between judges and reporters who refuse to disclose their sources in court, is an example of problems reporters confront while serving their audience in the face of opposition in the courts.

In the case of the courts, some states have passed so-called *shield laws* that allow reporters to stand on moral principle by refusing to disclose sources and still avoid being jailed for contempt of court. The decision from Minneapolis still puts journalists on notice that breaking a promise, even for a good cause, may be punished by the courts.

These examples still leave a question hanging of whether stories should be run without the naming of sources. In examples of classic stories, Woodward and Bernstein used the famous Deep Throat as an anonymous source in their series on the Richard Nixon White House, which ran for months in the early 1970s; similarly, as we noted in the previous chapter, the *Seattle Times* used eight anonymous women as the sources of its story accusing Sen. Brock Adams of sexual harassment and abuse as the time for his reelection bid approached.

On the other hand, many editors declare they will not run a story unless the source is identified by name and other important data. The decision whether to identify sources is a difficult one, for audiences have a right to know who is making a particular statement in order that that person's credibility may be assessed; audiences should be treated fairly and not be asked to take such information at face value. The naming of sources and their credentials is a mark of respect for audiences and their ability to assess information.

JOURNALISTS AS INTERMEDIARIES FOR SOURCES AND AUDIENCE

On the other hand, in the continuing war between journalists serving as intermediaries for their audiences and sources whose power relies on their ability to control the information distributed about them, journalists greatly increase their chances of keeping audiences well informed if they can use reliable but confidential sources who do not want to be named. In the process, of course, they place their own reputations and credibility on the line. This requires them to be extra careful before passing on rumors or materials that merely seem to have titillation value for audiences or may attract viewers or readers for its shock value.

REACTIONS TO COMPLEX CLASSIC CASES

The *Seattle Times* confronted this issue and felt the compelling stories, offered independently by the eight women, justified accepting sole responsibility for the harm done to Sen. Adams. The eight women had requested their names not be used for fear of retribution from a politically powerful (and popular) elected official. Nevertheless, several years later, and despite the destruction of Sen. Adams's political career, it remains a "he said–she said" scenario with no conclusive ending.

Such is the nature of moral decision making. Smoking guns were found to vindicate anonymous source usage by the *Washington Post* in the case of President Nixon. Neither the *Seattle Times* nor the *Portland Oregonian* can know for certain if its stories were accurate. Without a public airing of the story of sexual harassment, Sen. Packwood was reelected. The accusations, however, surfaced in another newspaper, and Oregon's senator spent nearly two years defending himself as other, similar charges surfaced before he finally resigned from the Senate.

JOURNALISM AND THE COURTS

Media relationships with the courts have been stormy throughout the history of the new democracy. They are two powerful social forces in conflict. The media have an informal power granted by immunity from regulation and a moral mandate to keep society effectively informed. The courts and the justice system have the responsibility to administer society's justice, both criminally and in civil disputes. Collisions occur when the media, in fulfilling their moral responsibilities, gather and distribute information the justice system feels is likely to obstruct the meting out of justice.

It is natural for judges to feel their function—that of assuring a fair trial—is more important for immediate purposes than the function of the media in gathering and distributing information that would endanger a fair trial. At the same time, the same principle that muddies the waters of privacy invasion creates an emotional favorite in the battle: Who would argue against a fair trial? This emotional response sometimes acts on citizens in such a way that they would be willing to give away rights to a public trial (guaranteed by the Sixth Amendment to the Constitution) in order to keep information from the public that would foul a fair trial (not guaranteed by the Constitution.)

ENSURING FAIR TRIALS AMID MEDIA PUBLICITY

Certainly, most journalists would not want to despoil a trial and victimize either the defendant or the justice system, but still they have neither a legal responsibility nor a moral obligation to assure a fair trial. That obligation falls on the courts, which have an array of tools at their disposal to assure fair trials despite media publicity. Courts may change venues, impose gag orders on officers of the court, declare mistrials and order new ones, and instruct jurors at length about their responsibilities to the fair-trial principle. Journalists, on the other hand, must keep their eye on the important public information function. Their job is often complicated by a confidentiality-preserving justice system that sees its function enhanced when done in secret or with a minimum of public scrutiny. Nevertheless, journalists have laws in their favor to help in their confrontations with the criminal justice system: Court and some police records tend to be open to inspection, most court proceedings are open, and often publicity holds some attraction for lawyers and police officers who are willing to speak out.

If journalists leave it to the courts to protect their domains within restrictions of the law and still hope to pursue their main objective—finding and publishing accurate information on the case at hand—the adversarial relationship should work to the mutual advantage of both and of the public at large. If one or the other fails in the responsibility, the system is subject to abuse. The courts and police would gladly do without public scrutiny, except when they need public help of some kind (in finding witnesses or locating suspects), so it would not be difficult to cloak the entire justice system in secrecy if it were not for energetic journalists. Similarly, a justice system disinclined to be scrutinized appeals to public emotions about fair trials and often requires journalists to be increasingly imaginative and resourceful in seeking out information.

RELUCTANT SOURCES: BUSINESS AND POLICE

Business is probably the only other steady source of information more reluctant than the criminal justice system to disclose information to journalists. Therefore, when covering business and when talking to police and court officers, journalists can take it for granted that they are talking to reluctant sources who only want to disclose a portion of the information they have. The difference here is that police and court officers are often clearly reluctant to disclose, almost challenging reporters to dig further.

CLASSIC CASE IN JOURNALISM: O. J. SIMPSON CRIMINAL TRIAL

The "public circus" of the O. J. Simpson trial for the murder of his wife and her friend is cited as a hallmark for deplorable court coverage that endangers a fair trial. While the question of whether the trial was fair, given the defendant's acquittal, is arguable, a number of public benefits clearly emerged that justified the anarchical coverage. From a journalistic view, the Simpson trial offered many Americans their first opportunity to see the workings of the justice and trial system from beginning to end, providing a priceless lesson in the mechanics of a criminal trial. It also returned spouse abuse to the public agenda and chronicled unconstitutional police "short cuts" and errors in investigations.

As in real life, not everyone connected with the trial was glorified, but the general result was a typical instruction in criminal justice. Also, the problem of spousal abuse (which Simpson inflicted on his wife) was given new life on the public agenda in the wake of disclosures about that stormy relationship, providing for a renewal of the discussion of personal power and its use. Similarly, an intriguing (and unwanted) view of the weaknesses of a Los Angeles Police Department investigation demonstrated both the techniques and their results in influencing juries, an effective civic lesson for viewers. The trial also humanized a judge (judges, as a class, prefer more of a pedestal environment), prosecuting attorneys, and defense lawyers.

SOCIAL ELEMENTS OF FAIRNESS

With only this superficial look at the Simpson trial, it is clear that ensuring a fair trial was not the only social element involved. Had journalists acceded to the wishes of judges, police, and prosecutors for the sake of providing a fair trial, the instructional and social value of the coverage would have been very different. If this were the case, it must also be acknowledged that attitudes toward the system, toward lawyers, and toward the police might also have been very different. One could argue, excitement of a circus atmosphere aside, that the Simpson trial was a power redistribution exercise in which critically important social institutions were described and depicted in ways that more typified the reality of their role in society than the idealized visions of pontifical, distant judges; idealistic lawyers; and flawless police investigators.

Those who watched or read about the trial are not likely to view these groups in the same way again. That, of course, is the job of the journalist—to create an image in people's minds that will match the image they encounter, whatever the consequences to the institutions they examine.

The moral obligation to be accurate in creating that image still applies, of course, even in situations in which journalists are accused of sacrificing accuracy to promulgate rumors in the absence of authoritative information about court affairs. The mandate to cover the system still does not allow distortions, making it important for journalists to be as certain as they can of this information and their sources.

Checklist for Ethical Decision Making: Journalism

Journalists, to assure they will consider diligently the ethics of their actions, may want to adopt a checklist. Such a list will not ensure that an ethical decision will always be made, but it will tend to ensure that the decision is a thoughtful one, increasing its likelihood of being good. Thus, journalists may want to ask themselves the following questions:

1. Is this topic important for my audience? Will the information help a substantial portion of my audience make better decisions in their lives?
2. Once the story is published, am I willing to have my audience know of the techniques I used to gather the information?
3. Can I justify the harm this story will do to individuals by citing the benefits of the story that offset the harm?
4. Have I checked the accuracy of the information contained in the story, and am I willing to stake my reputation that it is a truthful account?
5. Have I developed enough diverse sources that the various shadings of opinion are represented in the story?
6. Does the tenor of my story tend to serve a source's interest more than it does the interests of my audience?
7. Which of my unconscious biases may have directed my work on this story? Did I work to offset those biases?

SUMMARY

Neutrality is expected of the media, but often this is hard to deliver when there are clashing advertising and business interests. Additionally, power and position can harm a reporter's coverage on a story. Accuracy and fairness are additional issues, but there are myriad factors that rest within the rubric of journalism ethics. Social forces for representation are also paramount. Most individuals want to be represented in the public dialogue. Yet often opinions and even story topics do not represent the views of many. A public sometimes expresses feelings of powerlessness that extend from the perception that no one in the media speaks to its various points of view. Media need to represent all significant groups in their stories and presentations. This chapter focused on the ethical problems in journalism. The next chapter is dedicated to ethics in the persuasion areas: advertising and public relations. We will note many similarities in the baseline ethics, but differences in the expectation and scope of the professions.

MORAL REASONING QUESTIONS

1. What are the viable alternatives to a pluralistic social system that appears to do such harm to innocent, private people and families?
2. Why can it be said journalists have moral obligations to be less concerned about the news organizations they work for than the audiences they serve?
3. What is meant by the observation that good journalists level the power "playing field" with their stories?
4. What happens when minorities are not as well qualified as mainstream newsroom job applicants? Should minorities be hired to provide diversity in the newsroom?
5. Of what value to moral discussions in the newsroom are the traditions of the past?
6. Is it ethical to repeatedly victimize people who are already suffering (e.g., suicides, sexual assault, and false accusations) by putting their names in a story that will embarrass them?

CONTEMPORARY CASE IN JOURNALISM: HOMETOWN NEWS

You are distributor of a chain of free weekly newspapers, each serving a different community in a cluster of suburban towns, with your front pages carrying the slogan "Home town journalism at its best." Your issues have extensive coverage of local high-school sports, which is not provided by regional dailies, and you cover city and county government extensively. In your role as publisher, you decree that none of the six newspapers you publish will promote either the gay lifestyle or abortion and that no stories will be written for your papers which appear to support or be sympathetic to either of those topics.

Your papers are distributed free to 120,000 households and businesses in the county. Advertising has increased in the two weeks since you announced the policy, and you declare in the wake of announcing the policy that now "everyone has a clear understanding of our beliefs, and we feel we are by far a better paper." However, more than 12 reporters and editors have resigned in protest.

1. What are the moral issues involved in announcing this policy?
2. Does a newspaper purporting to be a community newspaper have a moral right to exclude favorable mention of community groups and issues from its columns? Why?
3. Is it morally correct for citizens in a community to provide support for a newspaper that excludes such groups, even if the community generally supports the newspaper's position? Why?

CONTEMPORARY CASE IN JOURNALISM: SMALL-TOWN FOOTBALL

A sports reporter in a small community is assigned to cover the football team of the university located in that community. The community views the success of the team as their success and has a huge emotional investment in the fortunes of the football team. The coach, who has had great success in ten years there, is an icon in the community and could probably be elected mayor if he wished.

In covering the team, you eat from a lavish free buffet in the press box on home game days, travel with the team at a discounted air and hotel rate on road trips, and consider yourself to be a good friend to the coaches and the athletic director.

Your editor assigns you to interview a former star who, midway through his senior season four years ago, sustained a painful injury that ended his college (and prospects for a professional) football career. The former player tells you the university was very solicitous of him after his injury and paid his medical bills. However, he became dependent on painkillers and could not break the dependency, declaring that he was badly addicted. He asked the university to pay for treatment of the dependency, but the university refused and cut off all support, including physical rehabilitation. He tried to find an attorney who would represent him in a suit against the university to force payment for dependency addiction, but no lawyer in town would help him. A lawyer from a town several miles away gave him some encouragement, but after talking to the local judge, he said he could not help.

He told you of three other former players who also sustained injuries, were still in town, and had similar experiences. You located and talked to two of them. They encountered generally the same rebuff from the university, and both confirmed their own dependency on painkillers, as well as infirmities from their football days that kept them from holding jobs.

Your editor discourages you from pursuing the matter, reminding you that you would not find much public support for a story that detailed criticism of the football program or its coach. Furthermore, of course, you would not be assigned to cover the football team, thereby losing the perks.

1. Is this a problem serious enough to warrant a news story about the plight of former players? Why?
2. Can the responsibility be placed on the editor if the reporter drops the story, arguing that he would cover it, but the boss is the boss? Why?
3. Shouldn't community values prevail? If the community loves the football team and its coach, should the reporter be the one to criticize the program?
4. How serious would the university's misdeeds have to be to warrant criticism by the newspaper?
5. Should it matter that the newspaper would probably lose advertising if the story ran, not to mention circulation? Why?

CONTEMPORARY CASE IN JOURNALISM: ILLEGAL BORDER ACTIVITIES

You are a television news reporter in San Diego. One Saturday night, you go to the border station between the United States and Mexico to watch teenagers (who can legally drink in Mexico) come across the border, staggering with drink, claim their cars from parking lots, and scream their tires as they drive down the freeway toward home. You film them as they walk along the side-walk, leaning on the fence for support, many vomiting in the gutter.

A parking lot attendant tells those driving out of her lot that she will report them to the police if they drive in that condition. Border patrol officers, on the other hand, say it is not their job to enforce drunk-driving laws, and police on the scene are not in enough force to be able to slow the flood of drunk drivers.

1. *Should you take down license numbers of drunk drivers and turn them over to police?*
2. *Is it appropriate for you to become an agent of the police in this matter of clear public danger? Why?*
3. *Should you ignore the problem and just do a story as assigned despite the dangers presented by these drunk drivers?*
4. *Who is the more ethical person, the parking booth attendant or the border patrol officers who say they cannot help? Explain your position in terms of an ethical system of duty, rights, virtue, utilitarianism, or relationships.*

SELECTED SOURCES

Black, J., Steele, B., & Barney, R. D. (1999). *Doing ethics in journalism: A handbook with case studies* (3rd ed.). New York, NY: Allyn and Bacon.

Elliott, D. (1986). *Responsible journalism.* Beverly Hills, CA: Sage Publications.

Lambeth, E. B. (1992). *Committed journalism: An ethic for the professional* (2nd ed.). Bloomington, IN: Indiana University Press.

Merrill, J. C. (1977). *Existential journalism.* New York: Hastings House.

Merrill, J. C. (1994). *Legacy of wisdom: Great thinkers and journalism.* Ames, Iowa: Iowa State University Press.

Schudson, M. (1995). *The power of news.* Cambridge, MA: Harvard University Press.

7

ADVERTISING AND PUBLIC RELATIONS: ETHICAL PERSUASION

CONTEMPORARY CASE IN PUBLIC RELATIONS: PUBLIC DENIALS

Salt Lake Olympics Committee (SLOC) executives immediately and vigorously denied they offered bribes—a predictable response to a news story suggesting the committee bribed International Olympic Committee members for favorable votes in Salt Lake City's bid to be the 2002 Winter Olympics site.

Likewise, lawyers for O. J. Simpson denied publicly that their client had killed Simpson's wife and her male friend. President Clinton emphatically denied having had sex with Monica Lewinsky. It was later shown in the 2002 Winter Olympics and Clinton cases that the respective bribery and sexual encounters apparently did occur, contradicting the denials. In the O. J. Simpson case, the lawyers were not proven wrong in criminal court, but a civil trial found that O. J. Simpson had violated the rights to life of the two victims.

Along the same lines, commercial media messages are designed to make it appear as though the product they are promoting is very nearly perfect, that it has no weaknesses and is much better than competing products. The denials and product hypes, both very common public messages, seem to be an important part of a competitive, adversarial society in which the give and take of public discussion and the public opinions such discussions produce may be more important than the truth. This philosophy lies at the center of the roles of public relations and advertising professionals.

Chapter 6 emphasized the power of journalists who control and distribute information. This chapter explores ethics in advertising and public relations—the persuasion professions. As individuals finds themselves making critical decisions based more on mediated information than on direct experience, those who provide that information are under increasing critical scrutiny. This chapter focuses on the practitioners, consumers, and ethicists who are concerned about developing some methods of ensuring that reliable and valid information is being provided by professional persuaders. Many consumers feel deceived or manipulated by advertising promising product performance that is not delivered. Should we advocate enforceable discipline for deceptive persuaders as a way of reassuring society that messengers and messages can be trusted? Both public relations and advertising are professional industries protected by the First Amendment. Chapter 6 noted that freedoms exist to make an open marketplace of information possible. The topics of lying and deception are foundational in the discipline of ethics and philosophy. As will be discussed in this chapter, it is also foundational in building a media profession based on innovation, trust, and honesty.

Although deceptions certainly appear to violate or at least distort the creed of truth telling, which is a fundamental doctrine of virtually any society, it does suggest the importance of other elements. Without discounting the importance of truth, perhaps these actions are even more important in specific circumstances. The common ground between a public denial in the face of accusations and the public promotion of a product or idea is that both are intended to be persuasive, to give their adherents a leg up in the battle for public favor. Such lies and deceptions are generally formulated and distributed by individuals skilled at public persuasion, the essence of their profession; they are successful in their field to the extent they are successful in persuading others to favor their clients.

PERSUASION: A MORALLY ACCEPTABLE GAME

The impact of these value conflicts can be better understood by looking at the professional persuasion process as a type of game—a very important game. In many games, behaviors that fall outside the normal boundaries of behavior are encouraged. For all their violations of norms, they fulfill a socially beneficial purpose and are accepted by society at large as moral and generally doing more good than harm.

Football is an example of a violent game that society justifies morally because it entertains. In this game, players do things for which they would be harshly criticized if they were done on the streets in everyday life. On the playing field, for example, a 350-pound lineman may smash a 200-pound linebacker to the ground with impunity as long as he is playing within the rules. Alternatively, a quarterback may deceive an onrushing lineman by pretending to hand the ball off to a running back, but keeping it to run in the opposite direction.

The first player has violated a moral principle of *do no* (physical) *harm*, while the quarterback has caused the rushing lineman to believe something the ball carrier himself did not believe (that the quarterback no longer had the ball), a deceptive act on its face. Both are generally unethical, but are nevertheless entertaining, and therefore socially acceptable in a game with special rules.

Let the lineman smash a little old lady to the ground on the sidewalk outside the stadium after the game and see how well it is tolerated. Professional persuaders in advertising and public relations can be as harmful and deceptive as football players or participants in many other games; their professional activities are part of a socially beneficial (even necessary) game, one whose noble purposes surpass the entertainment value of football.

COMPETITION IS KEY

As in most games, competition is a key element, and a democratic society thrives on competition. Competing manufacturers, from makers of light bulbs to automobiles, little by little improve the quality of their products over the years as they work for and promote an edge on their competitors. In this climate, product development snowballs over time into marvels not anticipated when they were first developed.

Today's automobile is a far better machine than the Model-T Ford of the early twentieth century, and light bulbs now give much more light, last longer, and are relatively cheaper than their predecessors of, say, the early 1930s. It is generally accepted that competition entails some deception, much as the quarterback's feint is acceptable on the playing field.

DECEPTION

In advertising and public relations, the use of deception is usually most apparent in the selective distribution of information. The advocate for a product or cause trumpets favorable information, leaving audience members to find for themselves any negative information that would enable them to make a truly informed decision. If it is acceptable that the distribution of selective information is generally ethical, the moral question for professional persuaders, then, revolves around the boundaries of persuasion, the thresholds beyond which persuaders ought not go if they are to avoid doing unnecessary harm to their audiences.

Less Than Strictly Factual Information

In examining the use of persuasion and its frequent bedfellow, deception, in a democratic society, two lines of inquiry suggest themselves. First, if society deifies competition, must it also accept a sliding scale of truth as parties jockey for competitive position and for advantage? Second, if absolute Truth is often not self-evident, must participants in a democratic society rely upon truth (with a lower-case "t"), rather than knowledge, to make informed decisions?

The Federal Trade Commission, acknowledging that strict adherence to facts is neither necessary nor practical in advertising, leaves official room for "hype"—that is, the expression of qualitative opinion. Qualitative opinions are arguable and subjective, "my toothpaste is best," for example. Unless the facts are clear, most utterances are qualitative, despite the personal feelings of the speaker. For example, how do you decide for everyone which toothpaste is "best"? The capital "T" of *Truth* creates an important distinction in our discussion for it implies that Truth is out there somewhere in all cases, but is difficult, if not impossible, to identify in most significant instances.

The Approximate Truth

Mere mortals, for all the generalizations made about Truth, must fall back on being satisfied with approximate truth in specific instances. The role of public discussion is to tease out truth with the hope that it will approximate the larger Truth we must all confront sooner or later. Whatever the public rhetoric, the search for Truth is often second in importance, standing in the shadow of the drive for results.

The operative rationale here, of course, is that competition encourages deception in qualitative speech and produces a better society in the long run, despite immediate feelings to the contrary. Each must make his or her own argument as to what constitutes a better society, but the fact remains we have collectively selected competition—and its persuasive "evils"—as the means of achieving whatever we decide is "better."

Competition Is Desirable

Certainly, not everyone agrees that competition is better, and much public debate revolves around keeping competition—viewed as desirable—while eliminating that handmaiden to competition, persuasion and its attendant deceptions. Psychological benefits are important in this equation. If you are persuaded a product will benefit you, the psychic benefits may be worth the price, no matter what the physical benefit. As a practical matter, differences between Fords, Chevrolets, and Toyotas are more psychological than actual, offering emotional joy, rather than the assurance of being the "best."

Neither O. J. Simpson's defense team, nor the prosecution team after a certain point in the investigation, were particularly interested in finding the Truth of whether O. J murdered Nicole Simpson and Ronald Goldman; however, each had the primary goal, even the honorable social responsibility, of persuading jurors toward a certain outcome. At some point in the process of investigation and putting a case together, prosecution officers said, "We don't know whether Simpson did it, but we think we can present enough evidence to jurors that they will agree that he committed the murders."

Truth

Presenting a Credible Truth

To put it baldly, the important question, in the absence of eyewitnesses, was not whether O. J. Simpson committed the murders (a Truth element), but whether sufficiently compelling evidence could be presented through credible witnesses so a jury of peers would agree with the prosecution (a persuasion task). Once the defense legal team was assembled, on the other hand, O. J. Simpson's guilt or innocence (Truth) was not a question. The task of the team was to win acquittal (persuasion, again). And Mr. Simpson had the right to a team of lawyers that would drive for his acquittal with all its combined professional and persuasive skills, no matter what his ultimate culpability.

The right to representation is critical in a competitive, adversarial society. With Truth an uncertain element in the equation, the persuasive skills of the prosecution and defense are the means we have chosen as a society to bring us to as near a semblance of truth as we are likely to find. The conflict in the O. J. Simpson case was a formal one in a court of law mandated by the legal system, yet it has enough commonality with everyday lives outside the boundaries of a courtroom to serve as a graphic illustration of the role that Truth plays in everyday lives.

The Importance of Truth

It is not that Truth is unimportant. What kind of a society would reject altogether the concept of Truth as a virtue? Such a society would decay and crumble from the mistrust that would corrode virtually all social relationships. Yet we must live with the uncertainty that what we know may not be the truth and that we often need to search further to raise the probabilities that we have Truth. This is so whether we are searching for a marriage partner or a reliable automobile.

Many of our individual problems lie in the vast gray area of unknowns and preferences. We choose to call many things that are merely unknowns or preferences *Truth* because of a need for reassurance and stability in our lives. As a practical matter, however, calling something true when, in fact, it will turn out not to be true gets a lot of people in trouble and tends to reinforce the importance of truth telling as a social value.

Classic Case in Media: Pamela Anderson and Companion

Pamela Anderson, the sexy former star of the television show Baywatch, for example, declared the "truth" when she married rock star Tommy Lee, by saying that this was the man with whom she would spend the rest of her life. In less than a year, Ms. Anderson filed for divorce after a series of domestic confrontations with her husband. Certainly, she must have believed this marriage would last forever when she said it would, but it turned out not to be the truth. She wanted to persuade skeptics this was a good marriage in the entertainment world of transitory relationships, and perhaps she had the need to try to persuade herself about it also.

Given, then, the hazy nature of Truth, this society, for all its love of—and lip service to—truth, has opted for confrontation and advocacy as the best way of providing some assurance that alternatives will be introduced into the marketplace. It is in this way that individual best guesses may be made with some assurance that a truth-finding process has occurred, rather than that truth will be accepted as a given. This cements our commitment to the importance of truth by assuring introduction of alternatives into the open marketplace of ideas—a nod toward not only the elusive nature of truth but also its importance.

PERSUASION SHOWS A COMMITMENT TO TRUTH

The alternative, of course, is that truth will be defined by those with power. Raw power defined the truths of property, leadership, social roles, and even individual upward mobility in the primitive social systems. Later, possession of "superior wisdom" and raw power were used to define truths that governed individual lives, conditions from which generations have fled their homelands searching for alternatives.

Some mental and emotional gymnastics are needed to recognize that approval of persuasion, including some deception, is society's way of cementing its commitment to Truth as a premiere virtue, however elusive it may be. Yet persuasion is the task that advertising and public relations people, as well as lawyers, politicians, lobbyists, and salespersons, take on as professionals.

IDENTIFYING BOUNDARIES

When the social climate rejects alternatives and persuasion, many who have the power to define and distribute their own truths are further empowered when their self-serving truths are validated by default. Therefore, it is important to examine the moral aspects of persuasion and, as long as persuasion (and its attendant deception) are such an implicit part of our system, to work toward identifying boundaries of deception rather than inveigh against persuasion, or its frequent synonym "manipulation," as a legitimate social goal or tool.

In the communication industry, public relations and advertising are the two areas with a specific involvement in the process of persuasion (hence, deception). Unfortunately, discussions of ethics in these areas seldom acknowledge that there is not only a socially acceptable, but even a socially necessary, role, for the persuasion function in a democratic, participatory society.

It is widely accepted that the deception inherent in advocacy or persuasion is harmful, adding another item to the list of socially justifiable harms professional communicators inevitably do.

The Philosophers on Lying

Blatant Lies

As we have seen, the search for Truth is a murky one. At the other end of the scale, lying, there is also ambiguity and misconception. It is important to have a realistic understanding of the role of lies in daily life, especially if one intends to enter the persuasion profession. When looking at persuasion and lies from a philosophical viewpoint, one might expect clear-cut approaches against any persuasive tactic that could be deemed a lie. But since we have reflected on the nature of Truth and approximate truth, what about lies? These are questions ethicists and philosophers have studied for centuries.

Contemporary Case in Public Relations: The House Organ Exaggeration

Genelle and her husband were interviewed regarding the highly emotional, premature birth (26 weeks' gestation) of their daughter, Linnea. The interview was conducted with a house organ for charitable services at the hospital. The writers determined that Genelle's story needed embellishing, so they added a quote to it. Genelle said: "We will always be thankful—very thankful—for the hospital's Newborn Intensive Care Unit, the memorial funds that helped to lead the way, and the many special, caring doctors and technicians"; to which the house organ writer added: "We will always be grateful for something else, too—the charitable care that the hospital gave us. We lacked adequate insurance and our own financial resources fell far short of the amount needed to pay the bill. The hospital covered it from its charitable care account" (Deseret News, August 23, 1993, p. B1).

None of the information contained in the added statement was true. Genelle's insurance company paid the entire $130,004.99 bill. Genelle and her husband paid an extra $300; the hospital paid nothing. The hospital apologized, and even mailed correction letters to the 1,300 individuals, mostly contributors, who received the publication. The mistake did not escape full public attention, however. A local newspaper ran the story in a prominently placed column.

The writers for the house organ had lied. The emotional story needed something to compel readers to donate, so a quote was added. It was a lie—one that hurt the parents, the hospital, the reputation of the house organ, and perhaps the charitable arm of the hospital.

This is the type of lie philosopher Tony Coady talked about when he stated: "Dishonesty has always been perceived in our culture, and in all cultures but the most bizarre, as a central human vice. Moreover, the specific form of dishonesty known as lying has generally been scorned, and the habitual liar treated with contempt" (1992, p. 17).

But Coady did not stop with scorn for the blatant lie. He teases us with the notion that not all lies are major infractions. Indeed, he believes that some lies are mere deceptions that may be acceptable in society:

> We should note that this perception is consistent with a certain hesitancy about what constitutes a lie and with more than sneaking suspicion that there might be a number of contexts in which lying is actually justified (1992, p. 17).

Coady is not alone in his view that there may be justifiable contexts for lying or deception and that not every situation will be as clear-cut as the house organ incident. Jean Jacques Rousseau believed there are situations when the truth is undefined. "To lie without advantage or disadvantage to oneself or others is not a lie; it is not falsehood but fiction" (Rousseau, 1953); additionally, Henry Sidgwick considers circumstances under which the code of honor prescribes lying (Bok, p. 272).

GOVERNMENT LIES

Is it different if the government does not tell the complete truth if it needs to persuade its citizens that all is well? There are numerous cases where presidents, senators, generals, governors, cabinet members, and other government officials believed that lying was proper. They may have turned to Plato, who gave support for some lies in saying:

> It is the business of the rulers of the city, if it is anybody's, to tell lies, deceiving both its enemies and its own citizens for the benefit of the city; and no one else must touch this privilege (Bloom, 1987, p. 139).

Presumably Plato would have supported the efforts of the media during the Reagan Administration to convince the public that there was nothing to the so-called Iran-gate scandal. Similarly, would the revered philosopher have nodded approvingly at the U.S. military's information effort during the Persian Gulf War that focused media and public attention on the "smart" missiles' precision without noting that such high-tech wonders accounted for only 7 percent of the bombing? (1993, Baker, p. 196).

Even Ludwig Wittgenstein told his students that "Lying is a language-game that needs to be learned like any other one" (1968, p. 249). If, phenomenologically speaking, we each make our own constructs of reality, is it possible to find we have created our worlds of fictions, myths, and lies? The possibility certainly cannot be dismissed.

In communication professions some individuals jest that this particular culture of liars exists solely in the media professions. However, philosopher F.G. Bailey believed that perhaps the whole society condones deception. He wonders how our society, or others, can ever exist without lying. "The notion of 'clear-cut lies' is not so much a guide to good conduct as a label, one more weapon with which to commit rhetorical assault and battery" (1991, p. 7).

ACTS OF GOOD WILL: BOK

Ethicist Sissela Bok believed there is no instance when it is appropriate to lie. Bok tells us that "a liar often does diminish himself by lying, and the loss is precisely to his dignity, his integrity" (1983, p. 46). Moreover, Gandhi related that everyone has access to truthfulness if they will but use it:

> Truthfulness is the master-key. Do not lie under any circumstances whatsoever, keep nothing secret, take your teachers and your elders into your confidence and make a clean breast of everything to them (Bailey, 1991, p. 7).

Many media professionals would agree with Gandhi's premise, but are there limits to how successfully his theory can be applied in this field? How would Gandhi's advice work in the case that follows?

CONTEMPORARY CASE IN PUBLIC RELATIONS: THE GOODWILL GIFTS

An agency is employed by a major sporting goods company. Smith, the account executive, is asked to give gifts, such as watches and other memorabilia, to journalists covering a major sporting event. What does Smith tell the press corps about these gifts? Would Smith ever consider giving journalists cash instead of the gifts? To what degree should Smith be expected to disclose the full extent of his gift giving to the journalists when distributing the memorabilia? Should the journalists be faulted for accepting these gifts?

Certainly, no lies have been told in this case, but in practicing one aspect of persuasion, has either deception or concealment occurred, or are the gifts a harmless gesture? Why? A "return of favor" by the journalists may not be imminent. But perhaps "goodwill" articles will be expected.

CONTEMPORARY CASE IN PUBLIC RELATIONS: THE STUDENT NEWSPAPER COMPENSATION

In one instance when the "goodwill" reasons were voiced, a university's sports information department paid expenses so a sports reporter from the school newspaper could accompany the basketball team on a road trip. The team performed poorly, losing both games, and the reporter wrote a negative story that blamed the coaching staff. The enraged coach took out his frustrations on the sports information department's director, who angrily confronted the reporter. *When the reporter responded that he was an objective observer entitled to his own viewpoint, the sports information department director exploded, saying, "But you weren't supposed to be an objective observer. Through the public relations fund, we paid your way." Few bestowers of gifts or gratuities would be as candid about the quid pro quo nature of such generosity (1994, p. 251).*

LIES CAN PROTECT OR INSPIRE: SOLOMON

Philosopher Robert Solomon has a diverse view on the fine lines of truth, deception, and lies, when he argues numerous sides to the questions involved in the tangled web of lying:

> Not all untruths are malicious, and not all deceptions are lies. The truth hurts, and sometimes it destroys. Lies can protect and inspire and deception can serve noble ends (1993, p. 4).

Solomon also believed that often the truth can produce significant agitation.

> Not just for the perplexing reasons long advocated by epistemological skeptics but rather because of the self-fulfilling and sometimes self-denying features of our beliefs about ourselves and those aspects of the world that matter most to us (1993, p. 5).

CONTEMPORARY CASE IN PUBLIC RELATIONS: CLEANUP OF UNITED WAY

Consider the public relations firm that was asked to clean up the image of the United Way after William Aramony, a 22-year president of the charity trust, resigned in disgrace. The PR firm was asked to respond in image-friendly ways to such questions as: Is it not true that Aramony received $463,000 yearly in salary and benefits and was entitled to $4.4 million in pension benefits? Is it not true that he used to fly on the supersonic Concorde *and used chauffeured limousines when he traveled? Is it not true that he created several for-profit spinoff organizations, one headed by his son? (Baker, 1993, p. 196)*

A media persuader certainly should not deny the problems the press is reporting. But the practitioner's job is likely to immediately focus on the good currently being done through local chapters of United Way. The practitioner's job is to emphasize that the charitable contributions must not decline or thousands of individuals will be hurt. There is nothing to gain by trying to persuade the public that this corporation is without blemish. In fact, the public relations practitioner would probably not be sure if he or she would personally want to contribute to the charitable fund. Yet the public relations professional would be obligated to divert public attention from the focus on Aramony and demonstrate the value of contributing to this organization. Is this practice deceptive? Is it defensible?

WHEN ALL LIES ARE HARMFUL

Some philosophers were not afraid of truth telling. Socrates supposedly died in the name of truth. For Francis Bacon, truth is "the sovereign good of human nature," and for Milton, truth has a "bright countenance" (Bailey, 1991, p. 3). Solomon reminds us that other philosophers have staked their very reputations on truthfulness. Epictetus, the early Stoic, defended, above all, the principle "not to speak falsely." In more modern times, Immanuel Kant took the prohibition against lying as his paradigm of a "categorical imperative," the unconditional moral law. According to Kant, there could be no exceptions, not even to save the life of a friend. Even Nietzsche took honesty to be one of his four "cardinal" virtues, and the existentialist Jean-Paul Sartre insisted that deception is a vice, perhaps indeed the ultimate vice (Solomon, 1993, p. 8).

Sissela Bok's philosophy on lying is theoretically similar to those of some of her predecessors. Bok believes that often individuals dismiss lies by saying they do not matter. "More often than not, they do matter, even where looked at in simple terms of harm and benefit. . . . Many [lies] are not as harmless as liars take them to be" (1983, p. 71). If we were only to read these

statements from ethicists of the past and present, we might assume that lying, for ethicists and communication practitioners alike, is wrong and that
truth telling is right.

CHOOSING NOT TO SEE THE TRUTH

Rather than the truth being manifest throughout an individual's life, as
Kant and Bok maintain, Sir Winston Churchill believed that often telling
the truth became a situational matter of convenience or inconvenience for
governmental persuaders. He stated that "Men occasionally stumble over
the truth, but most of them pick themselves up and hurry off as if nothing
had happened" (Van Ekeren, p. 213).

CONTEMPORARY CASE IN PUBLIC RELATIONS:
CORPORATE PERSUADER

*An internal audit in a Fortune 500 company found that one of its senior
executives had been cheating on his expense account. This executive was making almost $1 million per year, yet was pilfering unallowable minor expenses.
The board of directors decided to cover up any implications of wrongdoing and
let the executive immediately retire. The public relations officer was expected to
publicly announce the early retirement of the senior executive and the celebra-
tion of a good career. The deception was planned for two reasons. First, it was
to protect the corporation from implications of mismanagement or wrongdoing. Second, it was done to allow the executive to finish his career in a positive
light rather than a tarnished one.*

*The Wall Street Journal reporters questioned the early retirement, but
were unable to learn the reasons for it. The public relations officer gave only
information on the positive career, and corporation officers as well as the
executive believed reputations were preserved. This situation clearly involved
deception in that information was withheld, and reporters and others were
given information on retirement rather than on the fraud. The facts of this
situation are now buried in the private histories of both the corporation and
the executive.*

Was it appropriate for this information to be buried? The public relations officer, as an employee of the board of directors, was told to announce the incident as merely a retirement. The structure of deception was clearly outlined. If the press had been able to find the implications of fraud, the corporation certainly would have addressed it at that time. However, the board of directors of the corporation were unwilling to expose themselves and the corporation to the harm that comes with claims of mismanagement. The public relations officer was a major player in the deception. He still believes it was right to protect the corporation and the executive from embarrassment.

What would Immanuel Kant tell the corporate persuader? Kant declared: "A lie is a lie . . .whether it be told with good or bad intent. . . . But if a lie does no harm to anyone and no one's interests are affected by it, is it a lie? Certainly." (1785/1930/1963, p. 228). Kant believed truthfulness is a duty, an "unconditional duty which holds in all circumstances" (ibid). According to the categorical imperative, if there is even one case in which it is acceptable to lie and honesty can be overridden, then the "perfect" status of the duty not to lie is compromised. Kant was most strident in not allowing for even a seemingly innocent lie, one which could save a life instead of causing harm, for example. He merely asserts that if something terrible happens it is not your fault. The terrible act is something wholly unjustified in the first place (Kant, 1949, pp. 92–96).

LEAKING THE TRUTH: THE WHISTLE BLOWER

Media persuaders who value the truth may find themselves in a whistle blower's role, particularly if they are asked to suppress information of vital public interest. The Public Relations Society of America (PRSA) Code of Professional Standards advises that:

> A member shall: Be honest and accurate in all communications. Act promptly to correct erroneous communications for which the member is responsible. Investigate the truthfulness and accuracy of information released on behalf of those represented. . . . Avoid deceptive practices. (PRSA, 2000, p. 6)

If a member is asked by a client or an employer asks individuals in a persuasion assignment to do what they know is not truthful, they should quit. This is a noble course of action; however, when one's livelihood is threatened, practical considerations may prevail over idealism.

In that case, the media profession practitioner's only recourse may be to "leak" the information to the media for the public good or perhaps in hopes that the client or organization can be pressured into a more socially responsible posture.

Widespread acceptance of the clear declarations by Kant and Bok that condemn lying and the qualifying pronouncements of Coady, Wittgenstein, and Plato that acknowledge the utility of some lies inevitably thrust professional persuaders into a quagmire of public suspicion and distrust. Yet their roles are central and critical in society, and the strict truth telling of full disclosure is not an option, even as it is not an option with most of us in our personal lives.

Social Responsibility

Increasingly, a more complex society invests greater power in those who possess and use information. In this climate, information gatherers and distributors take a central role in the public consciousness. As individuals find themselves making critical decisions based more on mediated information than on direct experience, those who provide that information are under increasing critical scrutiny. The very nature of society widens the distance between the consumer and information mediators, making the process of obtaining day-to-day knowledge increasingly impersonal.

Among other effects, increasing complexity often denies individuals opportunities to match mediated images against the reality the images are intended to mirror. Each individual may not be able to talk directly with a candidate, but individuals must make a decision and vote, therefore relying on the media and on word of mouth from others for information.

Receiving Reliable and Valid Information

Consumers and ethicists are concerned about developing some assurance of reliable and valid information from their professional communicators. Communicators join surgeons and generals on the list of those whose competence is critical. It is likely that most consumers have felt deceived or manipulated by product information that promised one thing and delivered another. For example, advertising for an automobile may promise, and even deliver, psychological rewards to its owner while failing to fulfill mechanical promises.

TRUSTING THE MESSENGER

A natural first reaction to ensure a higher level of reliability is to advocate enforceable discipline for manipulative persuaders as a way of reassuring society that messengers and messages can be trusted, as surgeons can largely be trusted. Such reactions are responsible for current discussions within the field suggesting government licensing to elevate professional credibility and prestige.

The reality is that both public relations and advertising are professional industries protected by the Constitution's First Amendment, which declares that Congress shall make no law restricting freedom of speech. That freedom exists to make possible an open marketplace of information but would be bargained away in an effort to ensure public credibility and goodwill. If the persuasive, selective speech of the public relations or advertising professional is protected by law and, to some extent by (a reluctant) society, it is helpful to examine the unique roles of these professional communicators—roles that may often appear destructive and unethical. As with the surgeon, however, public relations and advertising counselors can indeed claim they do make vital social contributions. Once a role is defined, a set of ethics may be set in place, as surgeons are guided by ethical considerations in their respective specialties.

ADVANCING OUR CULTURE

A meaningful moral justification of public relations and advertising roles acknowledges that the foundation of American public philosophy is one of advocacy and adversarial relationships. It may not have been intended, and we may feel uncomfortable with it, but the American people and their institutions have, for more than 200 years, collectively decided that social benefits emerge when people arrive at collective judgments about public issues through public debate.

This is a pluralistic social characteristic that sets the stage for the moral confrontation between the two virtues of competitive public advocacy, in which some deception is necessary and healthy, and truth telling, in which deception is unforgivable. Certainly, the results are debatable, and the validity of objective discourse should be scrutinized, but the system itself is a utilitarian reality that permeates all aspects of American life.

In addition, it appears that an advocacy system tends to correlate strongly to higher living standards (literacy, life expectancy, education level, per capita income, etc.), suggesting that the relatively mild civil conflict inherent in the United States' social system results in substantially great-er benefits for its members. The adversarial system is virtuous in American society because it encourages each party to find and present its most per-suasive evidence. Presentation of that evidence, in turn, provides the sub-stantive basis for American decision making, right or wrong.

Rare is any class of people that does not, in one way or another, accept a moral obligation to advance the cause of a culture to which it feels loyalty. Lawyers are advocates for their clients—with an overriding obligation to protect the interests of that client in an adversarial society. Therefore, an ad-vocate arguing a reverse position, such as a prosecutor or defense attorney, is charged with the obligation of identifying and disclosing the weaknesses in the opposition's case while in turn advancing his or her own case. Each participant in the process has a specific assignment.

One legal scholar identifies the dilemma in which most of us find our-selves as advocates, citing the discomfort of a defense attorney. The crimi-nal defense attorney, however unwillingly in terms of personal morality, has a professional responsibility as an advocate in an adversarial system to ex-amine the perjurious client in the ordinary way. In other words, the defense, in gaining acquittal, must accept the testimony—truth or fiction—of a client and present it as truth to the court.

The Moral Limits of Advocating for the Client

Just as a lawyer serving a client has conflicting duties imposed by society and profession, it appears logical that a public relations or advertising coun-selor finds a legitimate conflict between society and client. Public relations and advertising counselors, as professional advocates, may be said to have roughly the same obligations to their clients as lawyers. The analogy is not an original one. Public relations pioneers Edward Bernays and Ivy Lee both claimed—three-quarters of a century ago—that public relations practition-ers are expected to serve as lawyers in the court of public opinion.

Lawyers are adversaries/advocates in the formalized courts of law, and public relations counselors and advertising people argue their cases as advocates/adversaries in the court of public opinion, a calling created and expanded in recent years by the explosion of media development whose moral boundaries its practitioners are still in the process of identifying. Whatever we may have learned about the United States as a nation of law, this country is, in the end, still most responsive to public opinion.

Thus, the public relations professional finds himself or herself wearing the mantle of single-minded advocate in the arena of public opinion. He or she should not apologize for it. Indeed, professional persuaders morally contract to acquire detailed, unthreatened knowledge of the client's business and to vigorously defend the client in public arenas without publicly disclosing personal reservations about client motives or performance. The adversarial system in this context assumes that self-interest will drive the range of participants to introduce virtually all significant viewpoints into the public dialogue.

On the other hand, reasoning together in a cooperative search for truth—even if it were feasible in today's complicated society—may restrict the system, excluding important affected parties: when adversarial process has been ignored in the operation of the courts, as in the days of the Star Chamber, human rights diminished and governmental repression increased. Yet there are limits, perhaps legal limits and certainly moral limits, to advocacy behavior. A recent *Chicago Tribune* analysis of prosecutors in the United States accused them of hiding evidence or twisting the truth in order to convict innocent people, noting that "winning has become more important than doing justice." If so, of course, this suggests an egoistic, rather than altruistic, drive on the part of prosecutors. Ever the advocate, the president of the National District Attorneys Association declared in response to the findings that he believes the great majority of prosecutors in this country are truly dedicated to doing their jobs in the proper fashion. He may not have lied, but his response to the specific findings was masked. Similarly, public relations and advertising ethics practices must revolve around the necessities of adversarial process in a participatory democracy, but with attention to moral limits.

A much longer discussion than we have room for here will be necessary to persuade most people about the essential civic role of public relations. However, if the advocacy/adversarial role described above for the advertising counselor is accepted, subsequent questions logically revolve around definitions of moral boundaries for these professional persuaders as honorable advocates.

WHAT ARE THE MORAL LIMITS OF PERSUASION?

The moral task for persuaders is to decide which thresholds must not be crossed in the persuasion process. For example, when you know that what you are saying about your company is an outright lie, you should find it very difficult to mount a moral defense of that action. While introduction of a variety of views is important, known lies merely obscure whatever truth may emerge, masking the truth and delaying its emergence. Although a prosecutor has a responsibility to earn convictions of those believed to be guilty, that same prosecutor must not do as the *Chicago Tribune* charged, that is, conceal evidence suggesting innocence or present false evidence in order to gain convictions and an enhanced reputation. Such behavior uses the prosecutor's inordinate state power to punish the powerless innocent.

The *Chicago Tribune* story noted that 381 defendants nationally had homicide convictions thrown out because of prosecutor behavior, including 28 death-row inmates who were freed. Beyond that, a 1999 Los Angeles investigation was examining up to 3,000 cases in which convictions were secured by police officers who planted evidence, lied under oath, and in other ways distorted the process by unacceptably crossing an investigative line.

Similarly, professional communicators should find a threshold division between disseminating information they can reasonably expect to be accurate and distributing that which they know is false. To withhold from consumers information that would save them from substantial harm would appear to cross the line. Frank Deaver, writing on the problems of finding truth, helps persuaders apply some principles to their search for the threshold by noting that professional persuaders owe their basic allegiance to a corporate or institutional employer, rather than to the public; in other words, to selective persuasion rather than to objective information. This is different than journalists, whose moral loyalty is to audience.

Loyalty to Client or Profession?

Primary loyalty to something other than society appears acceptable in an advocacy society because the persuader is hired to advance the cause of a client within that society, an act that in turn benefits society. Loyalty to the client is professionally obligatory until the threshold is crossed and more harm than good would result from that client loyalty. The persuader has a loyalty obligation to society to do no unjustifiable harm, and lying is harmful beyond the competitive harm of legitimate advocacy.

Deaver notes that persuaders, in their highest callings, tell "the truth, but inevitably not the whole truth," (1990, p. 171) with the intent to persuade.

In any case, no persuader is likely to tell the entire truth about clients because the client has areas of legitimate secrecy. This is comparable to the journalistic mandate to find what can be found and to publish if it is in the audience's interest. On another level, Deaver talks of "non truths told without intent to deceive" (1990, p. 143). Such "non truths" are common, though their use tends to get lost in rhetoric about truth telling. Deaver further reminds us that

> the earthly ministry of Jesus Christ was characterized by the telling of many parables. Technically speaking, Christ's parables conveyed untruths, but they were told for the purpose of revealing truths, and they were understood to be only examples. (1990, p. 173)

Deaver thus places persuaders in the middle of a continuum whose lower end consists of deceit, "white lies" and blatant lies—with intent to deceive, even if for purposes thought justifiable. The top of the continuum is the Truth we all seek.

The Message Must Be Likely to Be True

Deception seems to be the operant threshold, defined by philosopher Sissela Bok as causing others to believe as true something you yourself do not believe. Such a definition also probably ought to include a mandate to the persuader to avoid ignorance as a basis for making the decision. That is, to argue that you lied because you did not (bother to) know whether it was truth is not morally defensible.

As an autonomous moral agent, the persuader would still be under a moral obligation not to do unjustifiable harm, an obligation that includes making every effort to determine whether the message one is distributing is likely to be true. *Harm* is a relative term because competition inevitably creates harm; therefore, harm must be viewed as a given with an admonition to avoid unjustifiable harm.

Justifiable and Unjustifiable Harm

Deontologists who argue that individuals ought not be trusted to distinguish justifiable from unjustifiable harm (hence the reason for rules), should recognize such discretion is exactly what is conferred by the First Amendment, and is one reason why the communications professions must rely on moral, thoughtful practitioners. The test may still be one of whether the powerless are victimized by the deception. It is difficult to conceive of a situation in which victimizing the innocent works to one's advantage (e.g., I hurt you for your own good), yet reason suggests the possibility should be left open for rare instances.

One who abandons the pretense of moral agency, or whose conscience demands fealty to authority, may be satisfied to distribute messages merely because he or she was so ordered. Authoritarian organizations exist in which information is not shared; orders are merely handed down and underlings are expected to obey without question. Such an organization does not allow for the use of moral agency, except for efforts at using professionalism and credibility to urge the client toward a more morally defensible action. The professional communicator must still recognize that the client may demur, in which case the moral problem of loyalty to a flawed client arises.

ETHICAL DECISION MAKING

It is common in academic programs to encourage professionals to build up a personal fund that would allow them the satisfaction of resignation in order to search for a more morally acceptable position. However, an alternative would be to remain and accumulate enough credibility and value in the organization to change the culture from one that mandates information policies to one that allows the influence of professional communications skills to enhance the company's position in the marketplace through better performance and communications practice.

This is one of the areas of individual decision making that recurs for autonomous moral agents. To leave before assessing the possibilities for influencing the culture may be an egoistic act that is ultimately difficult to defend, while to remain in the face of an intractable system would cause loss of the individual's ability to act with moral autonomy. Thus, neither the action of staying with the hope of bringing about change nor of leaving in despair may be universally advisable.

Good judgment is required in such instances—judgment that returns us to recognition that development of a moral philosophy serves one better than reliance on moralizing. As professional persuaders confront morally problematic situations, it is helpful to have a principle-based list of questions to ask themselves. This ensures a thoughtful process of decision making, rather than reliance on intuition as a guide.

CONFLICT OF INTEREST

Professional persuaders necessarily have two masters. They should be loyal to their clients or employers, and they have a corollary loyalty to society to not cause unnecessary harm. The nature of persuasion is such that audiences will be deprived of some information. The nature of these conflicts suggests the need for persuaders to identify their thresholds, as discussed above. However, because of divided loyalties, conflicts of interest are an ever-present possibility for professional persuaders and are often particularly intense for third-party professionals, such as advertising agency personnel who develop and place advertising in the media for clients. Because agencies are trusted by clients to act in the best client interest in message and media selection, their professional skills give them great leeway in the placement of commercial messages. Because media outlets themselves are very competitive, it is natural for them to bring pressure on agencies to select their medium in the placement of commercial messages, but if they are to act as autonomous moral agents, their decisions should be thoughtful and well-informed.

It is not uncommon for media outlets to offer agency executives a wide range of inducements, from free trips around the world to gifts for the home, to persuade them to favor their medium over others. These gifts are intended to call attention of agency executives to the medium, but they may also have the effect of creating both an actual conflict of interest and a perceived conflict of interest for the agency if the inducements are accepted.

The two considerations in conflict of interest have to do with both whether the conflict does in reality shift loyalty from client to someone else and whether it appears to shift that loyalty. Both are deadly for a professional persuader intent on building and maintaining professional credibility. When a conflict occurs, the client, who should expect the agency to be loyal, loses some of that loyalty and, when inducements are involved, the agency may be seen as placing advertising on the basis of inducements, rather than in media that will best serve the client's objectives. The moral obligation is to serve the client, who presumably pays well for loyalty, rather than to shift loyalties to others, collecting from both the client and the medium offering gifts.

MAKING REASONED DECISIONS

Professional persuaders, as well as other communicators, have a huge capacity for doing harm through thoughtless and selfish professional efforts.

Even the most conscientious may inadvertently harm audiences with thoughtless actions or because they yield their moral autonomy to clients and employers. If society is to be served by its communications professionals, and if they are to act as autonomous moral agents, their decisions should be thoughtful and well-informed.

The following checklist provides self-test questions to help assess the ethics of most common activities in the field. Note the first item in the checklist includes the words "substantial harm" on the assumption that persuaders will cause more harm than journalists to the vulnerable. Although some harm to the defenseless appears inevitable in a competitive society, the professional persuader bears a moral obligation in common with the journalist to avoid causing unnecessary harm. Each person needs to thoughtfully evaluate the tolerable social limits of such harm. The cumulative decisions of the professions will determine, to a substantial degree, the quality of society.

Checklist for Ethical Decision Making: Public Relations and Advertising

Checklist for persuasion ethical decisions (not necessarily in order of importance):

1. Does my client/cause make a legitimate public contribution? Do I know enough about my client/cause and its products/ideas that I can advance my client/cause effectively while still protecting the public from substantial harm? What is my obligation here? Why?
2. Can I justify merely passing on what my client wishes me to say (a bulletin board function for a professional communicator in news releases or in commercial messages), or do I have a professional responsibility to assess the credibility and effects of what the client wishes to do?
3. Have I verified the information my client wishes me to distribute to determine its truth? Am I realistically satisfied my client has been honest with me? Why does it matter?
4. Who or what will be harmed by this action?
5. Do, or should, those who are harmed have the means to defend themselves in the public arena? Are vulnerable innocents more than incidentally affected by my messages?
6. Have I assured myself that my messages contain truthful statements?
7. Are there statements I have omitted that would help my audience avoid physical or catastrophic psychological harm?

8. The presentation of selective truth involves some misleading. Have I moved beyond normal misleading with positive or arguable statements into misleading with statements I believe are false?
9. On principle, does my client have a right to be heard publicly, whatever negative feelings I may have about the cause/product?
10. Is unease I may feel about what I am called upon to do based on principle or on tradition (e.g., naming competitors or opponents in copy or not being publicly critical of competitors)?
11. Have I identified the difference between making false statements in support of my client's product/cause and merely providing, selectively, supportive information which is true?

Summary

This chapter examined the complex notion of truth telling in the persuasion professions. Some persuasion professionals may work in sports, others in entertainment, and some in marketing a variety of products that are designed for sale. Ethics is an area that presumes that truth telling should be paramount in an individual's life. But sometimes it is hard to know if one is being told the Truth or the approximate truth. Often the approximate truth is a combination of stories and events told through the eyes of a media professional.

One section of this chapter focused on what philosophers have said about persuasion and using lying as a means to persuade. Once again, there is no clear statement as to which one path to follow to avoid deception and lies in the persuasion business. Ethics will often lead us down a road of rational justification where we believe we will find a lovely answer to our ethical problem. Sometimes we may find that answer. Other times we expect to find that answer gift-wrapped. Those pretty boxes do not exist, however. Making ethical decisions often requires time, energy, rational thought, and sometimes mistakes.

Sometimes deception is used by media organizations to bring about what they believe would be a greater good. This chapter attempted to clarify that the moral task for persuaders is to decide which thresholds must not be crossed in the persuasion process. The ethical decision-making checklist provided details eleven essential points in maintaining an ethical approach to media persuasion.

The final chapter focuses on the history of ethics in the media professions. Central to the discussion are individuals who have impacted the profession in terms of freedoms, innovations, scholarship, and technological advances. The final chapter also notes the current scholarship in field of media ethics and examines the future of media practices in light of cyberspace.

Moral Reasoning Questions

1. Should you reserve the right to tell "white lies," while expecting others to be honest with you?
2. If you are certain in your own mind that gifts from media do not influence your decisions as you serve clients, is it appropriate for you to accept a five-day skiing vacation in the Canadian Rockies from a television station?
3. How can truth be said to be less important than an obligation to vigorously defend a client's misdeeds before the media?
4. Provide an example of an instance in which a lie might inspire or protect someone. What is your personal moral belief about this?
5. What philosopher might help you decide it is acceptable to deceptively persuade for a greater cause?

Contemporary Case in Advertising: New Job, Small Agency, Lousy Assignment

As a brand new advertising graduate in a very competitive job market, you accept a position as an account executive in a small agency. You have brought with you, enhancing your value, a unique software package you developed as an undergraduate that works with a popular spreadsheet in producing calculations valuable in identifying target audiences and their habits. You are the only person in the agency, so far, who is able to utilize the software. You are the third person in the firm, in addition to two partners. The basic business of the agency has been in the field of political campaigning, with your agency representing the dominant political party in your area, an account that provides the vast majority of the company's income. The agency has a few retail accounts to tide it over between election campaigns, but political campaigning is its stock in trade. With a general election two months away, the political party has sent the list of candidates to the agency. They range from a U.S. Senator to a county auditor. Among other candidates, you, as the new person, are assigned a person of questionable character who is the party's candidate for lieutenant governor of the state (the equivalent to the vice president in national politics). This person, as the party leaders and your bosses will tell you, is an embezzler, an adulterer, and a liar, among other things. The party has shielded his deplorable actions from public view because he has been a faithful party foot soldier for 15 years, and this position will be his reward. Furthermore, of course, the party offers, and the agency has accepted, a package—all (the candidates) or none. Your job is to get this liar, thief, and adulterer elected to public office. The resources of the agency are available to you, but you are the primary executive responsible for this candidate.

1. *Assuming you are morally outraged by this assignment, what should you do? Should you resign yourself to fulfilling this onerous responsibility ("That's the way the system works!"), or should you refuse and leave the agency? Why?*
2. *What are the consequences to others in either of these scenarios? Are there options for acting honorably between these two extremes?*
3. *Is it morally defensible to leave the agency and the political party in a crisis at a critical time in the election process? Is it morally defensible to accept the judgment of the party and promote whoever survives its process? Why?*
4. *Does it make any difference that this is a largely insignificant position and only becomes important if the governor dies or is forced from office?*
5. *On the other hand, you may feel comfortable placing such a character in public office. Why? Spell out your justification, citing the moral principles that allow you to do it.*

CONTEMPORARY CASE IN ADVERTISING: GAMBLING BROCHURE

As the only college intern working for a semester in a metropolitan area agency, you are given the task, on your first day, of producing a mailer brochure promoting sexually-oriented stage shows and gambling attractions at a hotel casino in a neighboring state—casino gambling is illegal in your state and the type of entertainment offered is not generally available in your state. The brochures, offering three-day bus excursions from your area to the casino, will be mailed to a list of men, all over 65 years of age. Your supervisor, in handing you a file folder containing photographs of nude, or nearly nude, showgirls and dancers for use in the brochure, explains this short-term contract job was inherited in a merger of agencies, and everyone finds it distasteful. The contract will not be renewed once it expires in a year. Technically, you are appropriately qualified to do this job, but you have strong negative feelings about both casino gambling and sexually-oriented entertainment. Additionally, you are not that excited about pandering to dirty old men; however, you do hope to work for this, or another local agency, once you graduate.

1. *Would it make any difference whether you were a male or a female intern with this assignment? Why?*
2. *Does it make a difference that the activities promoted are legal, though not in your own state?*
3. *What are your options and the benefits/consequences of each?*
4. *What are the altruistic moral arguments in an open information society for refusing to accept this assignment? Who will be harmed? Is that harm unjustifiable because it strikes at vulnerable innocents?*
5. *Is there any justification for accepting the assignment but producing an ineffective brochure?*

Contemporary Case in Public Relations: The Trucking Company's Safety Problems

As public relations director for a large interstate trucking company, you must respond publicly to a rash of traffic mishaps in which your company's trucks have been involved. A state public safety director has accused your company of negligence in truck maintenance, citing three instances of faulty brakes found in your trucks in his state in the past six months. Your company's president assures you that maintenance procedures keep the trucks in faultless condition and that the company's trucks are among the safest on the road.

1. *As you stand before television cameras to defend your company, is it appropriate to say your president has assured you the trucks are safe?*

*Or must you speak as the company, declaring that the trucks are safe,
placing your personal integrity behind the statement?*

2. *What harms are done by your act of passing along the president's
denial? What are the benefits?*

3. *Is there a threshold that is morally indefensible for you to cross in your
announcement and defense of your company? Why?*

4. *Should your consideration of the dangers posed to innocent people by
faulty truck brakes be a part of your presentation?*

SELECTED SOURCES

Bailey, F. G. (1991). *The prevalence of deceit.* Ithaca, NY: Cornell University Press.

Baker, L. W. (1993). *The credibility factor: Putting ethics to work in public relations.*
Homewood, IL: Business One Irwin.

Barney, R. D. & Black, J. (1994). Ethics and professional persuasive communications.
Public Relations Review, 20, 233–248.

Bivins, T. H. (1987). Applying ethical theory to public relations. *Journal of Business
Ethics, 6,* 195–200.

Bivins, T. H. (1988). Professional advocacy in public relations. *Business and Professional Ethics Journal, 6,* 82–91.

Bivins, T. H. (1989). Ethical implications of the relationship of purpose to role and
function in public relations. *Journal of Business Ethics, 8,* 65–73.

Bloom, A. (Trans.) (1968/1991). *The Republic of Plato,* 2nd ed (p. 139). New York:
Basic Books.

Bok, S. (1978). *Lying: Moral choice in public and private life* (pp. 272–275). New York:
Vintage Books. (Bok provides an appendix with excerpts on lying from several
philosophers, including Sidgwick.)

Bok, S. (1983). *Secrets: On the ethics of concealment and revelation.* New York: Vintage Books.

Coady, C. A. J. (1992). The morality of lying. In St. James Ethics Center: *To tell a lie:
Truth in business and the professions.* Sydney, Australia: St. James Ethics Center.

Deaver, F. (1990). On defining truth. *Journal of Mass Media Ethics, 5,* 168–177.

Englehardt, E. E., & Evans, D. (1994). Lies, deception and public relations. *Public Relations Review, 30*(3), 251.

Gandhi, M. (1931/1991). Young India. In F. G. Bailey (Ed.), *The prevalence of deceit*
(p. 7). Ithaca, NY: Cornell University Press.

Kant, I. (1785/1930/1963). *Lectures on ethics* (p. 228) (L. Infield, Trans.). New York:
Harper & Row.

Kant, I. (1949). On a supposed right to lie from benevolent motives. In L. W. Beck
(Ed.), *The critique of practical reason and other writings in moral philosophy* (pp.
92–96). Chicago: University of Chicago Press.

Public Relations Society of America. (2000). "Member Code of Ethics 2000."

Rousseau, J. J. (1782/1953). *Reveries of the solitary walker* (p. 176) (J. M. Cohen, Trans.). New York: Penguin Books.

Solomon, R. C. (1993). What a tangled web: Deception and self-deception in philosophy. In M. Lewis & C. Saarni (Eds.), *Lying and everyday life*. New York: Guilford Press.

Van Ekeren, G. (1988). *The speaker's sourcebook* (p. 213). Englewood Cliffs, NJ: Prentice Hall.

Wittgenstein, L. (1968). Notes for lectures on "private experience" and "sense data." *Philosophical Review, 77,* 249.

8

THE HISTORY AND FUTURE OF MEDIA ETHICS

CONTEMPORARY CASE IN JOURNALISM:
STAGING THE NEWS

Wendy Bergen, an award-winning TV news reporter in Denver, Colorado, was found guilty of three felony charges related to staging a dogfight for a TV news series. Fired along with Wendy were veteran television photographers Jim Stair and Scott Wright. Bergen's three convictions were for staging a muzzled dogfight for her ratings-week series Blood Sport; *for conspiring to arrange the illegal match; and for obstructing justice while trying to mask the truth about the series. Bergen has given up the notion of ever working in journalism again, as has one of the photographers, Jim Stair. "I think the system for reporting needs to be changed. I would like to see just news. We shouldn't have to worry about ratings and commercials for ads," said Bergen. She then asked that "we" be omitted from her quote, acknowledging that she is no longer a journalist.*

    The history of mass media ethics does not offer moral theory or a model of ethical decision making to someone like Bergen. The history does, however, afford her the ability to understand the processes of the First Amendment that have survived as individuals, governments, and commercial enterprises have tested its boundaries. Media history can be helpful in informing Bergen and others that numerous media professionals have made similar mistakes; some were punished and others were not. The history of mass media ethics is long and distinguished, and it is a topic that was set aside for the final chapter of this book because it weaves together the ideas of the important thinkers, contributors, workers, educators, and professionals who have shaped the fields of the media professions and ethics. This chapter also includes a discussion of current academic work in media professions and concludes with a look at the future—the ethical challenges of the cyberspace age.

History

Developing better ethical practices within media is not a new topic. Indeed, it has roots that can be traced back to at least the seventeenth century and, perhaps, to tribal views of the distributors of news. As the practice of distributing news developed, so has our understanding of the moral responsibilities of mass media. The industry and courts have forged a number of principles over time, leaving an indelible imprint on society. They have also created a number of expectations. Throughout each era, new rules were fashioned for the mass media industry either from within the industry or externally. For example, when Joseph Pulitzer and William Randolph Hearst competed for readers, they created a major stir in the country as articles on divorce, death, and money covered the pages of their newspapers. Practitioners in public relations went through much ethical soul-searching in 1985. Anthony Franco, the president-elect of the Public Relations Society of America (PRSA) accepted the presidency while under investigation for securities violations. He did not reveal this information to the 13,000-member society when he took office and subsequently resigned the position.

There are other interesting incidents in advertising and public relations with ethical implications; however, many of the major historical events that have influenced mass media ethics happened within the field of journalism. When journalists made major breakthroughs in achieving freedom of the press, these freedoms had a major impact on other areas of media ethics. In fact, press freedom has been a contentious topic since the colonial period.

The Colonial Period

Zenger

As restrictive British laws were transplanted to America and even leaders of the new nation disagreed on whether a free press would serve the needs of a democracy, the granting of press freedom was an uncertainty. During the colonial period of this country, many writers and publishers were concerned about being jailed for printing publications that contained information deemed controversial by British rulers. The first individual to test press freedoms through the courts was a German immigrant, John Peter Zenger. In 1743 he was jailed and tried the following year for the crime of seditious libel. As editor for the *New York Weekly Journal*, Zenger had criticized New York Colonial Governor William Cosby. Zenger's attorney, Andrew Hamilton, argued that the criticisms of Cosby were true and, therefore, did not constitute libel. The prosecution did not claim Zenger's comments were lies; it merely stated that the truth of the comments exacerbated the crime of seditious libel. Andrew Hamilton did not argue his case on a free press foundation per se; instead, he focused on the right of an average citizen to complain about an incompetent government. The jury found in favor of Zenger.

Jefferson and Hamilton

Thomas Jefferson agreed with the legal precedent in Zenger's case, and in 1787 Jefferson made a plea for liberty and freedom of the press based on writings from the Enlightenment philosophers, primarily Hobbes, Kant, Locke, and Rousseau. In a statement to Edward Carrington regarding the need for the people to be the "censors" of their government, Jefferson said:

> The way to prevent these irregular interpositions on the people is to give them full information of their affairs through the channel of the public papers, and to contrive that those papers should penetrate the whole mass of the people. The basis of our government being the opinion of the people, the very first object should be to keep that right; and were it left to me to decide whether we should have a government without newspapers, or newspapers without a government, I should not hesitate a moment to prefer the latter. (Jefferson, 1939, p. 93)

Jefferson admonished the press to act as watchdogs of the government and to seek truth always. As an anti-Federalist, Jefferson believed that liberty and freedom were part of a press that was unfettered by any government impositions.

As a Federalist, Alexander Hamilton did not hold this same reverence for unlimited press freedoms. Hamilton believed that unregulated power in the hands of any one organization other than the government was foolish. In *The Federalist Papers*, he strongly advised press controls.

What signifies a declaration that "liberty of the press shall be inviolably preserved?" What is the liberty of the press? Who can give it any definition which would not leave the utmost latitude for evasion. I hold it to be impracticable; and from this, I infer, that its security, whatever fine declarations may be inserted in any constitution respecting it, must altogether depend on public opinion, and on the general spirit of the people and of the government. (Hamilton, 1987, No. 84)

Madison, Boller, de Tocqueville

James Madison and William Boller strongly supported the Jeffersonian ideal. George Washington, a Federalist, threw his support behind Hamilton in the press freedom discussion. In an early rendition of the Bill of Rights, Madison's recommendation on press freedom was as follows:

The people shall not be deprived or abridged of their right to speak, to write, or to publish their sentiments; and the freedom of the press, as one of the great bulwarks of liberty, shall be inviolable. (Levy, 1997, p. 48)

In 1766 William Boller said that a press must have the ability to examine and write about public happenings. He believed it to be an absolute right of free people in a free country (Boller, 1767). People of Jefferson's day expected publishers to seek liberty, truth, and virtue and to do so was in fact ethical.

With underpinning from the work of Jefferson, Madison, and Boller, Tunis Wortman wrote *A Treatise Concerning Political Enquiry and the Liberty of the Press* in 1800. In this work, he supports freedom of the press and further ties the values of society to the values that must be held by the press:

The Press is undeniably possessed of extensive influence upon Government, Manners, and Morals. Every exertion should, therefore, be employed to render it subservient to Liberty, Truth and Virtue. (1800, p. 273)

Alexis de Tocqueville's *Democracy in America,* published in 1848, also gives strong imperatives for media practitioners. He writes about a strong and independent country, placing the morality of the press as an essential foundation in America. "We should underrate [newspapers'] importance if we thought they just guaranteed liberty; they maintain civilization" (p. 517).

During the industrial and progressive eras of the 1850s and beyond, many publishers discovered the wealth the media industry could provide. As newspapers started making large profits, philosophies of the press became more market driven and began developing the tools necessary for large increases in circulation and profits. These tools included "high speed linotypers and presses, typewriters, metal for type, telegraphy to make news instantaneous, swift transportation. . ." (Bessie, 1938, p. 23).

A press critic of the time, Simon Bessie believed literacy and naiveté were important factors in the increase in profits in the media industry, describing "a great reading public of simple tastes and rudimentary education" (1938, p. 23). An attitude emerged during this time that the media could help individuals to be better-educated and finer citizens.

JOURNALISM BECOMES AN ACADEMIC DISCIPLINE

Because of ethical concerns regarding press freedom, in the 1850s university educators and journalists began discussing higher education requirements for journalists. If journalistic writings did in fact have a far-reaching impact on society, they felt that journalists as well as their professors should be trained for this moral responsibility. In 1856 George Lunt suggested journalism education with guidelines in ethics as the impetus.

> I am sure, I should be glad to see a college, or a commission established, to settle upon a firmer and fairer basis the theory of editorial qualifications . . . to raise the standard of instruction, in ethics, as well as in learning, amongst those, whose duty and whose privilege it is to teach. (Lunt, 1857; Dicken-Garcia, 1989, p. 218)

The first college journalism course was set up by Robert E. Lee in 1867 at what was then known as Washington College. In order to get students into the program, Lee offered scholarships to any students taking the journalism course who wanted "to make practical printing and journalism their business life" while working an hour a day at a college printing plant. A solid portion of this curriculum was the ethical implications inherent in the profession.

In 1871, Yale University set up a new curriculum under the umbrella of the School of Journalism. Required courses were in political science, history, and British literature. Yale University faculty had not intended the term *journalism* to refer to newspaper and printing work, and no courses in editorial or news writing were offered. Instead, they underscored the general need for writing and disseminating ideas in printed form (Hudson, 1873, p. 24).

It was the Washington College and Lee course in journalism that became the model for other colleges and universities rather than the Yale University curriculum, and journalism courses were subsequently started at Kansas State College in 1873, followed by Cornell University in 1875, University of

Missouri in 1878, University of Denver in 1882, Temple University in 1889, Iowa State University in 1892, University of Pennsylvania in 1893, Indiana University in 1893, University of Kansas in 1894, University of Michigan in 1895, and University of Nebraska in 1898 (Mirando, 1993, p. 7).

THE AGE OF SENSATIONALISM

The age of sensationalism began at the end of the nineteenth century and lasted two decades into the twentieth century as politicians, publishers, and educators examined media ethics and media professionalism. The two periods used to highlight the age of sensationalism are known as **yellow journalism** and muckraking.

Yellow Journalism

Joseph Pulitzer and William Randolph Hearst were the most notable publishers of the time. Some historians believe that yellow journalism was initiated with Pulitzer's philosophy in the *World*, a New York City newspaper. He believed that the common person wanted to read about crime, sports, fashions, romance, and scandal, and that is what his paper printed (Drewry, 1989). Although Pulitzer enjoyed sharing his opinions through the editorial page, his true genius is seen in his approach to journalism. Not only were the reports in newspapers sensational, but headlines were also greatly enlarged, as were photographs and drawings. Sunday supplements and comics were also very popular. The name *yellow journalism* came from the color used in a popular comic strip title "The Yellow Kid" (Emery, 1984, p. 285).

William Randolph Hearst copied most of Pulitzer's techniques in the *San Francisco Examiner*. However, Hearst often went a step beyond reporting the news; he created it. On one occasion his *New York Journal* obtained a court injunction that stalled a gas company's request for a city franchise. Pleased by the success, the paper adopted the motto, "While Others Talk, the *Journal* Acts" (Emery, 1984, p. 286). As publisher, Hearst not only determined what values were best for the city, but also imposed those values. Furthermore, the newspaper's scope of interest was not confined to covering local news as war became an interesting prospect for the country and tabloids of the time. Some media critics hold Hearst responsible for starting the Spanish-American War. Hearst's papers not only ran sensational stories about Cuba and Captain-General Valeriano Weyler, but Hearst, his editors, and reporters also attended the war:

The newspapers fought the war as determinedly as they had fostered it. Some 500 reporters, artists and photographers flocked to Florida, where the American army was mobilizing, and to the Cuban and Puerto Rican fronts. . . . Leading the *Journal's* contingent was the publisher himself, who exuded enthusiasm as he directed the work of his staff of twenty men and women, reporters, artists and photographers, including a motion picture man. (Emery, 1984, p. 293)

The sensational journalism trend soon involved an estimated one third of the metropolitan dailies in 1900, and it took about another ten years for a new philosophy in journalism to take over. The sensationalism of newspapers fighting each other to expand their audiences and the public reactions are interesting forerunners of today's trends in which media are fighting to recapture audiences. Journalism's evolution during the early years of the twentieth century provides a fascinating study of ethics on the move.

The Muckrakers

Numerous critics wrote scorching indictments of the members of the press who participated in yellow journalism. Yet during this time some publications started a reform movement fostered by an ethic that held that social responsibility was fundamental in covering the news. The reporters and writers of this era were dubbed **muckrakers** by Theodore Roosevelt. Noted muckraking included Ida Tarbell's investigations into unethical practices at Standard Oil, Lincoln Steffans's writings on civic corruption, and Samuel Hopkins Adams' attack through *McClure's* magazine on the patent-medicine trade. Upton Sinclair exposed and criticized the press in *The Brass Check: A Study of American Journalism*. Sinclair's exposé is still a controversial classic in examining the ethics journalists and publishers should possess.

The muckrakers did not just expose corruption. Through editorials, they also appealed to the American conscience, contending that the American people were socially responsible for the widespread corruption. They urged the American people to abandon their complacency and truly insist on strong morals in government and businesses. The following 1904 excerpt is from an editorial by Lincoln Steffans on personal, business, and political corruption:

And it's all a moral weakness; a weakness right where we think we are strongest. Oh, we are good, on Sunday, and we are 'fearfully patriotic' on the Fourth of July. . . . We break our own laws and rob our own government, the lady at the custom-house, the lyncher with his rope, and the captain of industry with his bribe and rebate. The spirit of graft and lawlessness is the American Spirit. (Emery, 1984, p. 325)

Roosevelt wanted to blame problems of corruption on a sensationalistic press, but the muckrakers would not accept the Roosevelt characterization. During the muckraking years, the press demanded more social responsibility from business, government, medicine, and itself. However, at the same time, the public and government were demanding more professionalism from the press. The passage of the 1906 Pure Food and Drug Act followed shortly after the publication of numerous magazine articles exposing corruption in business, medicine, and government.

After the publication of another Upton Sinclair book, *The Jungle*, the government accepted more responsibility in controlling the substances in food and medicines, particularly. This 1906 novel, set in Chicago, portrays immigrant workers in unsanitary meat-packing houses. In 1912, the federal government passed the Newspaper Publicity Law, requiring that all advertisements be clearly marked as such. In 1914, the Federal Trade Commission was created to oversee practices in businesses and trades, including newspapers and other media. Publications supporting the writings of muckrakers in a sense reflected a social role designed to establish the morality of the new century.

The criticism of the media and the citizenry by Steffans, Sinclair, and Tarbell may have been a factor that brought the discussion of newspaper ethics into the academic media arena. In one of the first books on media ethics, Nelson A. Crawford opposed Sinclair's views of a degenerate and failed press system. He reminded Sinclair that improper reporting was not just something done by the liberal press. He maintained that the conservative press made its share of mistakes in judgment, accuracy, and fairness (1924, pp. 72, 73).

ETHICAL REFORMS IN MEDIA AND ACADEMICS

In the 1910s, ethical reform in media still intermingled with academic advancement. The first Conference for the Teachers of Journalism (today's Association for Education in Journalism and Mass Communication [AEJMC]) was held in 1910. In the introduction to his book, *Newspaper Writing and Editing* (1913), Willard Bleyer reported that at this conference the challenge was issued that "Every professor of journalism must write a text-book on journalism in order to justify his claim to his title" (p. viii). Another notable happening of this period was Joseph Pulitzer's $2 million donation to establish a graduate school of journalism. A year after his death, Columbia's

Pulitzer School of Journalism opened in 1912. Also by 1912, 31 colleges offered journalism courses (Emery, 1987, p.3).

THE ETHICAL LEGACY OF THE 1920S

The 1920s was a time of major discussion in media ethics. The first six textbooks in media ethics were printed, as practitioners and academics determined the place of ethics and morality in the arena of the capitalist. Because the media industry is the only area of business protected by the Constitution through the First Amendment, a vigorous discussion of the limits of this privilege erupted.

Frederick Lewis Allen related events of 1920s in his historical account, *Only Yesterday*. He sketched the environment that affected the media discussions, recounting how the United States went through some major upheavals during the 1920s. Women were constitutionally given the right to vote, yet a person's right to drink alcohol was constitutionally taken away. Three presidents held office during the decade, with one of the presidents, Warren G. Harding, dying under suspicious circumstances after only 2 years in office. Graft and corruption abounded in his administration, yet most of the public, pursuing wealth, ignored the charges in the Teapot Dome Scandal.

According to Allen, after pinching pennies during World War I, consumers were ready to spend money, particularly on new cars and radios. Morality among capitalists was equated with wealth. The majority of Americans desired money, sometimes engaging in unethical business practices to get it. Yet the moral perceptions of business changed dramatically with the crash of the stock market at the end of the decade.

Allen also notes the significant change of fashions in the 1920s, with hem lengths rising from the ankle to the knee and cotton stockings becoming an item of the past. Sexuality was prominent in magazine pages. Allen claimed that religious societies tried to reinforce and even legislate morality, yet the practices of a more open society continued (1931, p. 28–42). To match these freedoms, codes of ethical behavior were being written by various organizations, including newspapers, and enforcement of the codes became a focus of debates.

RECOMMENDING ETHICAL CONSIDERATIONS IN MEDIA

Into this decade of the 1920s came a significant philosophical work in journalism by Walter Lippmann entitled *Liberty and the News*. One chapter relates indirectly to press ethics. In the work, Lippmann maintained that the press needs morality because of its heavy influence on society. He stated that the business of journalism is to be more than honest; journalists must always be open to criticism and improvement. He advocates that mass media employees should abide by a strict code of behavior and professionalism. "The newspaper is in all literalness the bible of democracy, the book out of which a people determines its conduct. It is the only serious book most people read. It is the only book they read every day" (1920, p. 47).

Lippmann challenged the press to set its own regulations and codes, and he warned that if the press did not establish an ethical framework, Congress would do so. The following is Lippmann's suggestion for the press:

> The regulation of the publishing business is a subtle and elusive matter, and only by an early and sympathetic effort to deal with great evils can the more sensible minds retain their control. If publishers and authors themselves do not face the facts and attempt to deal with them, some day Congress, in a fit of temper, egged on by an outraged public opinion, will operate on the press with an ax. (1920, p. 76)

His second book, *Public Opinion,* published in 1922, considered a stronger rights base in its approach to morals, ethics, the media professional, and the individual. Lippmann allowed the press more room for professional judgment but warned that accuracy could be harmed by speculation about reasons for actions for which proper proof could never be found.

Another important mark of the 1920s was the publication of the *Journalism Bulletin,* which later became *Journalism Quarterly* (1929–present). In 1924 Lawrence Murphy was selected as the first editor. Murphy printed numerous stories in the journal supporting ethics courses in journalism. Murphy's plan outlined an ethics prerequisite course in which students thoroughly examined news values.

FIRST BOOKS ON MEDIA ETHICS

Also during this time, the first six books on media ethics were written (Nelson A. Crawford, *The Ethics of Journalism,* 1924; Thomas Lahey, *The Morals of Newspaper Making,* 1924; Leon Nelson Flint, *The Conscience of the Newspaper,* 1925; William Futhey Gibbons, *Newspaper Ethics: A Discussion of Good Practice for Journalists,* 1926; Paul Douglas, *The Newspaper and Responsibility,* 1929; and Albert F. Henning, *Ethics and Practices in Journalism,* 1932). The books have clear themes throughout, particularly in applied ethics situations. It is also interesting to note that after the sixth book was written, no more books with journalism ethics in the title appeared for another forty years.

The philosophical approaches of the authors generally fell into elaborations on liberal or communitarian systems of ethics. Some of the books advanced the view that reporters have a duty to uphold the principles of the country, the community, and the profession. Other books maintain that the most important focus of journalism is to distribute newsworthy information for the citizenry.

These six books contain over 70 topical discussions on media ethics, but, in common, advance theories on the following:

1. The newspaper's duties to society.
2. Binding codes of ethics, licensing, and professional requirements.
3. Crusading, editorializing, and expressing opinion within the newspaper.
4. Business practices and publisher's duties.
5. Suppression of news.
6. Conflicts in reporting crime and the courts.

PROFESSIONAL JOURNALS

In 1924 the first academic media journal, the *Journalism Bulletin*, was published. It featured an article on journalism courses in ethics in its second issue for the year. The article, written by L. N. Flint, posed questions similar to those that might be asked by a journalism ethics professor today. The article begins with the following quandary:

> A teacher of journalism who has had a class in ethics for a decade tells me that only rarely does one of his former students testify to having got anything out of the course that proved helpful in after years. (1924, p. 21)

Flint argues against merely lecturing in the classroom about ethics. Rather he believed in presenting case studies along with a writing laboratory approach to journalism ethics. "Nothing is more important, however, than that all these efforts to develop what may be called a practical course in ethics should be made in an atmosphere of idealism" (1924, p. 23). He concludes that ethics taught to young reporters strengthens their moral foundations and helps them once they are media practitioners.

Writings in ethics also continued with the help of a "generous grant" from an anonymous philanthropist to a group of journalism ethics scholars in 1928. According to Susan M. Kingsbury, lead researcher for the study, among those funded to conduct a critical analysis were "Bleyer, Cannon, Crawford, Flint, Gordon, Lee, Lippmann, Park, Salmon, Willey, Williams, and others" (p. 363). The enterprise involved directing a "quantitative, objective analysis" of journalism ethics. Their final project was to design instruments for measuring the social behavior of the press.

The project's results first appear in *Journalism Quarterly* in 1934 in a series of articles by Susan M. Kingsbury, Hornell Hart, and Associates. Entitled *Measuring the Ethics of American Newspapers,* Kingsbury and coauthors not only surveyed different foundational questions in journalism ethics, but also attack the notion of a binding code of ethics. The group's conclusion was that while ethics for a news organization are essential and should be based on Enlightenment philosophies. a national code of behavior would be harmful to the profession and the constitutionality of freedom of the press.

The articles later appear in her 1937 book, *Newspapers and the News.* One conclusion drawn in the book is as follows:

> What can be said at the present time, with scientifically grounded assurance, is that, though the ethical ideals avowed by newspaper associations are being violated continually, distinguished leaders are blazing the way toward better standards. (p. 6)

THE BASICS ABOUT CODES OF ETHICS

One reason for Kingsbury's research was political pressure. During the 1930s, Franklin D. Roosevelt's administration placed considerable pressure on the media industry to adopt codes of ethics as part of the National Reconstruction Act, as well as the National Industrial Recovery Act (NIRA). Newspaper editors and publishers were firmly opposed to the government's intervention; indeed, most newspaper editors preferred an informal code of ethics rather than a written one. The government reasoned that the American Medical Association and the American Bar Association had binding codes that accommodated their respective professions well. If journalism wanted to be considered a profession, it would need to adopt a code of ethics similar to those in the other professions. At the time, only three occupations were considered professions: medicine, law, and theology. Journalism, with or without a binding code of ethics, was destined to be the fourth. The following section explains the American history of codes of ethics and the concessions journalists were willing to make toward adopting a professional code.

JOURNALISM'S FIRST CODES OF ETHICS

In journalism, codes of ethics had been discussed since the writing of the Constitution. However, the first "code of conduct" for journalists was written by W. S. Lilly for the *Forum* in 1890. Editors and critics had toyed with the idea of listing rules, maxims, and duties for journalists, but it was not until 1911 that Will Irwin listed four areas of rules under his *Code of Ethics,* which was published in *Collier's Magazine.*

Two of the initial texts list codes of ethics in an appendix: Nelson Crawford in *The Ethics of Journalism* details seventeen different codes of ethics written by newspaper administrations, journalistic organizations, or individual philosophers. Leon Flint in *The Conscience of the Newspaper* lists twenty codes.

In 1923 a code of ethics was adopted by the American Society of Newspaper Editors (ASNE). The society was formed in 1922, and at its first meeting, in 1923, the membership adopted the code. At that time, ASNE's membership included more than three fourths of the editors and managing editors of daily newspapers for populations in excess of 100,000 in the United States. The association was interested in seven different areas of morality, which included the following:

1. Responsibility
2. Freedom of the press
3. Independence
4. Sincerity, truthfulness, and accuracy
5. Impartiality
6. Fair play
7. Decency

Sigma Delta Chi (SDX), the Society of Professional Journalists (SPJ), was formed in 1909 and developed the *SPJ/SDX Code of Ethics* in 1926, but neither the ASNE nor the SPJ/SDX codes were binding.

The codes were tested in 1929, when the ASNE recommended *Denver Post* Publisher Fred G. Bonfils be expelled from the profession for graft. Bonfils stifled stories his reporters had written about illegal oil leases associated with the Teapot Dome Scandal. Bonfils stood to make half a million dollars on the leases. The ASNE allowed Bonfils to resign on the grounds that the code was not legally binding. As a society, they could only encourage voluntary support of the "Canons of Journalism."

Because of Roosevelt's campaign for a binding code of ethics for journalists, the notion was discussed and debated at every meeting of the ASNE during 1933 and 1934. In 1933, an agreement was adopted that suggested rules for employment, but not a binding code of ethics. The ASNE was resolute that it would not modify rights of free speech nor the freedom of the press as constitutionally guaranteed.

PUBLIC RELATIONS, TV, AND RADIO CODES

Codes of ethics and professional standards for the practice of public relations were written by the Public Relations Society of America (PRSA) in the 1950s and revised in 1988. The National Press Photographers Association has an eight-point code of ethics. Their code concludes with the statement, "No code of Ethics can prejudge every situation, thus common sense and good judgement are required in applying ethical principles."

The Radio-Television News Directors have a code of broadcast news ethics. It was revised in 1987, and again in 2000. The American Advertising Federation has a brief code based on honesty, truth, and decency. (These codes appear in the Appendix.) The codes give resourceful, prudent, and professional counsel to media practitioners. Only the code of the public relations industry asks that persons report misdeeds of other practitioners and also be willing to testify at a hearing. The rest of the codes do not have any legal implications. Generally, the codes provide information on right and wrong behavior, acceptable and unacceptable actions, and situations that must be avoided for the sake of professionalism.

CODES OF ETHICS IN OTHER PROFESSIONS

In addition to the above-stated organizations, codes of ethics are incorporated in most professions, including most branches of communication. Codes of ethics have been established for the following organizations: American Society of Journalists and Authors, Inc.; Associated Press Managing Editors; American Advertising Federation; Association of Better Business Bureaus International; and the American Association of Political Consultants.

VIEWS ON CODES OF ETHICS

NO BINDING CODE OF ETHICS

The authors of the first books on journalism ethics worried that journalists would one day have to pass certain requirements to work within the media industry. Crawford believed that binding codes and professional licensing would be a result of a demand from practicing journalists rather than from the outside and believed the examining board would be composed of members of the profession. "A professional consciousness and the ethical and social implications flowing from this are necessary before any legal enactment can improve the status of journalism as a profession" (1924, Appendix 1).

Crawford however maintained that if the journalism profession decides to construct professional codes and standards, it must be done without enforcement by the courts or government. Any enforcement from either of these groups would be an infringement on the First Amendment and the concept of fourth estate.

Crawford reflected the view that ethics are best situated within the individual, rather than decided and enforced by the entire community. He expected the journalistic community to insist on the protection of rights for individuals within the profession as well as the community. He warned that binding professional guidelines could have a dire effect on the gathering and reporting of information.

SUPPORT FOR BINDING CODES OF ETHICS

William F. Gibbons in 1926 called for a binding code of ethics in journalism, contending that journalists are not called learned because the field of journalism is not a profession. He believed that a code would restrict entrance into the field of journalism and better define its boundaries. His justification is that law, medicine, and **theology** have binding standards of ethical conduct and that the media must do the same. He also contended that the code is necessary for the entire community and country.

> Ethical and spiritual advancement in the community is secured by bringing the popular conscience up to the standards of a vigorous or militant minority. The progress cannot be accomplished until the general intelligence of the body politic has been raised and the moral standard of the advanced thinkers has become the norm of the majority. (p. 50)

He cited individuals who maintain that the press demolishes legislation, dominates public opinion, and yet has no ideals or ethics. Gibbons also warned that anyone could buy a newspaper business and cited an example of a tyrannical Austrian ambassador who was not allowed to purchase the *New York Journal of Commerce*. Gibbons advocated a professional standard that would legislate who could and could not purchase newspapers.

Gibbons was perplexed as to why most journalists oppose all regulative measures, and found that unless journalists establish binding professional requirements, more severe restrictions through the legislatures and courts will follow.

Professional requirements, including binding codes, was a heated issue in the 1920s. Much of the debate regarding media codes of ethics reflects the political/ethical debates in communitarianism and liberalism (see Chapter 4). The communitarian writers believe it is an appropriate professional move to have requirements and restrictions. The move would give more credibility to the field of journalism. Liberals, however, will not trade liberty and press freedoms for a construct of "credibility," or even "norms."

FREEDOM OF SPEECH

In today's discussions on codes of ethics, freedom of speech is the reason most professional communication organizations refuse to adopt a binding code of ethics. Communication is viewed both professionally and legally as the only commercial profession that is protected by the U.S. Constitution. This concept was argued by Justice Potter Stewart in an address to the Yale University Law School.

> [T]he Free Press guarantee is, in essence, a structural provision of the Constitution. Most of the other provisions in the Bill of Rights protect specific liberties or specific rights of individuals: freedom of speech, freedom of worship, the right to counsel, and the privilege against compulsory self-incrimination—to name a few. In contrast, the Free Press clause extends protection to an institution. The publishing business is, in short, the only organized private business that is given explicit constitutional protection. (1975)

Even though it may appear to be problematic to award freedom of expression protection to private organizations, Stewart sees the alternative as unacceptable. He asserted the press could be relegated to the status of a public utility that is controlled in some part by the government. However, he stated, this is not the rights-based ethic given to the press by the founders of the Constitution. "Perhaps our liberties might survive without an independent established press. But the Founders doubted it, and, in the year 1974, I think we can all be thankful for their doubts" (ibid).

FREEDOM OF PRESS: HUTCHINS COMMISSION

Still impacting journalism ethics today is the work of the Hutchins Commission in 1942. This mammoth undertaking in academic scholarship on media ethics was also known as the Commission on the Freedom of the Press. The Hutchins Commission involved a distinguished group of scholars at the University of Chicago, with Chancellor Robert M. Hutchins as chair. It was funded by *Time* magazine's Henry Luce and the *Encyclopedia Britannica*. This group of scholars produced two books and numerous documents on media ethics. The Hutchins Commission compiled *A Free and Responsible Press* to help replace some of the worn-out rhetoric in journalism ethics. The Hutchins Commission believed that in the culturally pluralistic world of the 40s, a social responsibility theory of ethics would be most acceptable. They further recommended that journalism education be strengthened. Emphasizing that ethical standards for journalists must include professional standards, they recommended stronger analysis of numerous elements of a story, including background, context, analysis, interpretation, relevance, and thoroughness.

Hutchins Commission Recommendations

The Hutchins Commission, composed mostly of scholars, wanted to adopt a system of ethics that would guarantee freedom while at the same time affirm responsible professional goals. As an additional consideration, the Hutchins Commission did not want to alienate editors. The following are some of its recommendations:

1. The media should serve as "a forum for the exchange of comment and criticism." In other words, the public often felt alienated from the press. The Hutchins Commission recommended that editorial pages be open for divergent political views.
2. That the media provide "a truthful, comprehensive, and intelligent account of the day's events, in a context that gives them meaning." The Hutchins Commission warned that it was not appropriate just to repeat words said by someone; this was termed *false objectivity*. They emphasized that reporters must spell out the context of the news as well.

3. The press should be responsible for "the presentation and clarification of the goals and values of the society." This was a communitarian goal that many members of the press found hard to fulfill. Some
   editors and reporters believed it was not within their purview to explain goals and values for society.
4. The media should provide "full access to the day's intelligence." Fulfilling this requirement has always been easier said than done. In the
   1940s and 1950s, there was more news than the newspapers could
   print. In today's society, which is based on information and a profusion of sources, the problem is still extremely complex.
5. The media should project "a representative picture of the con-
   stituent groups in society." Media professionals were asked to represent all members of society, particularly minorities and
   underrepresented cultures.

Independent Commission to Continue Ethics Probe

Many concepts of ethical accountability were molded by the Hutchins
Commission and became the fabric for discussion and policy to follow. Another accomplishment of the group was a recommendation to establish an
independent commission to follow-up on the Hutchins Commission's
work. In its summary statement, the Hutchins Commission said:

> Freedom of speech and press is close to the central meaning of all liberty.
> Where men cannot freely convey their thoughts to one another, no other
> liberty is secure. Where freedom of expression exists, the germ of a free
> society is already present and a means is at hand for every extension of
> liberty. . . . At the same time, freedom of the press is certainly not an iso-
> lated value, nor can it mean the same in every society and at all times. It
> is a function within a society and must vary with the social context. It will
> be different in times of general security and in times of crisis; it will be
> different under varying states of public emotion and belief. (Commission
> on Freedom of the Press, 1947, p. 132)

Additional insights into the work of the Hutchins Commission were
voiced by two authors close to the project. William Ernest Hocking, a member of the Hutchins Commission, wrote *Freedom of the Press: A Framework
of Principles* (1947). The theme of his work was that the institutional press
was in need of reform. His book assisted in expanding guidelines and theories that would help keep the media free of government intervention yet foster support for professional growth.

Another advocate of media independence was Morris L. Ernst in *The First Freedom* (1946). Ernst, an attorney for the American Newspaper Guild, was active in the Hutchins Commission's discussions on media ethics. In *The First Freedom,* he stated:

> Press, radio and the movies are the weapons of liberty. They are the core of freedom, whether religious, economic or political. No conqueror has ever taken real freedom from a people if he has left to the vanquished their full rights of free expression. (p. 32)

Following the Hutchins Commission's reports, a handful of books were written in the 1950s and 1960s. By the 1970s a few more books and numerous articles were being written on the topic. In the twenty-first century the topic has become increasingly popular with the establishment of media ethics societies; journals, including the *Journal of Mass Media Ethics;* and hundreds of books.

MODERN MEDIA ETHICS

The history of mass media ethics is rich and distinguished, and it continues today, particularly with writings from the 1970s to the present. John C. Merrill started the process moving forward again in 1975 when he coauthored a text with Ralph D. Barney entitled *Ethics and the Press: Readings in Mass Media Morality.* It was the first widely published textbook to contain the word *ethics* in its title after a forty-year dearth. Another prolific author in mass communication ethics is Clifford Christians. Christians has tackled a variety of areas in mass media ethics; however, his theories, based on communitarian notions, generally posit that, because of Enlightenment theories, individuals are pushing for more rights yet at the same time are lacking an understanding of the need for community values. Christians, Merrill, and Tom Cooper have also tackled the issue of global needs in communication ethics.

Numerous authors have made contributions to mass media ethics through interviews, case studies, and media ethics theory. They include Jay Black, B. M. Swain, Lee Thayer, Lou Hodges, and John Hulteng. Some authors remind professional communicators of the importance of ethics through study, dialogue, and understanding the human condition, including Ralph Barney, Edmund Lambeth, H. Eugene Goodwin, Philip Meyer, Conrad Fink, and Richard Johannesen. Other authors express numerous views and help students and other through the analysis of ethics systems, including Philip Patterson, Lee Wilkins, and Deni Elliott.

Public Relations and Advertising Sources

Works on ethics are also being published in the fields of public relations and advertising. Authors who convey their ideas through case analysis and theory include Lee W. Baker, Tom Goldstein, Joyce Nelson, and Robert L. Dilenschneider. Some authors give personal experience combined with national topics, including Jerry terHorst, Jody Powell, and Edward L. Bernays. Strong ethical indictments of the persuasion professions come from books by Jeff Blyskal, Marie Blyskal, Patrick Jackson, Scott Cutlip, Allen Center, and Glen Broom.

The New Horizon: Cyberspace

Contemporary Case in Advertising: Cyberspace Ethics

Advertising groups have developed numerous mechanisms for gathering information on the Internet. Many advertising agencies use software devised by such companies as DoubleClick and Engage Technologies. The advertising agency will place banner ads on Web sites. An unsuspecting person surfing the Web may come across this type of Web site, and, once the banner ad is clicked, a cookie, a small bit of code that identifies the computer, will be placed onto the user's hard drive. Then, whenever the computer hits another Web site with another banner ad, the URL of that site is sent to the advertising agency, providing the agency with a partial list of the sites the computer has visited. This information, when accumulated for thousands, or hundreds of thousands of consumers, gives valuable clues to the advertising agency for businesses they service, including consumer interests and buying habits.

This tactic is not new. Mail order companies have kept track of their customer's habits for years in order to send them a particularly appealing catalogue. Is getting information about a person through the use of cookies an ethical practice? The user is unaware of the information being taken. Currently, those in advertising claim the practice is relatively harmless. One of the more notable consequences of cookie placement is that the consumer will receive banner ads that are more tuned to the consumer's particular interests. The solution to the quandary may be simple; why not make a notation at each cookie site asking the consumer if it is acceptable for information to be shared? Agencies do need more information in order to serve both their clients and their audiences better, but it is a question of whether powerless consumers are victimized by the practice.

A further ethical quandary involves the uses of information collected online. It may be a minor ethical infraction for the advertising executive to look inside a consumer's "brain," but is it something entirely different for the agency to distribute that information to anyone willing to pay the price?

The commercials that are sent our way may seem harmless enough. However, one reason for the unease and distrust that is felt for media is that as individuals we have been conditioned to believe that some information is not good for us to possess. That social conditioning combines with a widely and deeply held notion that our fellow human beings cannot be trusted to handle certain kinds of information well. The two, when added to a third notion that media are uncontrollable, and even out of control and needing pressures to be kept in bounds, explain a great deal of the public support for restraining press freedom and free expression.

CYBERSPACE IS CRITICAL TO MASS MEDIA

The newest area of mass media interest is cyberspace. Mass media have a need to study the ethical implications of cyberspace because of the limitless uses of the Internet, which uses the injunction of the First Amendment as protection for creation of text, images, pages, sites, links, and the next cyberspace event. The Internet may be used for commercial purposes or simply to share information; in either case, users demand the protection of freedom of speech. One day cyberspace is likely to dominate mass communication. If the ethical implications of usages of media in cyberspace are not studied now, it is likely they will be studied by those who need to correct careless mistakes made and harms brought about by media practitioners and others. Cyberspace may be the fastest-growing area of mass communication. Certainly, other disciplines also study technology, software, Web sites, Internet, and other aspects of computer use. Because an incredible amount of communication takes place via the Internet, it cannot be neglected within the discipline.

Cyber has become the shorthand expression for the computer world. On-line activities occur within the realm of cyberspace. Technologies dependent on or associated with computers are cybertechnologies. Usage of the word has grown. We shop at the cybermall, we are members in a cyberdemocracy, and those using these technologies are called cybergeeks, cyberpunks or cyber-junkies. Excessive users are said to have a cyberaddiction.

Where did the term originate? William Gibson used the word *cyberspace* in his 1984 novel *Neuromancer* to describe the technologically created reality that existed in the minds of characters who were physiologically hooked to computers. But perhaps Gibson was not responsible for coining the term at all. The word *cybernetics* originated in the 1960s with scientists and the government, who used the word to define information designed to control or govern systems and the environments that house them.

UNDERSTANDING THE IMPACT OF CYBERSPACE

As mentioned previously, being deprived of information, no matter what harm it does, limits the ability of citizens to make decisions that would help them flourish in their environment. Moreover, the participatory society is endangered when substantial numbers of people are not able to participate meaningfully with informed decisions. Some of the ethical problems identified with cyberspace include access, privacy, control, deception, health, environment, job displacement, anonymity, cyberaddiction and overuse, spamming, freedoms of expression, covert collection of personal data, copyright, commercialization, and even courtesy. There are also numerous criminal behaviors associated with cyberspace, including virus creation and hacking.

All these are areas in which power may be exercised over others under First Amendment protection and in the relative anonymity of the Internet; hence, the principles applied to all information collection and distribution tend to apply. Cyberspace magnifies ethics problems because of the huge amount of information that may now be distributed or the equally huge amount of personal information that may now be collected.

"Spamming," for example, which is an indiscriminate transmission of the same electronic message to many addresses that floods the Internet e-mail accounts of recipients and slows the overall system, has come under serious scrutiny recently for the inconvenience it causes while serving only the selfish purposes of the sender. In days gone by, the First Amendment protected the pamphleteer who distributed fliers by hand from house to house. Constitutional protections discouraged the use of local littering laws to prohibit such distribution.

Now, however, the cybernet pamphleteer, whether ideological or commercial, has a powerful distribution engine through which minimal effort and little cost is required to reach very large numbers of e-mail addresses. Whatever benefit accrues to the sender, it is at great inconvenience to most recipients; hence, the argument that those who would "spam" have at least a moral obligation (and perhaps an imminent legal one) to cull their address lists to include only those who are very likely to have an interest in the message. Similarly, the Internet system can be used to retain vast quantities of data on the buying habits and other characteristics of Internet users, including shoppers, with the information subsequently being used to direct persuasive messages at shoppers with the advantage of privileged knowledge driving the persuasion.

Both these practices, as well as the others listed above, raise the ethics question of whether someone with superior power (e.g., special skills in Internet usage) is harming vulnerable innocents (e.g., those who cannot lock "spam" from their e-mail without losing legitimate messages also and those who have no control over the contribution they make to persuader databases when they shop or browse on the Internet) for selfish purposes and to the detriment of those who are the targets of the techniques. The same applies to those who use the anonymity afforded by the Internet to distribute false messages, those who take orders and collect money over the Internet and distribute a product of lower value than the one promised and paid for, and so forth.

These special problems are created by the speed, scope, and anonymity of Internet usage, which requires special consideration that the power of the Internet will be used well and the protections of the First Amendment will not be abused. At the same time, it might be argued that Internet users need to develop the skills required to become competent users of the Internet to the extent that they graduate from being vulnerable innocents who are easily victimized. This would include being aware of how the information they provide is being used, and the development of the capacity to evaluate messages for their potential to victimize. The acceptance of moral obligations and behavioral adjustments of all Internet users will limit the abuses and keep the Internet free of various controls that often are suggested.

Diversity: Who Uses the Internet?

Contemporary Case in Cyberspace: Raymond's Lack of Access

Raymond lives in a small rural town. He has a disability and needs to keep in touch with governmental agencies to make sure his benefits are in order. He and his wife are the parents of four children and struggle to make ends meet. They do not have a computer, and they do not have access to the Internet. Raymond's benefits agency has told him that all services are now available online and that it will expedite the processing of his benefits if he will use the online service. Raymond still needs to use the telephone, but finds that he spends hours waiting for someone to take his call. He has asked the mayor of his town to set up a town computer, but the funds are not available. Raymond believes that the cyberworld is passing him by and that he will never have the funds to "climb on board."

It appears anyone can gain access who has the resources, but gaining access can be a problem for people such as Raymond. A 1995 Nielson survey found that over 37 million people have Internet access, and over 18 million individuals use the World Wide Web. Within recent years, surveys detailed that two thirds of all users were college graduates, usually male, and over 25% of these users had an income of over $80,000. With the rapid growth of the Internet, these numbers have changed and demographics are shifting.

In January 1999, a survey released by the Pew Research Center for the People and the Press reported that the exclusive and uppercrust group of Internet users was quickly changing faces. The Pew Center found that 40% of those online had never attended college, and 23% had an annual income less than $30,000. This results also showed that more women are using the Internet; 52% of new users were women and 48% were men (Hiebert, p. 399)

ISSUES OF INTERNET ACCESS

Ethical issues regarding Internet access definitely involve the notion that only the affluent are able to enjoy the benefits of cyberspace. Because the technology originated through scientific and governmental research, the Internet is now seen as belonging equally to all citizens. Nevertheless, citizens such as Raymond do not have computers and software to access the myriad options available through cyberspace. This may be our example of a widening information and participation gap between "haves" and "have nots" in America.

Washington, D.C., government offices have recently been identified as the national leader in providing dotcom services and states are being encouraged to follow suit. Most states now provide online postings for state jobs and the online transfer of benefits into accounts, such as welfare. Some states offer electronic tax filing, unclaimed property lists, and a variety of licenses. Most government agencies are pushing to make all government documents available on the Web. A form that may take five hours to complete and submit using phone calls and typewriters and standing in post-office lines could perhaps be completed in an hour through Web access to government sites.

The government still faces the problem of the lack of access to cybertechnology for the poor and the less educated. Government surveys find that several groups of disadvantaged citizens do not have access to personal computers, thereby experiencing falling levels of service and increasing levels of frustration. For example, consumers may have a simple question that they believe can be answered by telephone rather than a detailed search of Web sites. But attempts to find a human being at the other end of the phone can some days prove impossible. Consumer groups report individuals working through series of voice messages for days at a time before being able to receive a needed government service. It may be that a government office, proud of a series of online innovations, is still not helping the customers in desperate need of their services. Some consumer groups are continuing to work with the government on the issue of denied access through an overreliance on cybertechnology.

CYBERDEMOCRACY

Black activist and author, Abdul Alkalimat, has coined the phrase *cyberdemocracy* to describe the information divide in computer literacy, computer access, and computer information among races and socioeconomic classes. Alkalimat believes that a cyberdemocracy will depend on everyone having access and becoming active users of cybertechnology, just as literacy and universal education are today's prerequisites for democracy. "The current explosion of information technology is class based. The new concept being used to describe the growth of information rich and poor is the 'digital divide.' This is a critical problem" (January 19, 2001).

In a report by Hoffman and Novak, blacks were 75% as likely to use the Web as whites, but in 1998 they were only 60% as likely. In spring of 1997, 22.4% of whites (35.2 million) were using the Web compared with only 16.6% of blacks (3.9 million) having Web access. An interesting shift occurred in 1998, however, with 25.8% of whites (60.4 million) using the Web compared with 21.9% of blacks (5.2 million).

The principle of cyberdemocracy is being promoted in society by a variety of forces, especially e-commerce. It is very likely that computer access will become as readily available as telephone access (whites, 95.0%; blacks, 85.4%). This is suggested by free Web usage, free e-mail, and free Internet access being provided through institutions such as libraries, schools, and community computing centers. Universities are leading the way in requiring their students to join the cyberdemocracy. Computers are either issued to or required of many entering students, raising—for the twenty-first century—the standard of computer literacy. Universities are also expanding access, making participation possible 24 hours a day, seven days a week.

According to Alkalimat, "Blacks are not on the Web as much as whites, but it looks like they are trying to be" (2001). Black activists are working on projects to bring computer literacy to communities, including churches, doctor's offices, government waiting rooms, and other areas where community members are likely to congregate and use a computer. Alkalimat suggests that computers should be recycled and sent to community centers where individuals can learn basic computer skills.

Gaining access to a variety of free Web sites is also necessary for cyberdemocracy. As mentioned, much of today's communication occurs through free e-mail, and free Internet access to libraries, universities, and schools. Once basic computer access and literacy is achieved, a new world of free media access will open up. For example, there are numerous government health online services that provide free Web access. Although competing private industry services complain, these free services assure that vital information will be available to everyone who is online, not just those who can afford subscriptions to an exclusive online health service.

Part of this free access also involves the need for access to minority books, movies, magazines, and educational journals. Oftentimes, the works found on library Web sites are seen as "canons of enduring value" that frequently do not contain minority or female authors or contributors. Because of demands from activists, more minority authors and publications are available online. Underrepresented and minority populations need Internet access to cultural as well as educational materials.

PRIVACY

Increasing numbers of people are going to the Internet to get the news, buy groceries, reserve airline tickets, and even get medical advice. The convenience of going to the Internet for all these things is undeniable, but one also runs the risk of losing control of personal information. Privacy policies can usually let an Internet user know what information a Web site is gathering and how it is being used. Search engines, such as Excite and Lycos, often gather information on a user's "clickstream," which is a record of the sites a user visits. This background information gives companies an idea of which advertisements would interest particular users the most. However, some Internet companies have been hit with lawsuits claiming that they violated their own privacy policy by sharing personal information. If such allegations are correct, the companies could be convicted of fraud. Sometimes an online entity will work with a third party that does not have a privacy policy. People using that site may not be aware that their personal information is not covered by the privacy policy they think protects them.

SUMMARY

Media ethics has been tested and transformed by tumult, growth, war, economic turmoil, and amazing technological advances. Noted practitioners in the various media professions and interested governmental areas have carved the media systems we have today, complete with sweeping rights promised by the First Amendment. Media practices have advanced from trade areas to professional endeavors through academic disciplines and a strong scholarship focus. The media professions continue to grow and improve with help from the classroom as well as outstanding business models and innovations in delivery systems.

This chapter concluded with a focus on the growing cyberworld and its impact on the communication professions. To make reasoned, ethical decisions, a wide variety of information should be available to everyone. At present, millions of free Web and Internet sites are readily accessible. Yet computer access is not open and available to everyone. To have an informed public, the uses of technology need to be taught in a variety of venues, with multiple community sources open to all.

The final section of this book comprises two separate Appendixes. The first lists codes of ethics adopted by various media professional organizations. The second Appendix contains Web sites for a variety of media venues.

MORAL REASONING QUESTIONS

1. Which individuals from the colonial period had the greatest impact on the media of today? Explain.
2. Explain some of the complications inherent in the First Amendment to the Constitution. If you could change it, would you add more media freedoms or restrict media freedoms? Why?
3. Explain the difference between yellow journalism and the muckrakers. Who are the yellow journalists today? Do you approve of their work? Who are the muckrakers of today? Do you approve of their work? Examine and analyze.
4. Why are books, journal articles, and other scholarship important in the field of media ethics? How have books and journal articles advanced your particular field in mass media?
5. What are your views on codes of ethics? Should media organizations have binding codes of ethics? Is there a difference between a binding code of ethics for the newspaper industry and one for the advertising industry? Explain.

CLASSIC CASE: THE PHOTO OF NANCY AND RAISA

A photo of Nancy Reagan and Raisa Gorbachev appeared on the cover of Picture Week *magazine on November 25, 1985. The two presidential wives seemed to be quite friendly. The photo and the relationship, however, were fabrications. The photo of Nancy and Raisa was a composite, and their relationship was cool at the summit meetings they attended with their husbands.*

1. *Is it acceptable to make a composite photograph of an historic news event and pass it off as an actual document?*
2. *What are the ethical and historical implications of this composite photo?*
3. *Do codes of ethics need to be established regarding photographs? How will digital photography continue to make ethics in photography difficult?*

Classic Case: William Randolph Hearst and the Spanish-American War

Some historians cite the media for starting the Spanish-American War, as over 500 journalists covered the events. In particular, William Randolph Hearst is charged with inciting the conflict. Hearst's papers not only ran sensational stories about Cuba and Captain-General Valeriano Weyler, but over 20 editors, reporters, and artists also attended the war. Hearst led his newspaper's contingent. When he arrived, the American army was mobilizing on Cuban and Puerto Rican fronts.

1. *Are there times when the media has changed history? Do you believe that the Spanish-American War would have taken place as it did without the attention of the press?*
2. *Why were Hearst's tactics seen as particularly unethical? Would these tactics be seen as unethical today? Examine the ethical implications of sensational journalism.*
3. *How would a code of ethics have been helpful for Hearst and his newspaper group during that time? Would a code of ethics prevent a publisher or editor from covering a news story? Should it? What are the long-term implications of ignoring a code of ethics or ignoring the need for a thorough ethical analysis in the coverage of a major story?*

Selected Sources

Alkalimat, A. (2001) "Internet and Minority Discrimination." Paper given at AAC&U National Conference, New Orleans, La.

Alkalimat, A., Gills, D., & Williams, K. (1995). *Job?Tech: The technological revolution and its impact on society.* Chicago, IL: 21st Century Books.

Allen, Frederick Lewis (1931). *Only Yesterday An Informal History of the Nineteen-Twenties.* New York: Harper & Brothers, Publishers.

Bessie, Simon Michael (1938). *Jazz Journalism.* New York: E.P. Dutton and Co., Inc., p. 23.

Bleyer, Willard (1913). *Newspaper Writing and Editing.* Boston: Houghton Mifflin, p. viii.

Boller, William (1767). "Freeborn American." *Boston Gazette and Country Journal,* Mar 9.

Chenery, W. L. (1955). *Freedom of the Press.* New York: Harcourt, Brace.

Christians, C. G. (1977). Fifty years of scholarship in media ethics. *Journal of Communication,* 27, 19–29.

Christians, C. G., Ferre, J. P., & Fackler, P. M. (1993). *Good news social ethics and the press.* New York: Oxford University Press.

Commission on Freedom of the Press (1947). *A free and responsible press.* Chicago: University of Chicago Press.

Cooper, T. (1990). Comparative international media ethics. *Journal of Mass Media Ethics,* 5, 3–14.

Crawford, N. A. (1924) Do newspapers thwart criminal justice? *The Journalism Bulletin,* 1, p. 19.

Crawford, N. A. (1924). *The ethics of journalism.* New York: Alfred A. Knopf.

Davis, J., Hirschl, T., & Stack, M. (1997). *Cutting edge: Technology, information capitalism and social revolution.* London, UK: Verso.

de Toqueville, Alexis (1848/ 1969). *Democracy in America,* trans. George Lawrence, ed. J.P. Mayer. Garden City, N.Y.: Doubleday and Co., Inc. p. 517.

Douglas, P. F. (1929). *The newspaper and responsibility.* Cincinnati, Ohio: The Caxton Press.

Drewry, John Eldridge (1989). "Joseph Pulitzer," *The World Book Encyclopedia.* Chicago: World Book, Inc.

Emery, Edwin & Michael Emery (1984). *The press and America: An interpretive history of the mass media,* 5th ed. Englewood Cliffs, N.J.: Prentice-Hall, p. 285.

Emery, Edwin & Joseph McKerns (Nov., 1987). "AEJMC: 75 Years in the Making," *Journalism Monographs* no. 104:3.

Englehardt, E. E. (1994). Dissertation. *An interpretation of academic discourse in journalism ethics in the early twentieth century: A liberal and communitarian framework in Ethics.* University of Utah.

Ernst, Morris L. (1946). *The first freedom.* New York: The Macmillan Co., p. 32.

Flint, L. N. (1924). The course in ethics. *Journalism Bulletin,* 1, 2:21–24.

Flint, L. N. (1925). *The conscience of the newspaper.* New York: D. Appleton.

Gibbons, W. F. (1926). *Newspaper ethics: A discussion of good practice for journalists.* Ann Arbor, MI: Edwards Bros.

Goldstein, T. (1989). *Killing the messenger: 100 years of media criticism.* New York: Columbia University Press.

Hamilton, Alexander. (1987). "The Federalist No. 84," in Garry Willis, ed., *The Federalist Papers by Alexander Hamilton, James Madison and John Jay.* New York: Bantam Books.

Henning, A. F. (1932). *Ethics and practices in journalism.* New York: Long and Smith.

Heibert, Ray Eldon, & Carol Reuss (1998). *Impact of mass media: Current issues,* 4th ed. New York: Longman.

Hocking, William Ernest (1947). *Freedom of the press: A framework of principles.* Chicago: University of Chicago Press.

Hudson, Frederic. (1873). *Journalism in the United States.* New York: Harper, p. 24.

Jaska, J. A. & Pritchard, M. S. (1988). *Communication ethics: Methods of analysis.* Belmont, CA: Wadsworth.

Jefferson, Thomas (1939). Letter in *Thomas Jefferson on Democracy,* ed. Saul K. Padover. New York: Appleton-Century Company, Inc. p. 93.

Jenkins, T. & Om-Ra-Seti, K. K. (1997). *Black futurists in the information age.* San Francisco, CA: KMT Publications.

Kingsbury, Susan M., Hornell Hart and Associates (Sept. 1934). "Measuring the Ethics of American Newspapers." *Journalism Quarterly,* 11:3, p. 363.

Kingsbury, Susan M, Hornell Hart and Associates (1937). *Newspapers and the news: An objective measurement of ethical and unethical behavior by representative newspapers.* New York: G.P. Putnam's Sons, p. 6.

Lahey, T. (1924). *The morals of newspaper making.* Notre Dame, IN: Notre Dame University Press.

Lambeth, E. B. (1986). *Committed journalism: An ethic for the profession.* Bloomington, IN: Indiana University Press.

Lee, E. (1997). *The labour movement and the Internet.* London, UK: Pluto Press.

Levy, P. (1997). *Collective intelligence: Mankind's emerging world in cyberspace.* New York: Plenum Press.

Lippmann, Walter (1920). *Liberty and the news.* New York: Harcourt, Brace and House, p. 47.

Lunt, Georges (1857). *Three eras of New England* (Boston: N.P.) in Hazel Dicken-Garcia (1989): *Journalistic standards in nineteenth-century America.* Madison, WI: University of Wisconsin Press, p. 218.

Merrill, J. C. (1989). *The dialectic in journalism.* Baton Rouge, LA: Louisiana State University Press.

Merrill, J. C. (1977). *Existential journalism.* New York: Hastings House.

Meyer, P. (1987). *Ethical journalism.* New York: Longman, Inc.

Miller, S. (1996). *Civilizing cyberspace: Policy, power, and the information superhighway.* Reading, MA: Addison-Wesley.

Mirando, Joe (1993). "Journalism's First Textbook: Creating a News Reporting Body of Knowledge." Paper presented at the AEJMC 76th convention, August 14, 1993, Kansas City, Missouri, p. 7.

Pane, George Henry (1941). *History of Journalism in the United States.* New York: D. Appleton-Century Company.

Patterson, P. & Wilkins, L. (1991). *Media ethics issues and cases.* Dubuque, Iowa: William C. Brown Publishers.

Perelman, M. (1998). *Class warfare in the information age.* New York: St. Martins Press.

Schuler, D. (1996). *New community networks: Wired for change.* Reading, MA: Addison-Wesley.

Stewart, P. & Nimmer, M. B. (1975). Freedom of expression: The First Amendment speech and press guarantees. *Hastings Law Journal,* 26, 632–637.

Wortman, Tunis (1800). "A Treatise Concerning Political Enquiry, and the Liberty of the Press," in *Freedom of the Press,* 1800, (np) p. 273.

APPENDIX: SELECTED CODES OF ETHICS IN MASS MEDIA

- ◆ AMERICAN SOCIETY OF NEWSPAPER EDITORS (ASNE)
- ◆ ASSOCIATED PRESS MANAGING EDITORS
- ◆ GANNETT NEWSPAPER DIVISION
- ◆ RADIO-TELEVISION NEWS DIRECTORS ASSOCIATION (RTNDA)
- ◆ THE E. W. SCRIPPS COMPANY STATEMENT OF POLICY ON ETHICS AND PROFESSIONAL CONDUCT
- ◆ NATIONAL PRESS PHOTOGRAPHERS ASSOCIATION
- ◆ SOCIETY OF PROFESSIONAL JOURNALISTS (SPJ)
- ◆ SOCIETY OF AMERICAN BUSINESS EDITORS AND WRITERS
- ◆ PUBLIC RELATIONS SOCIETY OF AMERICA
- ◆ AMERICAN ADVERTISING FEDERATION
- ◆ AMERICAN ASSOCIATION OF ADVERTISING AGENCIES

AMERICAN SOCIETY OF NEWSPAPER EDITORS (ASNE)

ASNE STATEMENT OF PRINCIPLES

ASNE's Statement of Principles was originally adopted in 1922 as the "Canons of Journalism." The document was revised and renamed "Statement of Principles" in 1975.

Preamble

The First Amendment, protecting freedom of expression from abridgment by any law, guarantees to the people through their press a constitutional right, and thereby places on newspaper people a particular responsibility. Thus journalism demands of its practitioners not only industry and knowledge but also the pursuit of a standard of integrity proportionate to the journalist's singular obligation. To this end the American Society of Newspaper Editors sets forth this Statement of Principles as a standard encouraging the highest ethical and professional performance.

Article I

Responsibility

The primary purpose of gathering and distributing news and opinion is to serve the general welfare by informing the people and enabling them to make judgments on the issues of the time. Newspapermen and women who abuse the power of their professional role for selfish motives or unworthy purposes are faithless to that public trust. The American press was made free not just to inform or just to serve as a forum for debate but also to bring an independent scrutiny to bear on the forces of power in the society, including the conduct of official power at all levels of government.

Article II

Freedom of the Press

Freedom of the press belongs to the people. It must be defended against encroachment or assault from any quarter, public or private. Journalists must be constantly alert to see that the public's business is conducted in public. They must be vigilant against all who would exploit the press for selfish purposes.

Article III

Independence

Journalists must avoid impropriety and the appearance of impropriety as well as any conflict of interest or the appearance of conflict. They should neither accept anything nor pursue any activity that might compromise or seem to compromise their integrity.

Article IV

Truth and Accuracy

Good faith with the reader is the foundation of good journalism. Every effort must be made to assure that the news content is accurate, free from bias and in context, and that all sides are presented fairly. Editorials, analytical articles and commentary should be held to the same standards of accuracy with respect to facts as news reports. Significant errors of fact, as well as errors of omission, should be corrected promptly and prominently.

Article V

Impartiality

To be impartial does not require the press to be unquestioning or to refrain from editorial expression. Sound practice, however, demands a clear distinction for the reader between news reports and opinion. Articles that contain opinion or personal interpretation should be clearly identified.

Article VI

Fair Play

Journalists should respect the rights of people involved in the news, observe the common standards of decency and stand accountable to the public for the fairness and accuracy of their news reports. Persons publicly accused should be given the earliest opportunity to respond. Pledges of confidentiality to news sources must be honored at all costs, and therefore should not be given lightly. Unless there is clear and pressing need to maintain confidences, sources of information should be identified.

These principles are intended to preserve, protect and strengthen the bond of trust and respect between American journalists and the American people, a bond that is essential to sustain the grant of freedom entrusted to both by the nation's founders.

ASSOCIATED PRESS MANAGING EDITORS
CODE OF ETHICS

REVISED AND ADOPTED 1995

These principles are a model against which news and editorial staff members can measure their performance. They have been formulated in the belief that newspapers and the people who produce them should adhere to the highest standards of ethical and professional conduct. The public's right to know about matters of importance is paramount. The newspaper has a special responsibility as surrogate of its readers to be a vigilant watchdog of their legitimate public interests.

No statement of principles can prescribe decisions governing every situation. Common sense and good judgment are required in applying ethical principles to newspaper realities. As new technologies evolve, these principles can help guide editors to insure the credibility of the news and information they provide. Individual newspapers are encouraged to augment these APME guidelines more specifically to their own situations.

RESPONSIBILITY

The good newspaper is fair, accurate, honest, responsible, independent and decent. Truth is its guiding principle. It avoids practices that would conflict with the ability to report and present news in a fair, accurate and unbiased manner. The newspaper should serve as a constructive critic of all segments of society. It should reasonably reflect, in staffing and coverage, its diverse constituencies. It should vigorously expose wrongdoing, duplicity or misuse of power, public or private. Editorially, it should advocate needed reform and innovation in the public interest. News sources should be disclosed unless there is a clear reason not to do so. When it is necessary to protect the confidentiality of a source, the reason should be explained. The newspaper should uphold the right of free speech and freedom of the press and should respect the individual's right to privacy. The newspaper should fight vigorously for public access to news of government through open meetings and records.

ACCURACY

The newspaper should guard against inaccuracies, carelessness, bias or distortion through emphasis, omission or technological manipulation. It should acknowledge substantive errors and correct them promptly and prominently.

INTEGRITY

The newspaper should strive for impartial treatment of issues and dispassionate handling of controversial subjects. It should provide a forum for the exchange of comment and criticism, especially when such comment is opposed to its editorial positions. Editorials and expressions of personal opinion by reporters and editors should be clearly labeled. Advertising should be differentiated from news. The newspaper should report the news without regard for its own interests, mindful of the need to disclose potential conflicts. It should not give favored news treatment to advertisers or special-interest groups. It should report matters regarding itself or its personnel with the same vigor and candor as it would other institutions or individuals. Concern for community, business or personal interests should not cause the newspaper to distort or misrepresent the facts. The newspaper should deal honestly with readers and newsmakers. It should keep its promises. The newspaper should not plagiarize words or images.

INDEPENDENCE

The newspaper and its staff should be free of obligations to news sources and newsmakers. Even the appearance of obligation or conflict of interest should be avoided. Newspapers should accept nothing of value from news sources or others outside the profession. Gifts and free or reduced-rate travel, entertainment, products and lodging should not be accepted. Expenses in connection with news reporting should be paid by the newspaper. Special favors and special treatment for members of the press should be avoided. Journalists are encouraged to be involved in their communities, to the extent that such activities do not create conflicts of interest. Involvement in politics, demonstrations and social causes that would cause a conflict of interest, or the appearance of such conflict, should be avoided. Work by staff members for the people or institutions they cover also should be avoided. Financial investments by staff members or other outside business interests that could create the impression of a conflict of interest should be avoided. Stories should not be written or edited primarily for the purpose of winning awards and prizes. Self-serving journalism contests and awards that reflect unfavorably on the newspaper or the profession should be avoided.

GANNETT NEWSPAPER DIVISION

I. PRINCIPLES OF ETHICAL CONDUCT FOR NEWSROOMS

We Are Committed To:

SEEKING AND REPORTING THE TRUTH IN A TRUTHFUL WAY

- We will dedicate ourselves to reporting the news accurately, thoroughly and in context.
- We will be honest in the way we gather, report and present news.
- We will be persistent in the pursuit of the whole story.
- We will keep our word.
- We will hold factual information in opinion columns and editorials to the same standards of accuracy as news stories.
- We will seek to gain sufficient understanding of the communities, individuals and stories we cover to provide an informed account of activities.

SERVING THE PUBLIC INTEREST

- We will uphold First Amendment principles to serve the democratic process.
- We will be vigilant watchdogs of government and institutions that affect the public.
- We will provide the news and information that people need to function as effective citizens.
- We will seek solutions as well as expose problems and wrongdoing.
- We will provide a public forum for diverse people and views.

- We will reflect and encourage understanding of the diverse segments of our community.
- We will provide editorial and community leadership.
- We will seek to promote understanding of complex issues.

EXERCISING FAIR PLAY

- We will treat people with dignity, respect and compassion.
- We will correct errors promptly.
- We will strive to include all sides relevant to a story and not take sides in news coverage.
- We will explain to readers our journalistic processes.
- We will give particular attention to fairness in relations with people unaccustomed to dealing with the press.
- We will use unnamed sources as the sole basis for published information only as a last resort and under specific procedures that best serve the public's right to know.
- We will be accessible to readers.

MAINTAINING INDEPENDENCE

- We will remain free of outside interests, investments or business relationships that may compromise the credibility of our news report.
- We will maintain an impartial, arm's length relationship with anyone seeking to influence the news.
- We will avoid potential conflicts of interest and eliminate inappropriate influence on content.
- We will be free of improper obligations to news sources, newsmakers and advertisers.
- We will differentiate advertising from news.

ACTING WITH INTEGRITY

- We will act honorably and ethically in dealing with news sources, the public and our colleagues.
- We will obey the law.
- We will observe common standards of decency.
- We will take responsibility for our decisions and consider the possible consequences of our actions.
- We will be conscientious in observing these Principles.
- We will always try to do the right thing.

II. PROTECTING THE PRINCIPLES

No statement of principles and procedures can envision every circumstance that may be faced in the course of covering the news. As in the United States Constitution, fundamental principles sometimes conflict. Thus, these recommended practices cannot establish standards of performance for journalists in every situation. Careful judgment and common sense should be applied to make the decisions that best serve the public interest and result in the greatest good. In such instances, journalists should not act unilaterally. The best decisions are obtained after open-minded consultations with appropriate colleagues and superiors—augmented, when necessary, by the advice of dispassionate outside parties, such as experts, lawyers, ethicists, or others whose views in confidence may provide clarity in sorting out issues.

Here are some recommended practices to follow to protect the Principles. This list is not all-inclusive. There may be additional practices—implicit in the Principles or determined within individual newsrooms—that will further ensure credible and responsible journalism.

Ensuring the Truth Principle

"Seeking and reporting the truth in a truthful way" includes, specifically:

- We will not lie.
- We will not misstate our identities or intentions.
- We will not fabricate.
- We will not plagiarize.
- We will not alter photographs to mislead readers.
- We will not intentionally slant the news.

Using Unnamed Sources

The use of unnamed sources in published stories should be rare and only for important news. Whenever possible, reporters should seek to confirm news on the record. If the use of unnamed sources is required:

- Use as sources only people who are in a position to know.
- Corroborate information from an unnamed source through another source or sources and/or by documentary information. Rare exceptions must be approved by the editor.

- Inform sources that reporters will disclose sources to at least one editor. Editors will be bound by the same promise of confidentiality to sources as are reporters.
- Hold editors as well as reporters accountable when unnamed sources are used. When a significant story to be published relies on a source who will not be named, it is the responsibility of the senior news executive to confirm the identity of the source and to review the information provided. This may require the editor to meet the source.
- Make clear to the reporters and to sources that agreements of confidentiality are between the newspaper and the sources, not just between the reporter and the sources. The newspaper will honor its agreements with sources. Reporters should make every effort to clear such confidentiality agreements with the editors first. Promises of confidentiality made by reporters to sources will not be overridden by the editors; however, editors may choose not to use the material obtained in this fashion.
- Do not allow unnamed sources to take cheap shots in stories. It is unfair and unprofessional.
- Expect reporters and editors to seek to understand the motivations of a source and take those into account in evaluating the fairness and truthfulness of the information provided.
- Make clear to sources the level of confidentiality agreed to. This does not mean each option must be discussed with the source, but each party should understand the agreement. Among the options are:
  - The newspaper will not name them in the article.
  - The newspaper will not name them unless a court compels the newspaper to do so.
  - The newspaper will not name them under any circumstances.
  - All sources should be informed that the newspaper will not honor confidentiality if the sources have lied or misled the newspaper.
  - Make sure both sides understand what is being agreed to. For example: Statements may be quoted directly or indirectly and will be attributed to the source. This is sometimes referred to as "on the record." The information may be used in the story but not attributed to the source. This is sometimes referred to as "not for attribution" or "for background." The information will not be used in the story unless obtained elsewhere and attributed to someone else. This is sometimes referred to as "off the record."

- Describe an unnamed source's identity as fully as possible (without revealing that identity) to help readers evaluate the credibility of what the source has said or provided.
- Do not make promises you do not intend to fulfill or may not be able to fulfill.
- Do not threaten sources.

Handling the Wires

These Principles are intended to provide front-line guidance for locally generated material. Wire-service material already has been edited professionally. Gannett News Service observes these same Principles. The Associated Press has its own standards for the use of unnamed sources. Other wire-service standards may be lower. Additional scrutiny often is required, and further editing is encouraged. Ultimately, an editor must make a sound judgment about how to reconcile conflicts between wire-service and local-newsroom practices. Whenever possible, these Principles should prevail.

Being Fair

Because of timeliness or unavailability, it is not always possible to include a response from the subject of an accusation in a news story. Nevertheless:

- We should make a good-faith effort to seek appropriate comment from the person (or organization) before publication.
- When that is not feasible, we should be receptive to requests for a response or try to seek a response for a follow-up story.
- Letters to the editor also may provide an appropriate means for reply.

Some public records will identify persons accused of wrongdoing. Publication of denials is not necessary in such circumstances.

Being Independent

"Maintaining independence" helps establish the impartiality of news coverage. To clarify two points:

- News staff members are encouraged to be involved in worthwhile community activities, so long as this does not compromise the credibility of news coverage.

- When unavoidable personal or business interests could compromise the newspaper's credibility, such potential conflicts must be disclosed to one's superior and, if relevant, to readers.

Conducting Investigative Reporting

Aggressive, hard-hitting reporting is honorable and often courageous in fulfilling the press' First Amendment responsibilities, and it is encouraged. Investigative reporting by its nature raises issues not ordinarily faced in routine reporting. Here are some suggested procedures to follow when undertaking investigative reporting:

- Involve more than one editor at the early stages and in the editing of the stories.
- Question continually the premise of the stories and revise accordingly.
- Follow the practices outlined in the use of sources.
- Document the information in stories to the satisfaction of the senior editor.
- Have a "fresh read" by an editor who has not seen the material as you near publication. Encourage the editor to read it skeptically, then listen carefully to and heed questions raised about clarity, accuracy and relevance.
- Make certain that care, accuracy and fairness are exercised in headlines, photographs, presentation and overall tone.
- Evaluate legal and ethical issues fully, involving appropriate colleagues, superiors, lawyers or dispassionate outside parties in the editorial process. (For example, it may be helpful to have a technical story reviewed by a scientist for accuracy, or have financial descriptions assessed by an accountant, or consult an ethicist or respected outside editor on an ethical issue.)
- Be careful about trading information with sources or authorities, particularly if it could lead to an impression that you are working in concert against an individual or entity.

Editing Skeptically

Editors are the gatekeepers who determine what will be published and what will not be. Their responsibility is to question and scrutinize, even when it is uncomfortable to do so. Here are some suggested practices that editors can follow:

- Take special care to understand the facts and context of the story.
- Guard against assumptions and preconceived notions—including their own.
- Ensure time and resources for sound editing. Nothing should be printed that has not been reviewed by someone else. When feasible, at least two editors should see stories before publication. Complex or controversial stories may require even more careful scrutiny.
- Consider involving an in-house skeptic on major stories—a contrarian who can play the role of devil's advocate.
- Challenge conventional wisdom.
- Heed their "gut instinct." Don't publish a story if it doesn't feel right. Check it further.
- Consider what may be missing from the story.
- Consider how others—especially antagonists or skeptical readers—may view the story. What questions would they ask? What parts would they think are unfair? Will they believe it?
- Be especially careful of stories that portray individuals purely as villains or heroes.
- Beware of stories that reach conclusions based on speculation or a pattern of facts.
- Protect against being manipulated by advocates and special interests.
- Consider these questions: "How do you know? How can you be sure? Where is the evidence? Who is the source? How does he or she know? What is the supporting documentation?"
- Watch carefully for red flags that give reason to be skeptical of newsgathering or editing conduct.
- Don't be stampeded by deadlines, unrealistic competitive concerns or peer pressure.

Ensuring Accuracy

Dedication to the truth means accuracy itself is an ethical issue. Each news person has the responsibility to strive for accuracy at each step of the process.

- Be aware that information attributed to a source may not be factually correct.
- Be sure the person quoted is in a position to know.

- Be especially careful with technical terms, statistics, mathematical computations, crowd estimates and poll results.
- Consider going over all or portions of an especially complicated story with primary sources or with outside experts. However, do not surrender editorial control.
- Don't make assumptions. Don't guess at facts or spellings. Asking the person next to you is not "verification"—he or she could be wrong too.
- Improve note taking. Consider backing up your notes with a tape recorder when ethically and legally appropriate.
- Be wary of newspaper library clippings, which may contain uncorrected errors.
- Develop checklists of troublesome or frequently used names, streets, titles, etc.
- Understand the community and subject matter. Develop expertise in areas of specialized reporting.
- Reread stories carefully after writing, watching especially for errors of context and balance as well as for spelling and other basic mistakes.
- Use care in writing headlines. Do not stretch beyond the facts of the story.
- Follow a simple rule on the copy desk to double-check the accuracy of headlines: "Find the headline in the story." (For example, if the headline says, "Three die in crash," go to the story and count the dead and be certain they died in the crash.)
- Consider using "accuracy checks" as an affirmative way to search out errors and monitor accuracy. (Accuracy checks are a process by which published stories are sent to sources or experts asking for comment on accuracy, fairness or other aspects.)

Correcting Errors

When errors occur, the newspaper has an ethical obligation to correct the record and minimize harm.

- Errors should be corrected promptly. But first, a determination must be made that the fact indeed was in error and that the correction itself is fully accurate.
- Errors should be corrected with sufficient prominence that readers who saw the original error are likely to see the correction. This is a matter of the editor's judgment.

- Although it is wise to avoid repeating the error in the correction, the correction should have sufficient context that readers will understand exactly what is being corrected.
- Errors of nuance, context or tone may require clarifications, editor's notes, editor's columns or letters to the editor.
- When the newspaper disagrees with a news subject about whether a story contained an error, editors should consider offering the aggrieved party an opportunity to express his or her view in a letter to the editor.
- Corrections should be reviewed before publication by a senior editor who was not directly involved in the error. The editor should determine if special handling or outside counsel are required.
- Errors should be corrected whether or not they are called to the attention of the newspaper by someone outside the newsroom.
- Factual errors should be corrected in most cases even if the subject of the error does not want it to be corrected. The rationale for this is rooted in the Truth Principle. It is the newspaper's duty to provide accurate information to readers. An exception may be made—at the behest of the subject—when the correction of a relatively minor mistake would result in public ridicule or greater harm than the original error.
- Newsroom staffers should be receptive to complaints about inaccuracies and follow up on them.
- Newsroom staffers have a responsibility to alert the appropriate editor if they become aware of a possible error in the newspaper.

III. REINFORCING THE PRINCIPLES

Communicating Standards

Editors have a responsibility to communicate these Principles to newsroom staff members and to the public. They should:

- Ensure that sound hiring practices are followed to build a staff of ethical and responsible journalists. Such practices include making reference checks and conducting sufficient interviewing and testing to draw reasonable conclusions about the individual's personal standards.
- Provide prospective hires with a copy of these Principles and make acceptance of them a condition of employment.
- Conduct staff training at least annually in the Principles of Ethical Conduct.

- Require staff members at the time of hire and each year thereafter to sign a statement acknowledging that they have read the Principles of Ethical Conduct and will raise any questions about them with their editors.
- Communicate these Principles to the public periodically.

Being Accountable

Because these Principles embody the highest standards of professional conduct, the Gannett Newspaper Division is committed to their adherence. They have been put in writing specifically so that members of every Gannett Newspaper Division newsroom know what the Division stands for and what is expected of them. The public will know, too.

RADIO-TELEVISION NEWS DIRECTORS ASSOCIATION CODE OF ETHICS

The Radio-Television News Directors Association (RTNDA) Code of Ethics and Professional Conduct is a statement of guiding principles for the practice of electronic journalism. It cannot anticipate every situation electronic journalists might face. Common sense and careful judgment should be applied in all cases.

CODE OF ETHICS AND PROFESSIONAL CONDUCT OF THE RTNDA

The RTDNA, wishing to foster the highest professional standards of electronic journalism, promote public understanding of and confidence in electronic journalism, and strengthen principles of journalistic freedom to gather and disseminate information, establishes this Code of Ethics and Professional Conduct.

PREAMBLE

Professional electronic journalists should operate as trustees of the public, seek the truth, report it fairly and with integrity and independence, and stand accountable for their actions.

PUBLIC TRUST

Professional electronic journalists should recognize that their first obligation is to the public. Professional electronic journalists should:

- Understand that any commitment other than service to the public undermines trust and credibility.
- Recognize that service in the public interest creates an obligation to reflect the diversity of the community and guard against oversimplification of issues or events.
- Provide a full range of information to enable the public to make enlightened decisions.
- Fight to ensure that the public's business is conducted in public.

TRUTH

Professional electronic journalists should pursue truth aggressively and present the news accurately, in context, and as completely as possible. Professional electronic journalists should:

- Continuously seek the truth.
- Resist distortions that obscure the importance of events.
- Clearly disclose the origin of information and label all material provided by outsiders.

Professional electronic journalists should not:

- Report anything known to be false.
- Manipulate images or sounds in any way that is misleading.
- Plagiarize.
- Present images or sounds that are reenacted without informing the public.

FAIRNESS

Professional electronic journalists should present the news fairly and impartially, placing primary value on significance and relevance. Professional electronic journalists should:

- Treat all subjects of news coverage with respect and dignity, showing particular compassion to victims of crime or tragedy.
- Exercise special care when children are involved in a story and give children greater privacy protection than adults.

- Seek to understand the diversity of their community and inform the public without bias or stereotype.
- Present a diversity of expressions, opinions, and ideas in context.
- Present analytical reporting based on professional perspective, not personal bias.
- Respect the right to a fair trial.

INTEGRITY

Professional electronic journalists should present the news with integrity and decency, avoiding real or perceived conflicts of interest, and should respect the dignity and intelligence of the audience as well as the subjects of news. Professional electronic journalists should:

- Identify sources whenever possible. Confidential sources should be used only when it is clearly in the public interest to gather or convey important information or when a person providing information might be harmed. Journalists should keep all commitments to protect a confidential source.
- Clearly label opinion and commentary.
- Guard against extended coverage of events or individuals that fail to significantly advance a story, place the event in context, or add to the public knowledge.
- Refrain from contacting participants in violent situations while the situation is in progress.
- Use technological tools with skill and thoughtfulness, avoiding techniques that skew facts, distort reality, or sensationalize events.
- Use surreptitious news gathering techniques, including hidden cameras or microphones, only if there is no other way to obtain stories of significant public importance and only if the technique is explained to the audience.
- Use the private transmissions of others only with permission.

Professional electronic journalists should not:

- Pay news sources who have a vested interest in a story.
- Accept gifts, favors, or compensation from those who might seek to influence coverage.
- Engage in activities that may compromise their integrity or independence.

INDEPENDENCE

Professional electronic journalists should defend the independence of all journalists from those seeking influence or control over news content. Professional electronic journalists should:

- Gather and report news without fear or favor, and vigorously resist undue influence from any outside forces, including advertisers, sources, story subjects, powerful individuals, and special interest groups.
- Resist those who would seek to buy or politically influence news content or who would seek to intimidate those who gather and disseminate the news.
- Determine news content solely through editorial judgment and not as the result of outside influence.
- Resist any self-interest or peer pressure that might erode journalistic duty and service to the public.
- Recognize that sponsorship of the news will not be used in any way to determine, restrict, or manipulate content.
- Refuse to allow the interests of ownership or management to influence news judgment and content inappropriately.
- Defend the rights of the free press for all journalists, recognizing that any professional or government licensing of journalists is a violation of that freedom.

ACCOUNTABILITY

Professional electronic journalists should recognize that they are accountable for their actions to the public, the profession and themselves. Professional electronic journalists should:

- Actively encourage adherence to these standards by all journalists and their employers.
- Respond to public concerns. Investigate complaints and correct errors promptly and as with as much prominence as the original report.
- Explain journalistic processes to the public, especially when practices spark questions or controversy.
- Recognize that professional electronic journalists are duty-bound to conduct themselves ethically.
- Refrain from ordering or encouraging courses of action which would force employees to commit an unethical act.

- Carefully listen to employees who raise ethical objections and create environments in which such objections and discussions are encouraged.
- Seek support for and provide opportunities to train employees in ethical decision-making.

In meeting its responsibility to the profession of electronic journalism, RTNDA has created this code to identify important issues, to serve as a guide for its members, to facilitate self-scrutiny, and to shape future debate.

THE E. W. SCRIPPS COMPANY STATEMENT OF POLICY ON ETHICS AND PROFESSIONAL CONDUCT

INTRODUCTION

For purposes of this statement of policy, The E. W. Scripps Company and each of its subsidiaries will be referred to as the Company.

PURPOSE

The businesses in which the Company is engaged embody a public trust. We firmly believe that integrity and credibility are inherent to our success. It is essential that each of us maintains the highest standards of conduct. Every precaution must be taken to avoid any act, however innocent, that might appear questionable or improper to others. We have developed this Statement of Policy on Ethics and Professional Conduct to help each of us understand the importance of maintaining public trust and confidence.

While we cannot set forth covenants to prejudge every situation, we believe the following guidelines create a climate in which appearances of misconduct or improper activity are avoided.

GENERAL POLICY

The success of our Company is closely related to the level of confidence that the public has with our newspapers, television stations, entertainment endeavors and other business initiatives. The services we provide to the public place us in a position of trust. A high level of confidence and trust can be maintained only if we adhere to the highest standards of ethical behavior in the performance of our duties. We are committed to meeting those standards without compromise.

For the benefit of our customers, co-workers and shareholders, we shall conduct all phases of our business honestly and ethically, with our best skills and judgment.

RIGHTS AND RESPONSIBILITIES

General

As a matter of policy, the Company will strive to provide a work environment that allows employees to perform to their maximum potential. It is essential that the work environment remain free of age, racial, ethnic, religious or sexual bias and harassment of any kind. The Company is committed to maintaining a workplace that fosters mutual respect and promotes productive working relationships.

Equal Employment Policy

The Company is an Equal Opportunity Employer as a matter of law, ethics, and good business practice. The Company provides equal employment opportunities and bases its employment decisions on sound business reasons without regard to race, religion, color, national origin, gender, age, disability, or on any other basis which would be in violation of any applicable ordinance or law. The Company will make reasonable accommodations for qualified individuals with known disabilities.

Substance Abuse

Abuse of alcohol or use of illegal drugs interferes with effective and safe job performance, which is a matter of Company concern. Employees are prohibited from using, possessing, distributing, selling, manufacturing, or being under the influence of alcohol or illegal drugs while on the job. It is understood that some employees may at times be required to attend, as one of their duties, events where alcohol is served. While consuming alcohol on such an occasion is not prohibited, employees must observe legal, business and common-sense guidelines.

Personal Business

Employees may not conduct personal business under circumstances which might mislead the public into believing that person represents the Company. No employee may use his or her position for personal gain or in any way that is detrimental to the Company.

Personal Use of Company Assets

Employees may not use, or permit others to use, Company materials, supplies, equipment, funds or co-workers for personal purposes. Any exceptions must be properly authorized and, when applicable, appropriate provision must be made for reimbursement to the Company.

Plagiarism

No employee may submit the work of another person without complete attribution of the true source.

Safety, Health and Environment

The Company intends to provide safe operating procedures, to promote its employees' health, and to care and encourage regard for the environment among co-workers and in the community.

Compliance With Laws

All employees must comply with the letter and spirit of all applicable laws. All relationships with governmental and community officials must be conducted in strict observance of applicable laws.

CONFIDENTIAL/PROPRIETARY INFORMATION

General: Protecting Confidential Information

Depending on the nature of their work with the Company, some employees may have access to information about the Company that is either competitively sensitive or needs to be held in confidence until a public announcement is made. To protect such confidential information, and to comply with securities regulations, employees must exercise the utmost care to avoid inadvertent disclosure through public or casual discussion which may be overheard or misinterpreted.

News employees may obtain confidential information about the Company, which is given to them based on their relationship with the Company other than that of a reporter or editor. In such cases, the news employee should honor the Company's need for confidentially until such time as the Company releases it as public information.

Insider Trading

Trading or tipping in the Company's stock on the basis of non-public information about the Company is strictly forbidden. Violations are criminally punishable under federal and state securities laws.

If an employee is in possession of material non-public information regarding the Company, he may not trade directly or indirectly in the Company's securities or disclose (tip) any such information to another person. Material information is any information that an investor would consider important in deciding to buy, hold or sell securities of the Company. In short, any information that could reasonably affect the price of Company stock is material. Examples of matters that may be material include: earnings forecasts, preliminary financial results, possible acquisitions, dispositions or joint ventures, the acquisition or loss of a significant contract, dividend actions and stock splits, important product developments, significant financing developments and the status of labor negotiations.

Requests for Information/Public Discussion

Requests for information relating to the Company should be referred to the Corporate Communications and Investor Relations Department. Additionally, press releases prepared by Company employees should be reviewed by the corporate communications department prior to dissemination if, when taken as a whole, the information contained therein could reasonably be expected to affect the price of Company stock.

CONFLICTS OF INTEREST

General

A conflict of interest may arise if an employee engages in activities, or advances any personal interests, at the expense of the Company. It is up to each employee to avoid situations in which his or her loyalty may become divided. Common types of conflicts include: using the Company's proprietary information for any outside employment, assisting competitors, or competing against the Company.

Outside Affiliations/Competition With the Company

An employee may not serve as a director, consultant, agent or employee of enterprises which conduct or seek to conduct business with the Company or which compete with or seek to compete with the Company, except with the knowledge and written consent of the Company's Compliance Officer.

Employees may not, directly or indirectly, compete with the Company in any manner whatsoever, nor can they assist others in doing so. All part-time or freelance work which may be deemed in possible competition with the Company must receive prior approval from the employee's appropriate supervisor.

While having a second job is not prohibited, it must not encroach on the standard Company workday, interfere or conflict with the employee's regular duties, or necessitate long hours which may affect working effectiveness.

Company Directors who are not employees are expected to avoid affiliations which would violate the foregoing and to disclose, in writing, any such affiliations to the Executive Committee of the Company's Board of Directors.

Investments

An employee and any member of his or her immediate family may have no ownership interest* in enterprises which conduct or seek to conduct business with the Company or which compete with the Company, except an interest that has been properly disclosed.

Community Involvement

Employees are encouraged to become involved in the communities where they live, but should be aware of potential conflicts which could arise as a

---

*An interest in the form of publicly traded securities in such enterprises, so long as the interest does not exceed 1% of the outstanding shares of the company in question, does not have to be disclosed.

result of the Company's news business. Reporters and editors are in a unique position and must be particularly sensitive to potential conflict of interest issues.

Conducting Company Business

General

An employee may not represent the Company in any transaction between the Company and an enterprise in which the employee has an interest, unless approved by the president, publisher or general manager at the employee's property location.

Accounting and Record Keeping

Accuracy and reliability in the preparation of all business records is mandated by law and is of critical importance to the Company's decision-making processes. Each employee is expected to record and report all information accurately and honestly. It is very important that the Company's books reflect all components of all transactions. Employees are expected to cooperate fully with internal and outside auditors. Employees shall not make any misrepresentation or dishonest statement in conducting the Company's business.

Business Gifts, Meals, Services and Entertainment

Employees should not place themselves under an actual or apparent obligation to anyone by borrowing money or by accepting gifts, entertainment or other personal favors. In today's competitive business climate the offering or receipt of promotional materials or gifts is not unusual. However, it is contrary to the policy of the Company for an employee to accept a gift or gratuity when it is given with the expectation of reward or influence. Acceptance of any gift of substantial value could lead to misperceptions of conflict.

Company employees should consider whether a gratuitous transaction is consistent with accepted business practices and whether, in the view of an independent observer, public disclosure of the matter would embarrass the Company. It is always improper for an employee and members of the immediate family who live with him or her to request anything that could be construed as an attempt to influence the performance of duties.

The acceptance or giving of bribes, kickbacks or other remuneration to any government official, political party, corporation, individual or organization is always prohibited.

Political Activity

The Company remains independent in all political matters and will not make monetary contributions, directly or indirectly, to political campaigns or causes, or to political parties. Moreover, its officers will not make such contributions acting on behalf of the Company. Rare exceptions may be made to this prohibition, but then only if permitted by law and approved by the President of the Company.

Although the Company is independent in all political matters, employees are encouraged to register to vote, with party affiliations, and to vote. Employees may pursue their own personal political activities, but may not, either inadvertently or intentionally, represent their personal views or contributions to be those of the Company. Employees must avoid any suggestion that their relationship with the Company constitutes an endorsement of any kind.

Journalists and others working in newsrooms must abide by a more restrictive standard, given the disinterested neutrality from which news organizations must work. They must not serve in elected or politically appointed positions. They must not participate in political fund-raising, political organizing, nor other activities designed to enhance a candidate, a political party or a political-interest organization. They must not make contributions of record to political campaigns nor engage in other such activity that might associate an employee's name with a political candidate or a political cause.

Antitrust Considerations

The Company will comply with all laws pertaining to antitrust and competition. Such laws generally forbid any kind of understanding or agreement, whether written or oral, between competitors to fix or control prices, terms, conditions of sales, customers, markets, boycotts, or to engage in any other conduct that restrains competition. Since competition laws may be unclear in their application, employees must be sensitive to the possibility of legal concerns under these laws and must consult with corporate management when concerns arise during the consideration of any action of competitive significance.

Company Opportunities

No employee or director may divert an opportunity for the Company for his own benefit or for the benefit of any member of his immediate family. An "opportunity for the Company" is a business opportunity in the Company's line of business which the Company is financially able to undertake and which has not been rejected by a majority of the disinterested directors of the Company after full disclosure.

Work Product

All work produced during the course of employment belongs to the Company, and no further use, distribution or commercial exploitation of it may be made without prior written authorization.

E-Mail

The Company's Electronic Mail (E-Mail) system is part of the business environment and should be used for company purposes only. As with all Company documents, employees do not have a personal privacy right in any material that is created, received or sent from our E-Mail system. The Company reserves the right to monitor the E-Mail system to assure that its property is being used for business purposes only. E-Mail correspondence is discoverable in accordance with federal and state court rules.

Voice Mail

The Company's Voice Mail system is also part of the business environment and should only be used for company purposes. Employees do not have a personal privacy right in messages that are created or received. The Company reserves the right to monitor the Voice Mail system to assure that its property is being used for business purposes only. (It is understood that employees are likely to receive messages from family and friends, but personal messages should be kept to a minimum.)

Data Security

The Company is committed to the establishment and enforcement of effective information security. Information is a corporate asset and the Company and its employees must protect it from unauthorized modification, destruction, or disclosure, whether accidental or intentional.

Employees may have access to systems that require a password. Passwords must be kept confidential and must not be shared or disclosed with anyone inside or outside of the Company.

Personal Computer Software

The Company licenses the use of computer software from a variety of outside businesses. Any duplication of licensed software, except for backup purposes, is a violation of Federal copyright law. Software that an employee uses at her or his office may not be duplicated for use on any other personal computer without the express permission of the general manager, or information systems manager, at the employee's property location.

COMPANY STANDARDS AND ENFORCEMENT

Company Standards

Every person who is a part of The E. W. Scripps Company's family has some responsibility associated with the ethics program. The Company is responsible for implementation and making available to all employees a copy of this booklet. Supervisors must be aware of the company's policies on conduct and ensure that all employees under their supervision are aware of and understand the Statement of Policy on Ethics and Professional Conduct. All employees are responsible for seeking clarification or requesting an exception if they believe the application of a section of this booklet would be inappropriate or detrimental to the Company.

Organization and Procedures

The President of The E. W. Scripps Company is the Company's Compliance Officer and the Corporate Secretary is the Ethical Program Director. The Compliance Officer is responsible for the dissemination, execution and functioning of the ethical conduct program. The Program Director supports the Compliance Officer and is responsible for the functioning of the program.

Enforcement

The standards described in each of the foregoing sections will be consistently enforced. Employees who violate these policies may be subject to a full range of disciplinary measures, including suspension or termination, responsibility for financial damages and possible criminal prosecution. Questions about the interpretation or administration of these guidelines, or about the investigation and enforcement procedures, should be referred to the Ethical Program Director.

Monitoring the effectiveness of the program will be done on a continual basis by the Ethical Program Director, reporting to the Company's Compliance Officer.

NEED HELP?

Helpline

It has always been the Company's policy to conduct its business in an ethical manner. An employee should fully and promptly disclose to his or her direct supervisor in writing any violation or potential violation of these policies. If there is anything that an employee feels should be reported to the Company that he or she is unable for any reason to communicate through his or her supervisor, or is unable to resolve at the local operating level, that employee is encouraged to use the Company's Helpline. The Helpline augments established procedures. It was created to provide a confidential method for an employee to report any situation that he or she feels may not be in compliance with the Company's policies or with local laws and regulations.

The private Helpline can be accessed by calling 1-888-397-4911 (a toll-free number). This number will be answered only by the Ethical Program Director who will insure the matter is investigated, and that appropriate confidentiality is maintained. (If the Program Director is unavailable, a voice message may be left. Only the Program Director has access to this recording.) It is helpful if you leave your name when calling the Helpline so that a proper response can be made. However, identification is not mandatory. No retaliation will be made against any employee nor will notes be placed in an employee's personnel file regarding an inquiry to the Helpline.

Investigation of Reports of Unethical Conduct

Upon receiving a report of unethical conduct, whether from the Helpline or a direct report from an employee, the Ethical Program Director will contact the Compliance Officer to discuss an internal investigation.

The Program Director will maintain a record of each report of unethical conduct he or she receives, including the name (or the identification number if a name was not given) of the reporting employee, the date and time the report is received, a summary of the conduct reported, and summary of the action taken. Such records shall be maintained for a period of one year after the report.

1. The Phone Call

Every call will be logged-in by the Ethical Program Director (EPD). The EPD will take down as much information as the reporting person will provide, such as:

- Name of the reporting employee
- If the caller prefers not to give a name, he/she will be assigned a number and asked to call back the following day so that the employee can be advised of the action taken
- The date and time the report is received
- The employee's property location and department
- A phone number to contact the employee
- A summary of the conduct reported

If an employee makes a report directly to the Compliance Officer or the Ethical Program Director, the follow-up procedure will be the same as if a call was received on the Helpline.

2. The Investigation

Upon receiving a call, the EPD will begin an appropriate investigation. If there is some basis to believe that unethical conduct may have taken place, the EPD will contact the Compliance Officer and arrange for a confidential internal investigation. The reporting employee is to be notified of the action taken. At no time will copies of any report be filed in the reporting employee's personnel file.

3. Findings/Enforcement

All findings of unethical conduct shall be dealt with promptly. Penalties will be consistent with the employee's conduct and the circumstances surrounding that conduct. Discipline may be subject to a full range of disciplinary measures, including suspension or termination, responsibility for financial damages and possible criminal prosecution.

The Compliance Officer shall determine the penalty for any unethical conduct.

Before the determination to discipline or not to discipline the employee is made, the employee shall be advised in writing of the conduct determined to be unethical and the employee shall be given the opportunity to present evidence or to make a statement on his own behalf to the Compliance Officer.

The Compliance Officer or the EPD shall document all decisions regarding employee discipline for unethical conduct.

If there is a determination of unethical conduct, the Ethical Program Director will meet with the department manager and/or division head to determine a means to prevent future misconduct.

4. Monitoring the Program

Monitoring the effectiveness of the program will be done on a continual basis by the Ethical Program Director. The Company will take all reasonable steps to achieve compliance with its standards. Such steps include, but shall not be limited to: reminding employees of the program on a periodic basis, having a reporting system (Helpline) in place, utilizing internal auditing procedures, and sending insider trading reminders on a quarterly basis to officers of the Company.

NATIONAL PRESS PHOTOGRAPHERS ASSOCIATION CODE OF ETHICS

STATEMENT OF PURPOSE

The National Press Photographers Association (NPPA), a professional society dedicated to the advancement of photojournalism, acknowledges concern and respect for the public's natural-law, right to freedom in searching for the truth and the right to be informed truthfully and completely about public events and the world in which we live. NPPA believes that no report can be complete if it is possible to enhance and clarify the meaning of the words. We believe that pictures, whether used to depict news events as they actually happen, illustrate news that has happened, or to help explain anything of public interest, are indispensable means of keeping people accurately informed, that they help all people, young and old, to better understand any subject in the public domain. NPPA recognizes and acknowledges that photojournalists should at all times maintain the highest standards of ethical conduct in serving the public interest.

CODE OF ETHICS

The practice of photojournalism, both as a science and art, is worthy of the very best thought and effort of those who enter into it as a profession.

Photojournalism affords an opportunity to serve the public that is equaled by few other vocations and all members of the profession should strive by example and influence to maintain high standards of ethical conduct free of mercenary considerations of any kind.

It is the individual responsibility of every photojournalist at all times to strive for pictures that report truthfully, honestly and objectively.

As journalists, we believe that credibility is our greatest asset. In documentary photojournalism, it is wrong to alter the content of a photograph in any way (electronically or in the darkroom) that deceives the public. We believe the guidelines for fair and accurate reporting should be the criteria for judging what may be done electronically to a photograph.

Business promotion in its many forms is essential but untrue statements of any nature are not worthy of a professional photojournalist and we severely condemn any such practice.

It is our duty to encourage and assist all members of our profession, individually and collectively, so that the quality of photojournalism may constantly be raised to higher standards.

It is the duty of every photojournalist to work to preserve all freedom-of-the-press rights recognized by law and to work to protect and expand freedom-of-access to all sources of news and visual information.

Our standards of business dealings, ambitions and relations shall have in them a note of sympathy for our common humanity and shall always require us to take into consideration our highest duties as members of society. In every situation in our business life, in every responsibility that comes before us, our chief thought shall be to fulfill that responsibility and discharge that duty so that when each of us is finished we shall have endeavored to lift the level of human ideals and achievement higher that we found it.

No Code of Ethics can prejudge every situation, thus common sense and good judgement are required in applying ethical principles.

SOCIETY OF PROFESSIONAL JOURNALISTS CODE OF ETHICS

PREAMBLE

Members of the Society of Professional Journalists (SPJ) believe that public enlightenment is the forerunner of justice and the foundation of democracy. The duty of the journalist is to further those ends by seeking truth and providing a fair and comprehensive account of events and issues. Conscientious journalists from all media and specialties strive to serve the public with thoroughness and honesty. Professional integrity is the cornerstone of a journalist's credibility. Members of the Society share a dedication to ethical behavior and adopt this code to declare the Society's principles and standards of practice.

SEEK TRUTH AND REPORT IT

Journalists should be honest, fair and courageous in gathering, reporting and interpreting information. Journalists should:

- Test the accuracy of information from all sources and exercise care to avoid inadvertent error. Deliberate distortion is never permissible.
- Diligently seek out subjects of news stories to give them the opportunity to respond to allegations of wrongdoing.
- Identify sources whenever feasible. The public is entitled to as much information as possible on sources' reliability.
- Always question sources' motives before promising anonymity. Clarify conditions attached to any promise made in exchange for information. Keep promises.
- Make certain that headlines, news teases and promotional material, photos, video, audio, graphics, sound bites and quotations do not misrepresent. They should not oversimplify or highlight incidents out of context.

Society of Professional Journalists, Improving & Protecting Journalism, 16 S. Jackson St. Greencastle, IN 46135. Phone: (317) 927-8000; Fax: (765) 653-4631; spj@spjhq.orgwebmaster.

- Never distort the content of news photos or video. Image enhancement for technical clarity is always permissible. Label montages and photo illustrations.
- Avoid misleading re-enactments or staged news events. If re-enactment is necessary to tell a story, label it.
- Avoid undercover or other surreptitious methods of gathering information except when traditional open methods will not yield information vital to the public. Use of such methods should be explained as part of the story.
- Never plagiarize.
- Tell the story of the diversity and magnitude of the human experience boldly, even when it is unpopular to do so.
- Examine their own cultural values and avoid imposing those values on others.
- Avoid stereotyping by race, gender, age, religion, ethnicity, geography, sexual orientation, disability, physical appearance or social status.
- Support the open exchange of views, even views they find repugnant.
- Give voice to the voiceless; official and unofficial sources of information can be equally valid.
- Distinguish between advocacy and news reporting. Analysis and commentary should be labeled and not misrepresent fact or context.
- Distinguish news from advertising and shun hybrids that blur the lines between the two.
- Recognize a special obligation to ensure that the public's business is conducted in the open and that government records are open to inspection.

MINIMIZE HARM

Ethical journalists treat sources, subjects and colleagues as human beings deserving of respect. Journalists should:

- Show compassion for those who may be affected adversely by news coverage. Use special sensitivity when dealing with children and inexperienced sources or subjects.
- Be sensitive when seeking or using interviews or photographs of those affected by tragedy or grief.
- Recognize that gathering and reporting information may cause harm or discomfort. Pursuit of the news is not a license for arrogance.
- Recognize that private people have a greater right to control information about themselves than do public officials and others who

seek power, influence or attention. Only an overriding public need can justify intrusion into anyone's privacy.

- ◆ Show good taste. Avoid pandering to lurid curiosity.
- ◆ Be cautious about identifying juvenile suspects or victims of sex crimes.
- ◆ Be judicious about naming criminal suspects before the formal filing of charges.
- ◆ Balance a criminal suspect's fair trial rights with the public's right to be informed.

ACT INDEPENDENTLY

Journalists should be free of obligation to any interest other than the public's right to know. Journalists should:

- ◆ Avoid conflicts of interest, real or perceived.
- ◆ Remain free of associations and activities that may compromise integrity or damage credibility.
- ◆ Refuse gifts, favors, fees, free travel and special treatment, and shun secondary employment, political involvement, public office and service in community organizations if they compromise journalistic integrity.
- ◆ Disclose unavoidable conflicts.
- ◆ Be vigilant and courageous about holding those with power accountable.
- ◆ Deny favored treatment to advertisers and special interests and resist their pressure to influence news coverage.
- ◆ Be wary of sources offering information for favors or money; avoid bidding for news.

BE ACCOUNTABLE

Journalists are accountable to their readers, listeners, viewers and each other. Journalists should:

- ◆ Clarify and explain news coverage and invite dialogue with the public over journalistic conduct.
- ◆ Encourage the public to voice grievances against the news media.
- ◆ Admit mistakes and correct them promptly.
- ◆ Expose unethical practices of journalists and the news media.
- ◆ Abide by the same high standards to which they hold others.

Sigma Delta Chi's first Code of Ethics was borrowed from the American Society of Newspaper Editors in 1926. In 1973, *Sigma Delta Chi* wrote its own code, which was revised in 1984 and 1987. The present version of the

Society of Professional Journalists' Code of Ethics was adopted in September 1996.

Public Relations Society of America (PRSA) Member Code of Ethics 2000

Approved by the PRSA Assembly October, 2000

The PRSA Assembly adopted this Code of Ethics in 2000. It replaces the Code of Professional Standards (previously referred to as the Code of Ethics) that was last revised in 1988. For further information on the Code, please contact the chair of the Board of Ethics through PRSA headquarters.

Preamble

Public Relations Society of America Member Code of Ethics 2000

- Professional Values
- Principles of Conduct
- Commitment and Compliance

This Code applies to PRSA members. The Code is designed to be a useful guide for PRSA members as they carry out their ethical responsibilities. This document is designed to anticipate and accommodate, by precedent, ethical challenges that may arise. The scenarios outlined in the Code provision are actual examples of misconduct. More will be added as experience with the Code occurs.

The Public Relations Society of America (PRSA) is committed to ethical practices. The level of public trust PRSA members seek, as we serve the public good, means we have taken on a special obligation to operate ethically.

The value of member reputation depends upon the ethical conduct of everyone affiliated with the Public Relations Society of America. Each of us sets an example for each other—as well as other professionals—by our pursuit of excellence with powerful standards of performance, professionalism, and ethical conduct.

Emphasis on enforcement of the Code has been eliminated. But, the PRSA Board of Directors retains the right to bar from membership or expel from the Society any individual who has been or is sanctioned by a government agency or convicted in a court of law of an action that is in violation of this Code.

Ethical practice is the most important obligation of a PRSA member. We view the Member Code of Ethics as a model for other professions, organizations, and professionals.

PRSA Member Statement of Professional Values

This statement presents the core values of PRSA members and, more broadly, of the public relations profession. These values provide the foundation for the Member Code of Ethics and set the industry standard for the professional practice of public relations. These values are the fundamental beliefs that guide our behaviors and decision-making process. We believe our professional values are vital to the integrity of the profession as a whole.

Advocacy

- We serve the public interest by acting as responsible advocates for those we represent.
- We provide a voice in the marketplace of ideas, facts, and viewpoints to aid informed public debate.

Honesty

- We adhere to the highest standards of accuracy and truth in advancing the interests of those we represent and in communicating with the public.

Expertise

- We acquire and responsibly use specialized knowledge and experience.
- We advance the profession through continued professional development, research, and education.
- We build mutual understanding, credibility, and relationships among a wide array of institutions and audiences.

Independence

- We provide objective counsel to those we represent.
- We are accountable for our actions.

Loyalty

- We are faithful to those we represent, while honoring our obligation to serve the public interest.

Fairness

- We deal fairly with clients, employers, competitors, peers, vendors, the media, and the general public.
- We respect all opinions and support the right of free expression.

PRSA CODE PROVISIONS

Free flow of information.

Core Principle

Protecting and advancing the free flow of accurate and truthful information is essential to serving the public interest and contributing to informed decision making in a democratic society.

Intent

- To maintain the integrity of relationships with the media, government officials, and the public.
- To aid informed decision-making.

Guidelines

A member shall:

- Preserve the integrity of the process of communication.
- Be honest and accurate in all communications.
- Act promptly to correct erroneous communications for which the practitioner is responsible.
- Preserve the free flow of unprejudiced information when giving or receiving gifts by ensuring that gifts are nominal, legal, and infrequent.

Examples of Improper Conduct Under This Provision:

- A member representing a ski manufacturer gives a pair of expensive racing skis to a sports magazine columnist, to influence the columnist to write favorable articles about the product.
- A member entertains a government official beyond legal limits and/or in violation of government reporting requirements.

COMPETITION

Core Principle

Promoting healthy and fair competition among professionals preserves an ethical climate while fostering a robust business environment.

Intent

- To promote respect and fair competition among public relations professionals.
- To serve the public interest by providing the widest choice of practitioner options.

Guidelines

A member shall:

- Follow ethical hiring practices designed to respect free and open competition without deliberately undermining a competitor.
- Preserve intellectual property rights in the marketplace.

Examples of Improper Conduct Under This Provision:

- A member employed by a "client organization" shares helpful information with a counseling firm that is competing with others for the organization's business.
- A member spreads malicious and unfounded rumors about a competitor in order to alienate the competitor's clients and employees in a ploy to recruit people and business.

DISCLOSURE OF INFORMATION

Core Principle

Open communication fosters informed decision making in a democratic society.

Intent

+ To build trust with the public by revealing all information needed for responsible decision making.

Guidelines

A member shall:

+ Be honest and accurate in all communications.
+ Act promptly to correct erroneous communications for which the member is responsible.
+ Investigate the truthfulness and accuracy of information released on behalf of those represented.
+ Reveal the sponsors for causes and interests represented.
+ Disclose financial interest (such as stock ownership) in a client's organization.
+ Avoid deceptive practices.

Examples of Improper Conduct Under This Provision:

+ Front groups: A member implements "grass roots" campaigns or let-ter-writing campaigns to legislators on behalf of undisclosed interest groups.
+ Lying by omission: A practitioner for a corporation knowingly fails to release financial information, giving a misleading impression of the corporation's performance.
+ A member discovers inaccurate information disseminated via a Web site or media kit and does not correct the information.
+ A member deceives the public by employing people to pose as vol-unteers to speak at public hearings and participate in "grass roots" campaigns.

SAFEGUARDING CONFIDENCES

Core Principle

Client trust requires appropriate protection of confidential and private information.

Intent

- To protect the privacy rights of clients, organizations, and individuals by safeguarding confidential information.

Guidelines

A member shall:

- Safeguard the confidences and privacy rights of present, former, and prospective clients and employees.
- Protect privileged, confidential, or insider information gained from a client or organization.
- Immediately advise an appropriate authority if a member discovers that confidential information is being divulged by an employee of a client company or organization.

Examples of Improper Conduct Under This Provision:

- A member changes jobs, takes confidential information, and uses that information in the new position to the detriment of the former employer.
- A member intentionally leaks proprietary information to the detriment of some other party.

CONFLICTS OF INTEREST

Core Principle

Avoiding real, potential or perceived conflicts of interest builds the trust of clients, employers, and the publics.

Intent

- To earn trust and mutual respect with clients or employers.
- To build trust with the public by avoiding or ending situations that put one's personal or professional interests in conflict with society's interests.

Guidelines

A member shall:

- Act in the best interests of the client or employer, even subordinating the member's personal interests.
- Avoid actions and circumstances that may appear to compromise good business judgment or create a conflict between personal and professional interests.
- Disclose promptly any existing or potential conflict of interest to affected clients or organizations.
- Encourage clients and customers to determine if a conflict exists after notifying all affected parties.

Examples of Improper Conduct Under This Provision

- The member fails to disclose that he or she has a strong financial interest in a client's chief competitor.
- The member represents a "competitor company" or a "conflicting interest" without informing a prospective client.

ENHANCING THE PROFESSION

Core Principle

Public relations professionals work constantly to strengthen the public's trust in the profession.

Intent

- To build respect and credibility with the public for the profession of public relations.
- To improve, adapt and expand professional practices.

Guidelines

A member shall:

- Acknowledge that there is an obligation to protect and enhance the profession.
- Keep informed and educated about practices in the profession to ensure ethical conduct.

- Actively pursue personal professional development.
- Decline representation of clients or organizations that urge or require actions contrary to this Code.
- Accurately define what public relations activities can accomplish.
- Counsel subordinates in proper ethical decision making.
- Require that subordinates adhere to the ethical requirements of the Code.
- Report ethical violations, whether committed by PRSA members or not, to the appropriate authority.

Examples of Improper Conduct Under This Provision:

- A PRSA member declares publicly that a product the client sells is safe, without disclosing evidence to the contrary.
- A member initially assigns some questionable client work to a non-member practitioner to avoid the ethical obligation of PRSA membership.

RESOURCES

Rules and Guidelines

The following PRSA documents, available online at www.prsa.org provide detailed rules and guidelines to help guide your professional behavior. If, after reviewing them, you still have a question or issue, contact PRSA headquarters.

- PRSA Bylaws
- PRSA Administrative Rules
- Member Code of Ethics

AMERICAN ADVERTISING FEDERATION

ADVERTISING PRINCIPLES OF AMERICAN BUSINESS

Truth

Advertising shall tell the truth, and shall reveal significant facts, the omission of which would mislead the public.

Adopted by the American Advertising Federation Board of Directors, March 2, 1984, San Antonio, Texas.

Substantiation

Advertising claims shall be substantiated by evidence in possession of the advertiser and advertising agency, prior to making such claims.

Comparisons

Advertising shall refrain from making false, misleading, or unsubstantiated statements or claims about a competitor or his/her products or services.

Bait Advertising

Advertising shall not offer products or services for sale unless such offer constitutes a bona fide effort to sell the advertised products or services and is not a device to switch consumers to other goods or services, usually higher priced.

Guarantees and Warranties

Advertising of guarantees and warranties shall be explicit, with sufficient information to apprise consumers of their principal terms and limitations or, when space or time restrictions preclude such disclosures, the advertisement should clearly reveal where the full text of the guarantee or warranty can be examined before purchase.

Price Claims

Advertising shall avoid price claims which are false or misleading, or saving claims which do not offer provable savings.

Testimonials

Advertising containing testimonials shall be limited to those of competent witnesses who are reflecting a real and honest opinion or experience.

Taste and Decency

Advertising shall be free of statements, illustrations or implications which are offensive to good taste or public decency.

AMERICAN ASSOCIATION OF ADVERTISING AGENCIES

FIRST ADOPTED OCTOBER 16, 1924—MOST RECENTLY REVISED SEPTEMBER 18, 1990

We hold that a responsibility of advertising agencies is to be a constructive force in business.

We hold that, to discharge this responsibility, advertising agencies must recognize an obligation, not only to their clients, but to the public, the media they employ, and to each other. As a business, the advertising agency must operate within the framework of competition. It is recognized that keen and vigorous competition, honestly conducted, is necessary to the growth and the health of American business. However, unethical competitive practices in the advertising agency business lead to financial waste, dilution of service, diversion of manpower, loss of prestige, and tend to weaken public confidence both in advertisements and in the institution of advertising.

We hold that the advertising agency should compete on merit and not by attempts at discrediting or disparaging a competitor agency, or its work, directly or by inference, or by circulating harmful rumors about another agency, or by making unwarranted claims of particular skill in judging or prejudging advertising copy.

To these ends, the American Association of Advertising Agencies has adopted the following *Creative Code* as being in the best interests of the public, the advertisers, the media, and the agencies themselves. The AAAA believes the Code's provisions serve as a guide to the kind of agency conduct that experience has shown to be wise, foresighted, and constructive. In accepting membership, an agency agrees to follow it.

Creative Code

We, the members of the American Association of Advertising Agencies, in addition to supporting and obeying the laws and legal regulations pertaining to advertising, undertake to extend and broaden the application of high

---

ethical standards. Specifically, we will not knowingly create advertising that contains:

a. False or misleading statements or exaggerations, visual or verbal
b. Testimonials that do not reflect the real opinion of the individual(s) involved
c. Price claims that are misleading
d. Claims insufficiently supported or that distort the true meaning or practicable application of statements made by professional or scientific authority
e. Statements, suggestions, or pictures offensive to public decency or minority segments of the population.

We recognize that there are areas that are subject to honestly different interpretations and judgment. Nevertheless, we agree not to recommend to an advertiser, and to discourage the use of, advertising that is in poor or questionable taste or that is deliberately irritating through aural or visual content or presentation.

Comparative advertising shall be governed by the same standards of truthfulness, claim substantiation, tastefulness, etc., as apply to other types of advertising.

These Standards of Practice of the American Association of Advertising Agencies come from the belief that sound and ethical practice is good business. Confidence and respect are indispensable to success in a business embracing the many intangibles of agency service and involving relationships so dependent upon good faith.

Clear and willful violations of these Standards of Practice may be referred to the Board of Directors of the American Association of Advertising Agencies for appropriate action, including possible annulment of membership as provided by Article IV, Section 5, of the Constitution and By-Laws.

RESOURCES: WEB SITES IN MEDIA ETHICS

GENERAL

THE AMERICAN CIVIL LIBERTIES UNION (ACLU)

Web site on cyberliberties *(http://www.aclu.org/issues/cyber/hmcl.html)* covers cybercensorship, library blocking of Internet, and online privacy.
Codes of Ethics online: *http://csep.iit.edu/codes/codes.html*

ACCURACY IN MEDIA

www.aim.org is an organization "for fairness, balance and accuracy in news reporting"; this group is a non-profit, grassroots citizens watchdog of the news media that critiques inaccurate or biased news stories and attempts to establish accuracy on important issues that have received slanted coverage.

AMERICAN JOURNALISM REVIEW (AJR NEWSLINK)

www.newslink.org/ajrtoc.html is a joint venture between *American Journalism Review* magazine and NewsLink Associates, an online research and consulting firm. It includes features from the printed edition of AJR magazine, the worldwide online publication lists of NewsLink, and original content created especially for online readers.

AMERICAN SOCIETY OF NEWSPAPER EDITORS

www.asne.org/ideas/codes/codes.htm features a comprehensive list of codes of ethics of various organizations, as collected by ASNE. These include codes of ethical conduct from national associations, news organizations, and regional presses.

ASSOCIATION FOR EDUCATION IN JOURNALISM AND MASS COMMUNICATIONS (AEJMC)

www.aejmc.org is an international association of some 3,300 journalism/mass communication faculty, students, administrators, and professionals. International in scope, AEJMC's members come from more than 30 countries, with the majority working in the United States and Canada. Resources include research and publications by the AEJMC Media Ethics Interest Group.

ASSOCIATION FOR PRACTICAL AND PROFESSIONAL ETHICS

php.indiana.edu/~appe/ is maintained out of Indiana University. This organization is committed to encouraging high quality interdisciplinary scholarship and teaching in practical and professional ethics by educators and practitioners who appreciate the theoretical and practical impacts of their subjects. Organizational scope is interdisciplinary in nature, concerned with the study and teaching of practical and professional ethics in a variety of contexts and towards educating for civic and professional responsibility.

CAROL BURNETT FUND FOR RESPONSIBLE JOURNALISM

www2.soc.hawaii.edu/css/journ/cbfund.html has been administered out of the University of Hawaii's Journalism Department since 1981. The fund is an endowment from actress Carol Burnett to encourage responsibility in journalism, with an emphasis on ethics. Users have access to research and scholarship produced from this endowment that "support[s] teaching and research designed to further high standards of ethics and professionalism in journalism," and can make application for "awards to outstanding students who have demonstrated a strong sense of journalistic responsibility and integrity."

CIVIC PRACTICES NETWORK

www.cpn.org/sections/topics/journalism/index.html is the Civic Journalism section of CPN. Users may access essays that provide an overview of the civic and public journalism movement. CPN cases offer a city-by-city guide to public journalism projects across the United States, as reported by Project Public Life and the Press, the Pew Center for Civic Journalism, the Poynter Institute, Democracy Place USA, and other CPN partners. Includes access to the CPN **Journalism Bulletin Board.**

EthicNet

www.uta.fi/ethicnet is a project out of Finland that aims to provide a comprehensive databank offering basic information on media ethics for journalism students and teachers as well as scholars and practitioners. Included is a collection of codes of journalism ethics from most of the European countries, translated into English. The source and core of the collection resulted from numerous research projects of the Department of Journalism and Mass Communication, University of Tampere, and it has been extended and updated with information from various relevant sources.

IJNet

www.ijnet.org/EventArchive/1999/9/2-10.html is the International Journalists' Network. Organized and administered by the International Center For Journalists (ICFJ), an organization established in 1984 to improve the quality of journalism in nations where there is little or no tradition of independent journalism. An excellent electronic source for the latest media assistance news from Central and Eastern Europe, Russia, and the Newly Independent States as well as Latin America (en Español) and Africa. IJNet also provides both geographical and topical forums for journalists. Includes information on worldwide fellowships, grants, and national codes of ethics.

Columbia Journalism Review

www.cjr.org features current and archived issues of the journal. Archive includes full text of CJR issues back to July/August 1991. Users may access the CJR database to search a variety of media publications as well as several resource guides and hyperlinks.

Ethics Updates

http://ethics.acusd.edu/index.html is maintained out of the University of San Diego and is designed primarily to be used by ethics instructors and their students. It is intended to provide updates on current literature, both popular and professional, that relates to ethics. Comprehensive in scope, this resource offers an informative and authoritative look at classic works in moral philosophy including ethical theory, applied ethics, moral theory, ethical relativism, meta-ethical concerns, and virtue ethics. Of particular interest to the journalist, is the reference section on meta-ethics and moral pluralism that deals with specifically with the ep? of questions and contexts. A discussion forum extends from this section. An additional feature is *A Glossary of Terms in Ethics.*

FAIR: FAIRNESS AND ACCURACY IN NEWS REPORTING

www.fair.org is a national media watch group that offers well-documented criticism of media bias and censorship and advocates for greater diversity in the press.

FREEDOM FORUM ONLINE

www.freedomforum.org is a nonpartisan, international foundation dedicated to free press, free speech and free spirit for all people. The foundation focuses on four main priorities: the Newseum, First Amendment issues, newsroom diversity and world press freedom. An excellent resource for information pertaining to responsible journalism.

INDIANA UNIVERSITY INDEX TO JOURNALISM ETHICS CASES

www.journalism.indiana.edu/ethics features Journalism Ethics Cases Online, a set of cases that has been created for teachers, researchers, professional journalists and consumers of news to help them explore ethical issues in journalism. The cases raise a variety of ethical problems faced by journalists, including such issues as privacy, conflict of interest, reporter-source relationships, and the role of journalists in their communities. Users may browse entries by category or search case texts.

INSTITUTE FOR BUSINESS AND PROFESSIONAL ETHICS: DE PAUL UNIVERSITY

www.depaul.edu/ethics/ is the website of the Institute for Business and Professional Ethics, which was established in 1985 by a joint effort of the Colleges of Liberal Arts and Sciences and Commerce at DePaul University.

The Institute is one of the first ethics-related resources to pioneer a hypertext linked ethics network throughout the Internet. The mission of the IBPE is to encourage ethical deliberation in decision-makers by stirring the moral conscience and imagination. Their objective is to provide a forum for exploring and furthering ethical practices in organizations. Includes an excellent resource listing with hyperlinks.

JOURNAL OF MASS MEDIA ETHICS (JMME)

http://jmme.byu.edu is a publication website devoted to explorations of ethics problems and issues in various fields of mass communication, with emphasis on materials dealing with principles and reasoning in ethics. Users may access a variety of search tools and bibliographic information—including article abstracts and archival matter—from this site.

MEDIA ETHICS ONLINE

www.mediaethics.com is a comprehensive virtual catalog of media organizations, ethics codes online, directories, and scholarship. Catalog subset of **Web Ethics** highlights "cyberethics" or ethical concerns relating to journalism in digital media.

NATIONAL PRESS PHOTOGRAPHERS ASSOCIATION ONLINE

www.nppa.org is an organization dedicated to the advancement of photojournalism, its creation, editing and distribution in all news media. NPPA encourages photojournalists to reflect high standards of quality in their professional performance and personal code of ethics. Users may access a variety of resources linked to the homepage, including previews from *News Photographer Magazine,* event calendars, NPPA publications, educational resources, and leadership directories.

THE ON-LINE JOURNAL OF ETHICS (ISSN 1092-8286)

www.depaul.edu/ethics/ethg1.html is an online journal of cutting-edge research in the field of business and professional ethics. Users may access the full-text of current and archived issues.

POYNTER INSTITUTE FOR MEDIA STUDIES ONLINE

www.poynter.org is an institute dedicated to helping journalists fulfill their responsibility to empower citizens by informing them. Includes a comprehensive resource center for journalists, including, but not limited to, online editor services, tip sheets, Poynter Institute research, and a comprehensive hyperextension of professional resources catalogued by job classification.

RADIO-TELEVISION NEWS DIRECTORS ASSOCIATION

web.missouri.edu/~jourvs/rtcodes.html is maintained by Vernon Stone, of the Missouri School of Journalism. An excellent practical and historical resource, this site traces the evolution of, and amendments to, the RTNDA Codes of Ethics and Standards in broadcast journalism across half a century, from 1946 through the 1987 code in effect in 2000.

SOCIETY OF PROFESSIONAL JOURNALISTS. ETHICS IN JOURNALISM.

www.spj.org/ethics/index.htm is the website of the Society of Professional Journalists, the nation's largest and most broad-based journalism organization, dedicated to encouraging the free practice of journalism and stimulating high standards of ethical behavior. Website provides the SPJ Code, Ethics News, and ethics resources.

PUBLIC RELATIONS

http://www.business.com/directory/advertising/public_relations/research_ and_reference/ includes an online ads discussion list and focuses on professional discussion of online advertising strategies, studies, tools, and public relations.

CRISIS MANAGEMENT

http://www.business.com/directory/advertising/public_relations/reputation_ management/ includes several sites for crisis management in public relations for clients under attack by the media. This Web site also includes a general reputation management journal featuring a public relations quarterly, spring 1998 article on the future reconciliation of multicultural perspectives in public relations ethics that takes an in-depth look at culture-based ethics. It also shows how professional ethics should be applied and the differences among those of the past, present, and future.

ADVERTISING

ADVERTISING LAW AND ETHICS

http://advertising.utexas.edu/research/law/index.html
   This site from the Department of Advertising at the University of Texas at Austin includes information on the First Amendment, current issues, subliminal appeals, tobacco and alcohol, children, sweepstakes, and contests and lotteries.

ADVERTISING NEWS

http://www.business.com/directory/advertising/news/
   This Web site features articles on the slow growth of online advertising and the tobacco advertising ban that has been lifted in Europe.

BUSINESS AND ENTERTAINMENT NEWS

www.business.com/directory/media_and_entertainment/journalism/news/
   This Web site features articles on a reporter who was sent home from the Prince William Sound trip, a journalist who was pursued for hunting national secrets, and *China Times*.

AMERICAN JOURNALISM REVIEW ONLINE

http://ajr.newslink.org

COLUMBIA JOURNALISM REVIEW ONLINE

http://www.cjr.org

HINDMAN

http://ethics.acusd.edu/index.html
This Web site features Hindman on racism, deontology, virtue, utilitarianism, gender issues, and a list of periodicals.

ONLINE JOURNALISM REVIEW

http://ojr.usc.edu/
This Web site includes articles on making the Web an equal partner—
New York Times and its online presence and online news from the Democratic National Convention.

CENTER FOR DEMOCRACY & TECHNOLOGY

http://www.cdt.org/speech/
This Web site covers issues of child online protection, spamming, and free speech.

CAN WE TAPE?

http://dir.lycos.com/News/Media/Journalism/Issues/FirstAmendment/
This Web site features a state-by-state guide to laws governing recording conversations over the telephone, using hidden cameras, and the publication of illegal tapes.

DIVERSITY

1. Africana Studies, University of Pittsburgh: *http://www.pitt.edu/bjgrier/links.htm*
2. African and African Diaspora Studies, Tulane University: *http://www.tulane.edu/adst/links.htm*
3. Center for Afro-American and African Studies, University of Michigan (Ann Arbor): *http://www.umich.edu/iinet/caas/links/index.html*
4. Africana Studies Research Center, Cornell University: *http://www.library.cornell.edu/africana/index.html*
5. Center for the Study of Race, Politics and Culture, University of Chicago: *http://social_sciences.uchicago.edu/ucrpc/*

CLASS, CULTURE, AND CYBERSPACE

1. Donna Hoffman and Thomas Novak, *The Evolution of the Digital Divide: Examining the Relationship of Race to Internet Access and Usage Over Time*: *http://www2000.ogsm.vanderbilt.edu/*
2. Commerce Department: *http://digitaldivide.gov/*
3. Benton Foundation: *http://www.benton.org/Library*
4. Art McGee, *Class Culture and Cyberspace*: *http://www.igc.org/amcgee/e_race.html*
5. Abdul Alkalimat, *The Technological Revolution and Prospects for Black Liberation in the 21st Century*: *http://www.cyrev.net/Issues/Issue4/TechnologicalRevolutionAndProspectsforBlackLiberation.htm*

INFORMATION REVOLUTION WEB SITES

1. The Community Connector, School of Information, University of Michigan: *http://www.si.umich.edu/Community*
2. Information Technology in Africa: *http://www.sas.upenn.edu/AfricanStudies/AboutAfrican/wwtech.html*
3. cyRev: A Journal of Cybernetic Revolution, Sustainable Socialism and Radical Democracy: *http://www.cyrev.net/*
4. Media Lab, MIT: *http://www.media.mit.edu/*
5. H_Net: Humanities and Social Sciences Online: *http://www.h_net.msu.edu/*

LISTSERVS*

SOCIETY OF PROFESSIONAL JOURNALISTS

spj.org/ethics/listserv.htm is an online discussion group and mail list forum dedicated to the discussion of journalism ethics and its sociological, political, and cultural imports. Website (spj.org/ethics) communicates relevant information on SPJ ethic codes, ethics news, and resources. Users may

---

*Copyright 2001 by Lawrence Erlbaum Associates, Publishers. Published with permission. Appears in Walshe, E., "Digital Research in Media Ethics; An Annotated Webliography of Information Resources," in the *Journal of Mass Media Ethics,* Vol. 16, No. 4 (in press).

subscribe by sending a message to **majordomo@dworkin.wustl.edu** and in the body of the subscription request message, type **subscribe SPJ-ETHICS**.

JOURNETHICS

tile.net/listserv/journethicsethics.html is an ethics in journalism forum maintained out of the Missouri School of Journalism. Users may subscribe by sending a message to **listproc@lists.missouri.edu** and in the body of the subscription request message, type **subscribe JOURNETHICS**.

NATIONAL PRESS PHOTOGRAPHERS ASSOCIATION (NPPA) LISTSERV

www.ibiblio.org/nppa/online.html is sponsored by the National Press Photographers Association. This discussion group focuses generally on the profession of photojournalism, both print and electronic, and specifically on the members of the National Press Photographers Association (NPPA). Input is welcome from anyone interested in these issues. Users may subscribe by sending a message to **listserv@cmuvm.csv.cmich.edu** and in the body of the subscription request message, type **subscribe NPPA-L**.

ONLINE PRESS CLUB—JOURNALISM FORUM

www.jforum.org is the international press club on CompuServe. The site includes a mail list forum and discussion group devoted to global issues in journalism. Membership is free and exclusive to CompuServe users.

IJN JOURNALISM ETHICS FORUM

www.ijnet.org/ijnforum.html?Forum=ijnfl3 is the International Journalism Network's discussion group on important media issues and journalism training developments worldwide.

GLOSSARY

Absolutism. The belief that there are unequivocal mandates, known by humans, that must dictate their actions (ie., I must not lie, for the truth is always best).

Autonomous moral agent. One who makes moral decisions based on principle and reason and is relatively unaffected by pressures from peers, supervisiors, and others.

Categorical imperative. This concept refers to a command or law that is unconditional. Such a law instructs us to do something regardless of the consequences. According to Kant, this is the principle of all morality. Kant characterized it as the highest moral law and formulated it in several ways, one of which states that humans should be treated as ends, not means.

Code of ethics. A set of admonitions meant to guide a subscriber. Some codes are prescriptive and require compliance under threat of penalties. Other codes are advisory, suggesting principles to be considered in moral decision making.

Communicate. The process of transmitting information from one individual to another, or to others, with the expectation of a desired effect.

Communication. Interaction and exchange of information through a variety of methods including verbal and nonverbal.

Communitarianism. A political position that promotes the needs of the community over the individual.

Conflict of interest. When an individual or organization could unfairly act from a privileged position.

Deception. An intentional attempt to mislead.

Democracy. The political theory stating that the people are sovereign and have the right to rule.

Deontology. This term refers to ethical theories (such as Kant's) that stress the importance of the motive of doing one's duty as a determining factor in assessing the moral value of actions. It is the motive for, not the consequences of, actions that count.

Divine command. A theory holding that what makes an action morally right is the fact that God commands or wills it.

Duty. Something that is required of someone. For Kant a perfect duty must be performed whatever the circumstances.

Ethics. The study of morality and moral behavior.

First Amendment. The First Amendment to the Constitution: "Congress shall make no law respecting an establishment of religion, or prohibiting the free exercise thereof; or abridging the freedom of speech, or of the press. . ."

Foundationalism. The claim that rationality and knowledge rest on a firm foundation of self-evident truths.

Freedom of the press. The guarantee by the Constitution of unrestricted distribution of information. A freedom-of-the-press absolutist believes in the strictest sense that media should be completely unregulated.

Green-light journalism. Journalistic decisions based on a greater distribution of information under the principle that broad and open distribution of information is beneficial. A basic premise is: When in doubt, publish.

Hard determinism. The theory that every event has a cause and that this fact is incompatible with the existence of free will. Hence human beings should not be held morally responsible for their actions because it is impossible for them to do other than what they do.

Idealism. A metaphysical theory holding that only ideas (minds and mental events) are real, or that they are more real, valuable, and enduring than material things. In an ethical context, "idealistic" is sometimes used to refer to a person who lives by ideals or to a view based on principle.

Individualism. Holds that rights of individuals have primacy over normal needs of community. Necessary for development of moral autonomy.

Liberalism. The political philosophy that espouses individual choice within a political framework.

Moral reasoning. The decision-making process associated with decisions of right, wrong, harm, mutual aid, etc.

Moral skepticism. The position that doubts the existence of moral truth and the possibility of ethical knowledge.

Morality. A system of guidance designed to assist in living within a society.

Muckrakers. Journalists in the early twentieth century who sought to expose corruption in business, industry, and government.

Normative. This concept, often contrasted with descriptive, is used to refer to a type of reflection that seeks to discover the way things ought to be.

Objectivism. A view holding that there is some permanent framework for determining rationality, knowledge, truth, reality, and moral value. The opposite of relativism.

Personal Moral Theory. An individual's personal and professional views on daily moral choices.

Philosophy. This word derives from the Greek word for "love of wisdom." It has been defined in a variety of ways, one of which is the notion that philosophy is the rational attempt to formulate, understand, and answer fundamental questions.

Pluralism. The theory holding that there are many different realities and that they are not reducible to a single reality or to only two basic realities. Also used in a different context to refer to a society characterized by a variety of cultural groups.

Principle.   The underlying directive to moral decision making that influences action (ie., Respect for human reasoning powers [principle] may direct the telling of the truth [action]).

Privacy.   Relates to the right to private conduct that is of no concern to the public. Similarly, personal information to which there can be no right of public access.

Red-light journalism.   A philosophy that restricts distribution of information out of consideration for the status quo. Usually requires substantial documentation. Operating principle: If there is doubt, do not publish.

Relationship ethics.   An emerging system of ethics which focuses on the ability to make ethical decisions based on caring and sharing within a network of relationships.

Relativism.   A view that denies the existence of objective, transcultural moral values and/or standards of rationality. The only moral values and standards of rationality that exist are relative to either individuals or societies.

Rights.   One is allowed to perform an action and nobody should be allowed to prevent that action. Having a right doesn't mean one ought to do it, but that one is allowed to do if desired.

Rules.   Formal or informal conventions one is required or conditioned to follow.

Rumor.   Information that has yet to be verified fully.

Sensationalism.   Exaggeration and often adding more and more titillating emphasis to information.

Social philosophy.   The study of government, the state, and issues of social policy.

Social contract.   A theory of political sovereignty claiming that the authority of government derives from a voluntary agreement among all the people of a society to form a political community and to obey the laws laid down by the government they collectively select.

Social conflict.   Elements which bring about disturbances within a given society.

Social order.   A social condition of stability; one in which behavior of members of the order is highly predictable and is likely to contribute to a hospitable, nonthreatening social climate.

Theology.   The study of divine reality or God, sometimes divided into natural theology, which deals with possible knowledge about God based on the use of reason alone, and revealed theology, which claims knowledge about God based on special revelations.

Utilitarianism.   A moral theory holding that the value of an action resides in its utility or use for the production of pleasure or happiness.

Veil of ignorance.   A theory developed by philosopher John Rawls that involves the making of a decision as if one had no knowledge of their place in society.

Virtue.   Notions of moral excellence or uprightness. Ancient Greek philosophers defined virtues as those character traits that they thought made for a good person.

Yellow journalism.   A movement dating to the late 1800s in which news events were routinely overdramatized. The most notable yellow journalist was William Randolph Hearst.

INDEX